THE COLONIAL HORIZON: AMERICA IN THE SIXTEENTH AND SEVENTEENTH CENTURIES

Interpretive Articles and Documentary Sources
Edited by
WILLIAM H. GOETZMANN
University of Texas

ADDISON-WESLEY PUBLISHING COMPANY
Reading, Massachusetts / Menlo Park, California / London / Don Mills, Ontario

AMERICAN HISTORY IN FOCUS SERIES

Under the Editorship of
William H. Goetzmann

THE COLONIAL HORIZON:
AMERICA IN THE SIXTEENTH AND SEVENTEENTH CENTURIES
William H. Goetzmann, University of Texas

THE AMERICAN REVOLUTION:
THE ANGLO-AMERICAN RELATION, 1763–1794
Charles R. Ritcheson, Southern Methodist University

YEARS OF TURMOIL:
CIVIL WAR AND RECONSTRUCTION
John Niven, Claremont Graduate School

THE GILDED AGE: AMERICA, 1865–1900
Richard A. Bartlett, The Florida State University

THE AGE OF INSECURITY: AMERICA, 1920–1945
Robert A. Divine, University of Texas

Cover drawing by Herbert Caswell.

PREFACE:
THE AMERICAN HISTORY IN FOCUS SERIES

History is the recorded deeds, ideas, and emotions of men. Living history is the re-recording of these deeds, ideas, and emotions by interpreters in each new generation. *The American History in Focus Series* seeks to provide the student with what might be called "the varieties of living historical experience," from a mid-twentieth century point of view. Each of the major historical epochs in American history is brought into focus by means of modern interpretive articles written by major scholars in the field, scholars who may be said to be on "the growing tip" of historical knowledge. Their interests span a vast range of historical methods and commitments. Collectively, they represent the multiple points of view of political, social, economic, diplomatic, military, and intellectual historians—historians who are nonetheless very much products of our own times and affected by current interests. These selections are concerned in almost every instance with answering that simple but all-important question—"so what?"—as it relates to our historical heritage. Of what relevance has past American historical experience been to the total course of human development, to the emergence of American values, achievements, problems, and predicaments? How did I, a citizen of the United States, get to be where and what I am today with all the privileges, burdens, and responsibilities that are entailed? What experiences of quality and nobility of conduct can be noted in the past against which we can measure our own aspirations and behavior—for we can the better recognize quality in our own lives for having seen it somewhere before in the recent or distant past?! By portraying realistically the complexities, relativisms, and ambiguities in the interpretations of time past, the editors and authors represented in these volumes provide new perspectives for determining our cultural identity.

Each of the volumes concentrates on a major period in American history, from colonial times to the present. Each is structured around focal, interpretive articles of modern historians with several varieties of history represented. These focal articles are supplemented by important and revealing historical documents of the particular era with which the historian is concerned. These are samples of the kinds of materials out of which he has constructed his interpretation. They are intended to serve two purposes: first, to give today's student a "feel" for the language and perspectives of the people of earlier generations; second, to provide materials with which to *test* the generalizations of the modern interpreters—to provide a laboratory situation whereby the student may critically examine some of the interpreter's answers and hopefully even some of his questions. For serious historical study requires constant criticism of historical generalizations, and it is too little recognized that such criticism might properly begin with the question, "did the historian ask the right questions of the period?"

Given the above, it should be obvious that these are experimental books especially designed as tools for learning. They are neither exercises in belletristic virtuosity, nor are they "canned" problems where the rules are clear and for the clever, the answers pat. Rather they are intended to be sophisticated, broad-based springboards to future discussion. As an added dimension we have experimented with the addition of pictorial materials which are not intended as idle embellishment but should rather serve as integral parts of the text—as further documents of the time. These, too, when examined with care, afford points of focus.

In attempting to draw a distinction between the nature of science and the nature of history, an historian of science, Derek de Solla Price, makes a striking analogy. He sees science as a "many-brained" machine into whose circuits all of the latest "growing tip" discoveries, however limited, can be wired so that advances in knowledge can result without the necessity for retracing in detail the historical steps involved in previous discoveries. History, on the other hand, is a "single-brained" enterprise in which each historian has to go back over all the sources and interpretations of the past before making his own generalization.* The *American History in Focus Series* attempts to draw upon the advantages of both. For the individual student it is clearly a "single-brained" experience. But in assembling between two covers modern interpretations, along with documents from the past, both written and pictorial, we have attempted to provide the advantages of a "many-brained" approach as well, so as to encourage the student to examine the nature of historical enquiry as a process of thought, and to address himself to the problem of cultural identity in a changing world.

William H. Goetzmann
General Editor

---

* Derek D. Price, "Two Cultures and One Historian of Science," *Teachers College Record*, **64**, 7, April 1963, pp. 528–531.

ACKNOWLEDGMENTS

I wish to thank the following for their assistance in preparing this book for publication: Mrs. Charlotte Darehshori, Mr. Brian Dippie, Mrs. Phyllis O'Keefe, Miss Susan Phinney, and Miss Sara Speights, all of The University of Texas. I am grateful also to Stefan Lorant, for permission to use illustrations from *The New World: The First Pictures of America* (New York, Meredith Press, 1965); and to Allan I. Ludwig, for permission to use an illustration from *Graven Images: New England Stonecarving and its Symbols, 1650–1815* (Middletown, Conn., Wesleyan University Press, 1966).

TABLE OF TUDOR, STUART, AND HANOVERIAN MONARCHS
OF ENGLAND FROM THE AGE OF DISCOVERY
TO THE END OF THE SEVENTEENTH CENTURY

TUDORS	Henry VII	1485–1509
	Henry VIII	1509–1547
	Edward VI	1547–1553
	Mary I	1553–1558
	Elizabeth I	1558–1603
STUARTS	James I	1603–1625
	Charles I	1625–1649
	Oliver Cromwell	1649–1658
	(The Protectorate, 1653–1658)	
	Richard Cromwell	1658–1659
	Charles II	1660–1685
	James II	1685–1688
HANOVERIANS	William III	1689–1702
	(Mary, 1689–1694)	

CONTENTS

GENERAL INTRODUCTION *1*

I **ENGLAND AND THE NEW WORLD:**
   DREAMS, IMAGES, AND STRATEGIES

   INTRODUCTION *15*

   INTERPRETATION *17*
   Howard Mumford Jones, *The Colonial Impulse*

1 THE USES OF LEGEND *39*
   A Discourse of Sebastian Cabot

2 THE USES OF GEOGRAPHY *42*
   Robert Thorne's Picture of the World

3 THE USES OF HISTORY *50*
   John Smith on English Exploration and Settlement in the New World

4 THE PIRATE AS NATIONAL HERO *56*
   Sir John Hawkins in Africa and the Spanish Main

5 IN SEARCH OF EL DORADO *63*
   Raleigh's Voyage to Guiana in 1617

6 THE FIRST SCIENTIFIC VIEW OF VIRGINIA *69*
   Thomas Heriot's Report

7 AMERICAN ABUNDANCE 75
   John Smith on Virginia

8 VIRGINIA'S DARKER SIDE 77
   The Awful Trials of the Honourable George Percy in Virginia

9 JOHN SMITH ON NEW ENGLAND 79
   From the Spanish to the Dutch Model

II VIRGINIA: FROM COMPANY TO COLONY TO EMPIRE

   INTRODUCTION 83

   INTERPRETATION 85
   Herbert S. Klein, Virginia's Institutions

1 THE VIRGINIA CHARTER OF 1609 97

2 STARVING TIME IN VIRGINIA 101
   A True Declaration of Virginia

3 FREEHOLDING AND FREE ENTERPRISE 104
   The Virginia Company's Land Policy

4 A MORE POWERFUL GENERAL ASSEMBLY 107
   The Ordinance of 1621

5 THE MASSACRE OF 1622 109
   Failure of the Assembly's Indian Policy

6 GOVERNMENT BY ROYAL INSTRUCTIONS 113
   Instructions to Governor Yeardley in 1626

7 BEHIND THE SCENES OF ROYAL GOVERNMENT 117
   Samuel Mathews Intrigues against the Authorities
   in Virginia and Maryland

8 MERCANTILISM AND EMPIRE 120
   The Navigation Act of 1660

9 AMERICAN TOBACCO IMPORTED BY ENGLAND, 1616–1693 127

10 THE VIRGINIAN AS COSMOPOLITAN MERCHANT 127
    The Letters of William Fitzhugh

11 A NEW CIVILIZATION AND ITS DISCONTENTS 133
    Bacon's Rebellion, 1676

12 VIRGINIA SOCIETY AT THE END
    OF THE SEVENTEENTH CENTURY 139
    An Overview of the State and Government of Virginia

III MASSACHUSETTS BAY:
     THE SHIFTING STANCES OF PURITANISM

     INTRODUCTION 147

     INTERPRETATION 148
     Perry Miller, The Puritan State and Puritan Society

1 THE HISTORIAN'S HEROIC VIEW 160
   Edward Johnson's Wonder-Working Providence

2 A MODEL OF THE PURITAN STATE 169
   John Winthrop on the Aims of the Bay Colony

3   THE IDEA OF THE COVENANT   *179*
Peter Bulkeley on the Covenant

4   THE ANTINOMIAN CRISIS   *181*
Governor Thomas Hutchinson's Version of the Trial of Anne Hutchinson

5   THE CAMBRIDGE PLATFORM   *184*

6   THE CHRISTIAN CALLING   *187*
John Cotton on Puritan Economic and Social Ideals

7   THE PURITAN'S MORAL DECATHLON   *190*
Michael Wigglesworth's Diary

8   THE CHANGING NATURE OF NATURE   *197*
John Wise and Natural Law

9   "THERE SHALL BE A STINK"   *200*
Increase Mather Delivers a Jeremiad
on the Occasion of King Philip's War

10   THE DEVIL AMONGST THEM   *204*
Cotton Mather on Witchcraft and the Witchcraft Trials
Together with Judge Samuel Sewall's Profound Apology

GENERAL INTRODUCTION

In historical terms, the process which culminated in the establishment of North American civilization spanned most of the Renaissance and Reformation, the Age of the Scientific Revolution, and the emerging era of modern nationalism. It was part of a great break in historical continuity, the consequences of which man has not yet fully seen. In its simplest form, the story of America's beginnings is the story of the process whereby the technologically advanced civilization of Europe imposed its will upon, or, more accurately, came to terms with, a vast new environment. But the story is not a simple one. It is composed of a complex set of dreams fashioned by a traditional society in the throes of cultural revolution, and an even more complex set of realities which continually modified, baffled, and thwarted the energies of European civilization. The result was the emergence of a new society in America quite unlike anything envisioned in Europe.

When the first leaky vessels touched the islands of the Caribbean and the densely forested coasts of North America, the European explorer-conquerors did not even have a vocabulary to describe accurately what they saw and what they experienced. Resorting to convention and a strong propensity toward wish fulfillment, they called the inhabitants "Indians," an obvious misnomer. For a long time, their reports back home were either matter-of-fact in the style of Columbus or, as they warmed to their subject, richly fabricated visions of longed-for oriental splendor like those of Marco Polo. Even the earliest graphic representations of the North American New World, those by John White, seem excessively dependent on previous convention. They were clearly the products of the programmed imagination. But then, as the magnitude and significance of their discoveries dawned upon the Europeans, they began formulating new dreams, new strategies, and new plans for what they came to fully recognize as a New World. By a process of trial and error and continuous adjustment, the Americas came ever more steadily into focus. And as the forces of tradition combined with the newer revolutionary currents of the time to bring about this focus and adjustment, Europe, as well as America, slowly but surely became transformed. It became committed to increasing national rivalries, a scramble for material wealth, a habit of ruthless exploitation, and even, sad to say, ever more aggressive, competing forms of Christianity.

To study fully this process of global acculturation (the beginning of a chain reaction which is still going on) requires more than a recitation of discoveries and conquests since Columbus or, as it applies to the origins of the present-day

1

United States, a dutiful description of the Pilgrims of New England and the adventurers of Virginia. It requires some investigation of the beginning of the chain of events: it requires analysis of the dreams, the models, and the plans of the men who came to the New World, as well as knowledge of the details of their actual attempts to establish colonies. Therefore, in studying the roots of American civilization, one must go back beyond Plymouth or Jamestown, or even the lost tragic colony of Roanoke, and then forward through the seventeenth century, before one can begin even the sketchiest scenario of what is surely one of the most climactic events in world history.

ii

All of this is necessarily a large task. Fortunately for the student of United States history, it is possible to narrow the focus somewhat to the English experience, for it was English culture, though it came late to the New World and took, as it were, "the leavings," that became most relevant to the formation of American values, institutions, and modes of behavior. And if one is especially interested in beginnings, the focus can be narrowed even more— to the shores of Massachusetts Bay and Virginia—never forgetting that it is process rather than pageantry that is the point of interest. After decades of careful historical investigation, we now know that there was something more to the landing in New England than the Mayflower Compact and the discovery of corn. We also know that the plantations of Virginia did not just spring to life at the touch of mattock and spade; nor did the tradition of local representative assemblies and the assumption of inalienable individual rights appear at once obvious to that ragged company of gentlemen adventurers marooned in Jamestown's miasmal environs.

The entire English strategy with regard to the New World—indeed, the very forms of settlement—was in large measure dictated by England's world position as much as by the forces of English tradition, which themselves were rapidly weakening under the religious and secular reorganization instituted by the Tudors. England, as mentioned above, came late to the New World, despite the early work of the Venetian mercenary John Cabot, who made the actual rediscovery (after the Vikings) of North America in 1497. By the time England entered seriously into worldwide imperial competition, the Portuguese already had an African and East Indian empire which had begun to pass its peak. Magellan's expedition had circled the globe. Da Gama and Francis Xavier had carried trade and Christianity to India, the Spice Islands, and Japan. The Azores were a familiar Atlantic outpost. Pinzón and Cabral had discovered Brazil. And the Pope had conveniently divided the globe exclusively between Portugal and its major rival Spain. The latter's admirals and conquistadores, following Columbus and Cortez, had invaded the Caribbean, crossed over to the Pacific, conquered Peru and Mexico, and were, by the mid-fifteenth century, rapidly exploiting the mines of Mexico and the silver mountains of Central and South America. The transpacific Manila Galleon was in regular operation, and Coronado had begun his search for the golden cities of Cibola somewhere in the heartland of North America.

Upon all of this England could, for a long time, look only with envy, hoping that by nibbling around the edges of the Spanish and Portuguese empires she would in time become rich enough to discover another Aztec Tenochtitlan or Incan El Dorado or, better still, the sea passage to India by means of which she would gain control of world commerce. For England in the Great Age of Discovery was a poor country, inferior in wealth to the Hanse towns of the Baltic, the League of Augsburg in Central Europe, the Dutch, the Venetians, the Portuguese, and Spain. Whatever national expenditure she made on ships had to be spent on a navy to guard home waters and Channel ports against possible invaders from the Continent.

Still the New World success of Spain—especially the dazzling image of Cortez' conquest and the endless flow of bullion from South and Central America—remained always before the English. Moreover, the desire for material wealth became intertwined with religious strife as Protestant England rightly felt herself ever on the defensive against Catholic Spain. Fear of Spain was generated from many quarters: evidence of internal plots, the possibility of invasion across the Channel, the stirring of Irish revolt, and even, as it turned out, the very real threat of invasion from Spain itself. With wealth went power—the power to defend one's religion, one's commerce, one's self-respect in the marketplaces of the world. Thus competition for economic and political advantage became coupled with ideological motives in the minds of Englishmen. Add to these factors the Renaissance fashion of the gentleman adventurer who quested and competed not for profit alone, but because it was one's role—a role conveniently spelled out in books like Castiglione's *The Book of the Courtier,* imported from Italy, and epitomized in the behavior of Cortez and, later, Raleigh and Drake. These were only a few of the motives and circumstances that impelled the English to enter competition for the New World in the ways that they did.

Because of the lack of real governmental wealth and power, a premium was placed upon the individual adventurer; and so, characteristically, single men or small groups of men ventured out into the unknown. Richard Chancellor, for example, entered Russia from the north at Archangel and established trading relations with Czar Ivan the Terrible in 1553. His successor, Anthony Jenkinson, acting for the Muscovy Company which dates from 1555, traveled from Moscow to the Caspian Sea in 1557, opening trade along the way. Somewhat later, in 1581, the Turkey Company was founded, which in 1592 became the Levant Company. In 1600 the mighty East India Company was created by consent of Queen Elizabeth. These were all joint stock companies or partnerships made up of private individuals who pooled their limited resources and, with the help of a charter obtained from the Crown, gained an English monopoly of trading rights in various parts of the world. The Crown could, of course, supply little besides encouragement, and certainly no protection against foreign rivals.

In addition, rulers, particularly Elizabeth I, invested in private ventures, such as those of Hawkins and Drake, which had for their objectives slaving and plundering on the high seas and illicit trade in the Spanish Caribbean empire. Joint stock companies became the characteristic form of British imperial enterprise. It was this type of company, as represented by the Virginia Company of London and the Massachusetts Bay Company, which at last attempted settlement with such high hopes in North America—very nearly, so it seemed at the time, the only unexploited territory left on the globe.

iii

The earliest years of the colonists' experience in both Virginia and Massachusetts were of crucial importance. Professor Sigmund Diamond, in a brilliant article, has described in detail the process whereby the Company's plantations in Virginia were transformed into a functional colonial society between 1607 and 1624.* In the beginning, he observed, "Virginia was not established as a colony to take its place among the territories governed by the British crown; it was not a state, and properly speaking, it was not a political unit at all. It was property, the property of the Virginia Company of London, and it was established to return a profit to the stockholders of that company." Management of the Company property was under the control of the major shareholders or subscribers who sat in London. Authority to deal with immediate problems in Virginia was delegated to a council of seven gentlemen shareholders who sailed with the first expedition to Jamestown in 1607. These councillors fell out with one another almost immediately, and Captain John Smith, one of their number, made part of the trip to America under arrest. Thus began the first of a series of problems—that of leadership—which rendered the Company's strategy inadequate to meet the conditions of isolation in the New World. Factionalism, incompetence, imperfect grasp of Indian psychology, even the very makeup of the original contingent of settlers—all contributed to starving times and near disaster. The gentlemen on the expedition, who made up a large proportion of the settlers, refused to work even to

* See Sigmund Diamond, "From Organization to Society: Virginia in the Seventeenth Century," *The American Journal of Sociology*, **63**, March 1958, pp. 457–475.

obtain food, and at first the colony was wholly dependent on John Smith's ingenuity in securing food supplies from the Indians. Even elementary sanitation measures did not appeal to the gentlemen, and many died as a result. By the same token, lower orders of beings either had little to occupy their particular talents, such as goldsmithing and perfumery, or else felt scant incentive to work, since in a company-communal system there was no possibility of individual reward.

Under Governor Thomas Dale, Smith's earlier efforts at military organization of the colony were stepped up, and every person had his rigid status in what became an armed camp. Still this failed to stimulate incentive to work, and as time wore on and casualty lists mounted, even the incentive to emigrate from England waned. Convicts risked brutal public execution rather than be deported to the colony; and orphaned streetchildren preferred to beg in the alleys and backwashes of London rather than die of the "bloudie flixe" in the New World.

Thus the Company was gradually forced to alter its plans. Clearly there was no Tenochtitlan or easy gold in Virginia. There was likewise no really encouraging evidence of a passage to India. Hence, what was needed to make the colony pay were plain sturdy farmers who could work the tobacco plantations, rather than ideal Renaissance rakes. And so the Company began granting free land to stockholders, settlers, and even indentured servants, the produce of which was credited to the individual landholder. Company-communalism had very quickly given way to private individualistic enterprise on a relatively broad-based scale. Even further, in 1619, to cope with a widening divergence between the interests of Virginia and those of the London Council, a representative assembly was created. The Assembly had no real powers, since the local governor and the London Council could veto its measures; but it did act as a sounding board for colonial grievances, and it gradually acquired more powers.

The grant of free land, concessions to individualism, and a concomitant rise in social mobility, not to mention the illusion of at least some measure of self-government, greatly stimulated immigration to Virginia. After 1619, thousands poured in. Among the new people were women, and thus a bachelor barracks state became a family-oriented community. The result of all this, as Professor Diamond points out, was to create a series of multiple roles and hence interrelationships for each person. A frontier freeholder was at the same time a planter, a merchant, a politician, a family man, a fighter, or a trader, as the situation demanded. He was also, to some degree, a real estate speculator. The increasing multiplicity of roles for the individual led speedily to the transformation of Virginia from a company to a society with political, economic, and social interests distinct from those of the people back home in London.

This process of subtle transformation did not stop, however, with the dissolution of the Virginia Company in 1624. Even as a Royal Colony with the governor acting under detailed, explicit, and often wildly unrealistic instructions from the Crown and the Privy Council, transformation and development continued at an accelerated pace. The Crown and the Cromwellian government interfered relatively little before 1660. They could not afford to. As a consequence, the governors came to be held at bay, for the most part, by the leading colonial factions. The gentleman adventurer became the wealthy plantation merchant who took sides in factional disputes within the colonial government, whether as part of the Governor's Council or as a leader in the Assembly. Intrigue continued, and even broke out in spectacular fashion in Bacon's Rebellion in 1676.* If it can be said that the efforts of the Virginia Company to recruit a labor force by means of individual incentives paradoxically brought about the thwarting of its basic aim of carefully controlled economic exploitation and its eventual downfall, it can also be said that a continuation of these policies under Crown rule resulted in even greater frustrations for Britain. Large grants of land to favorites in Stuart times only enhanced the feeling of societal independence and self-interest. Thus the cutting edge of Britain's advance into the New World—individualism—shaped the basic institutions and values of a new society that was to arise in opposition to the mother country.

Except in the work of Professor Bernard Bailyn, the rise of this individualistic societal spirit in the later years of the seventeenth century has been largely neglected.† These developments can be seen, however, in the lives of the important colonial landowners and merchants. The chief characteristic of latter-day Virginia seems to have been the failure to bring commerce under control at a central shipping point. Jamestown had been a miserable failure in this respect, and Williamsburg was but a village. Consequently great landowners saw to their own needs and dealt directly with agents or factors in England. Political, economic, and family connections, not to mention their own holdings in Virginia, gave them great power and a feeling of independence from the local authorities. It also made them feel more than ever like Englishmen and hence equal if not superior to their friends, relatives, and agents in the mother country. Isolation cut two ways. It left a man free to bypass local

---

* Bacon's Rebellion was a "popular" uprising in Virginia led by Nathaniel Bacon. It arose over the question of governmental support for defense against the Indians, but it became a struggle between frontier farmers and the landed Tidewater gentlemen, who were led by Governor William Berkeley. See below, pp. 133–138.

† See Bernard Bailyn, "Politics and Social Structure in Virginia," in James Martin Smith, ed., *Seventeenth Century America* (Chapel Hill, N.C., University of North Carolina Press for the Institute of Early American History and Culture, 1959), pp. 90–115.

government if he chose to, and it also left him free to ignore, for long periods of time, regulations from the mother country. And yet, paradoxically, the latter-day seventeenth-century Virginian used this isolation or freedom to join enthusiastically in the worldwide network of commerce, and even to participate in the cosmopolitan culture that was emerging toward the end of the century. The great "isolated" families of Virginia became most emphatically part of a cosmopolitan world empire.

Attempts by the Crown to deal with the suddenly arising problem of empire proved to be disastrously narrow and reactionary. The Navigation Act of 1660, which attempted to bring colonial trade under control to the advantage of the mother country, only stimulated smuggling and other illicit activities, not to mention resentment from the depression that followed—the first genuine depression in American history. In dealing with the problem of empire, Britain proved to be hardly equal to her new cosmopolitan role, and instead adopted reactionary, provincial policies (see documents, Part II) that looked backward to the old days of struggle against Spain instead of forward to a modern powerful Atlantic community. She was guided by the only precedents available in the face of a new and truly revolutionary situation full of positive potential. A rigidity akin to that which ultimately defeated the Spanish imperialists set in.

iv

In New England a similar general process took place, but with very significant specific differences which are bound up with the phenomenon of Puritanism. From an initial planting of rigidly defined, isolated model religious communities (both at Plymouth and, ten years later, at Massachusetts Bay), the tendency was toward increased individualism, secular economic interests, and a juncture with the broadened currents of European thought. Nothing that the leadership in Massachusetts could do in any way seriously impeded these trends. Instead the reverse happened: the Massachusetts Bay and Plymouth communitarians found themselves increasingly anachronistic, forced into constant redefinition, and ultimately ignored. Yet in some ways it was their own revolutionary doctrines which brought about their downfall.

Like the Virginians, the people of Plymouth Plantation and Massachusetts Bay arrived in America not as members of a recognized colony, but rather as members of a company—the Virginia Company of London, and later the Massachusetts Bay Company. Of these two companies the most interesting in terms of lasting effects was the Massachusetts Bay Company, whose major migration to the New World took place in 1630. The leadership structure was similar to that of the Virginians in that the Governor and Councillors in Massachusetts were shareholders in the Company. They owed debts to other stockholders back in England. But there was a significant difference between their position and that of the Virginians. Thanks to the fact that the Massachusetts Bay people brought their charter with them aboard ship to the New World, the headquarters of the Company was, in effect, in Massachusetts Bay. This circumstance gave the settlers great initial independence, which they meant to take advantage of in building, as Peter Bulkeley and John Winthrop put it, "a city set upon a hill," which would be a model religious community offering an example of God-fearing right living to a corrupt world. In this way, by means of example, they hoped to bring about a Puritan revolution. And since someday they meant to carry these principles back to Europe, they carefully avoided any suggestion of a complete break with the Church of England, calling themselves instead "Non-Separating Congregationalists."

The Puritan enterprise was, from the beginning, company-communal in proportion to shares of stock held, though the leadership was largely made up of rather well-to-do but sober gentlemen adventurers like Governor John Winthrop. There was, in addition, a high percentage of Oxford and Cambridge men, and hence the radical Protestant clergy was well represented. Unlike the Virginians, the Puritans, almost from the outset, were able to recruit large numbers of people who fled from religious persecution. Moreover, though the enterprise was company-communal, the doctrine of the "Christian calling" demanded that people, under fear of God's wrath, maximize their talents through hard work which would contribute to the prosperity of the whole community. The leaders, and indeed the whole congregation, had a bargain or "covenant" with God to lead good lives and create a model community free of sin. If they kept this "covenant," they could expect salvation in the hereafter. If not, God's wrath would fall upon them in Old Testament fashion. Individual prosperity was a sign of maximizing one's talents and, presumably, of God's favor for doing so. Very soon, individual achievement began to outweigh the progress of the whole community. Interests, both material and spiritual, turned inward, and the Puritan leadership began to be forced to shift its ground. Consequently the history of seventeenth-century New England Puritanism is the confusing, but fascinating, story of the constantly changing accommodation of the Puritan dream to American and world reality.

Given the constantly changing postures of American Puritanism, it is doubtful whether anyone will ever completely understand its true nature, despite the monumental efforts of the late Perry Miller. The Puritans were Calvinists and wished, of course, to "purify" the Church of England—to strip down ceremonial practices, to rid themselves of hierarchy and ecclesiastical rank and privilege, to elevate the congregation, which, in turn, would elect or "call" the minister to it. They believed in original sin, predestination, divine providence, God's irresistible grace, and, in general, a Platonic view of the world which saw all nature as simply projected images of the mind of an all-powerful God.

It was a relatively simple doctrine, but it soon grew exceedingly complex. As more and more questions arose, the supplying of answers necessitated the creation of a whole new theology to replace the one the Puritans were in the process of discarding. A new world view based on Ramus' logic (a variety of Plato's dichotomous logic which rejected the Aristotelian syllogism) was adopted, and inevitably disputes arose over the details of its interpretation, the final resolutions of which usually required resort to "common sense" or empirical observation. Nice questions concerning the determination of the saved and the damned were constantly arising. And each Puritan lived out his life in endless self-examination in an effort to see if he were of the elect or not. If looking inward did not help, then one looked outward at nature for secret signs and indications. One anxiously read the emblems and symbols of the universe.

Out of uncertainty and disputation arose heresies and misguided enthusiasms. Arminianism was one; this was the idea of the Dutchman, Jacob Arminius, that you could work your way to salvation, as it were, with good deeds. It bore an ironic relationship to the covenant, since the doing of good deeds meant that you were keeping your end of the bargain with God. It was, however, anathema to the "orthodox" Puritan because it implied that an individual could somehow exercise control over his God, and hence conflicted with the dogma of predestination.

Antinomianism was another heresy. It was the idea that God in his infinite grace especially inspired select individuals with insight into his purposes and plans, including their own destiny. This smacked of the Catholic doctrine of sainthood. Moreover, it disturbed the stability of the theocratic order, and it could be misguided. It was contemptuously labeled "enthusiasm." Anne Hutchinson, one of its foremost exponents, was banished from Massachusetts.

The Puritan generally walked a tightrope of uncertainty between the awful chasms of Arminianism and Antinomianism, content to follow church and civil authorities and to depend on God's mercy as expressed through the vague reciprocity of the covenant theology.

It is not surprising that, as time wore on and internal religious disputes mounted (as in the case of Roger Williams),* the Puritan citizen thought less and less in terms of grace, election, and damnation and tended to concentrate on the hopeful possibilities of the calling. Meanwhile the political

---

* Roger Williams (1603–1683) was a Puritan rebel who came to Massachusetts Bay in 1631. Intolerant of every man's purity but his own, Williams caused so much trouble in the Bay Colony that he was eventually forced to flee to Rhode Island, where he became the leader of that colony. As Governor of the colony, Williams became extremely tolerant of all religious sects, saw eye to eye with the Cromwellian "united front" position, and befriended the Indian, from whom, he always maintained, the Massachusetts Puritans had stolen their land.

base of Massachusetts Bay broadened only slightly with the addition of some 109 freeholders as voters in 1631. While disputation rent the church, the citizen frustrated by the twin mysteries of theology and politics began to concentrate on commerce, trade, and material well-being.

In 1648 the church was forced to clarify and restate its doctrine in the Cambridge Platform. By 1662 the indifference of the younger generation ("teenagers" then as now) forced agreement by the elders to a "Half-way Covenant" designed to hold the church together. The children of the elect could now be baptized church members, but still could not receive the Lord's Supper unless they could prove genuine "sainthood" through a carefully documented religious experience.

Puritan commerce expanded. Sea captains, following their calling, ventured over the oceans and became more and more attached to the idea of wealth. In the course of their duties, some went to perdition at places like Jamaica, Barbados, or Surinam and other forbidden Gomorrahs. Little by little, New Englanders established complicated trading relationships with the West Indian Islands, Nova Scotia, Virginia, and other parts of the British empire. A triangular trade developed between these outlying points, New England, and Britain itself. And as this trade advanced, the New England merchants were forced to employ factors or agents in Britain, purchase British insurance for their cargoes, borrow British money, and maintain a "lobby" in the home government, whether Puritan or Royalist, that would protect them against arbitrary turns in mercantilist policy. Some married into important families to gain both wealth and influence.

In North America proper, Puritan pioneers moved west into the Connecticut River Valley, or south to New Haven and Providence Plantations, breaking off from the tightly knit towns and communities of the Bay. Timber cutters in New Hampshire's remote forests eventually supplied the major proportion of masts for the British fleet, and they did business within the empire without instructions from the Massachusetts Bay leaders. Individual enterprise and independence born of isolation prevailed, and the sturdy values of the Puritan model slowly but surely turned against it.

At the same time, back in England, the Puritans had triumphed in a great revolution at home under Oliver Cromwell. But they had prevailed not in terms of exclusiveness, but by means of what today might be called a "united front" against the Church of England. General tolerance among the splintered Protestant sects held sway in the New Model Army and the Cromwell government. Puritan power at home depended on it. The exclusivism, the rigidities, and the niceties of New England orthodoxy (however shifting and uncertain that was) became anachronistic. In Cromwell's words, the outposts of New England were "cold, poor, and useless." Like Australian marsupials stranded after the collapse of the land bridge, the New England orthodox congregationalists were left to breed alone, unaided, and to a very great extent ignored until the Restoration.

Then, with the Stuart Restoration in 1660, New England became the subject of repeated scrutiny by royal commissioners. Customs collectors, hostile to Puritan interests, began to do more than their duty in enforcing the series of Navigation Acts. In 1684 the Massachusetts charter was revoked and a royal government for New England was established under Sir Edmund Andros. This precipitated a revolt by the orthodoxy which resulted in the imprisonment of Andros and several royal officials. The imprisonment was, however, of short duration because the orthodoxy was slowly but surely losing its power—in the Empire and among its own people.

Given the shifts of individual interest, the changing homeland scene, and increasing internal doctrinal strife, the Puritans' holy mission was on the verge of being aborted. Orthodox or establishment ministers thundered jeremiad sermons warning of doom and damnation while at the same time they again shifted ground and composed the milder doctrine of "preparation for salvation." Still this was not enough, and the last weapon for enforcing church-communal discipline was employed—the witchcraft trials of 1692.

The witchcraft trials were the last stand of seventeenth-century New England orthodox Puritanism. Whether generated out of a cynical desire to hold the orthodoxy together, or out of a genuine feeling that in such a wicked, worldly, depressing time the Devil must indeed be abroad doing his work, the trials were a shameful failure, and Samuel Sewall, one of the presiding magistrates, had the courage to acknowledge them as such.

But what, after all, had happened to the Puritan dream in terms of historical experience? In New England, Puritan leadership had itself been isolated. The Mathers lost their hold on Harvard College and the intellectual establishment. The rich merchants, and much of the rank-and-file citizenry, farmers as well as the intellectuals, had joined the cosmopolitan community and had been carried along with the profound revolutions in commerce, Newtonian science, Lockean psychology, continental nature philosophy and materialistic individualism. As Boston, along with Philadelphia to the south, were to become the second cities in the emerging British Empire, so too were New England's people joining the world once again. Like the Virginians, they assumed direct relations with Britain in matters of business, church, family, education, and culture. The Puritan oligarchy, with its dreams, its models, its conservative accommodations and eventual reaction, had become, since the days of Cromwell, largely irrelevant.

1 / ENGLAND AND THE NEW WORLD: DREAMS, IMAGES, AND STRATEGIES

INTRODUCTION

The intellectual explosion of the Age of Discovery, which altered the knowledge and thought, if not the values, of Europe, was not confined to what might today be called "the intellectuals." A great many different kinds of men were involved, ranging from rulers and statesmen to cartographers, yeomen, court dandies, master mariners, religious zealots, and common pirates. Thus the historian who seeks to understand the age must turn to what seems like an infinite variety of sources for information—books, official documents, letters, maps, artifacts, and pictures of the time—weighing each of them as carefully as possible to determine their relevance in building up a true picture of what it must have been like to live in those times. He must also do this with an eye to fashioning a picture which has "shape" or "form": that is, an honest historical interpretation which yields generalizations useful—as great art is "useful"—to men of any age. The materials in the section which follows illustrate the difficult and special problems confronting the intellectual historian for whom almost every source is in some way relevant. They are intended to do no more than suggest the variety of approaches via the sources that it is possible to use in building up the kind of interpretation envisioned in the first part of the general introduction.

The focal article by Professor Howard Mumford Jones on "The Colonial Impulse" concentrates on one special part of the total picture of the times, but a shrewdly selected part which gets at the motivating forces behind the English drive for colonization. Professor Jones's choice of subject has enabled him to survey the vast range of existing promotional or advertising literature of the day which was designed to persuade people, to appeal either in print or by word of mouth to all walks of English life. The information which his study yields tells us a great deal about the hopes, dreams, objectives, prejudices, self-images, and limited knowledge of the English people of the time and their leaders. It also alerts us to the necessity of considering the authorship of the various kinds of appeals. Metaphorically speaking, if the New World and its possibilities are being described by a group not unlike the blind men who described the elephant, then clearly it matters whether the observer is in proximity to trunk, tail, or tusk—whether he is engaged in buying, selling, or condemning the beast.

The variety of sources open to the intellectual historian of the period is further indicated by the series of documents here included as supplements to Professor Jones's article. They include hearsay accounts of almost forgotten discoveries, geographical treatises, stirring tales of epic adventure, legal documents, promotional letters, scientific and emotional eyewitness observations, and opinions as to the proper course of broad national policy. Assuming their authenticity, the historian must assess the validity, accuracy, and utility of each. It should be evident that the documents have been ordered in a series which tends to reinforce the interpretation offered in the general introduction—namely, that the English adventurers approached the New World with a number of conflicting, often very complex, dreams and preconceptions that were sharply modified by actual experience.

INTERPRETATION

Howard Mumford Jones is Professor Emeritus in English at Harvard University. He received the Pulitzer Prize in 1965 for O Strange New World, a broad study of the impact of Elizabethan thought on American civilization. The selection printed here is from an article Professor Jones wrote in preparation for his book.

HOWARD MUMFORD JONES, *The Colonial Impulse*

1. THE KINDS OF "PROMOTION" LITERATURE

The drive to persuade settlers to emigrate to the New World left as its record the so-called "promotion literature" which accompanied English colonization in North America. This literature is not simple. It exhibits a wide variety of appeals, which varied from decade to decade and which occasionally contradicted each other. This changing emphasis was a function sometimes of international politics, sometimes of real or fancied economic and social alterations in the British Isles. To this aspect of promotion literature the attention of historians has frequently been directed, but perhaps less attention has been paid to the social and occupational distribution of the arguments in the propaganda. These varied with the class and status of the group to which the appeal was made. If arguments were sometimes contradictory, the contradiction was inevitable. Reasons which might move statesmen were not necessarily identical with those advanced by an explorer who wanted backing for some hazardous enterprise; and the interests of noble or mercantile investors in a joint-stock colonization scheme were not the same as those of the actual colonists. Ministers talked about the plantations from one point of view; military strategists from another; politicians from a third. The theories of an arm-chair writer, even if he were as well informed as the elder Hakluyt, differed *toto caelo* from the practical needs set forth by hard-bitten heads of actual settlements, like Captain John Smith. Moreover, whatever the power of the printed or the written word might be among the middle and upper

Howard Mumford Jones, "The Colonial Impulse: an Analysis of the 'Promotion' Literature of Colonization," *Proceedings of the American Philosophical Society*, **90**, May 1946, pp. 131–161. Reprinted with cuts as indicated by ellipses, and without the 38 footnotes and reference notes, by permission of The Viking Press, Inc., New York. This article became the basis for Chapter V of *O Strange New World*, © 1964 by Howard Mumford Jones.

classes, it must not be forgotten that the majority of Englishmen could not read—a fact which calls for severe scrutiny of certain hasty inferences drawn concerning this propaganda. Finally, it is important to remember that one of the principal purposes of "promotion literature" was to combat the flood of slander and malicious gossip about the colonies, of which almost every important writer complains.

Promotion literature falls into several categories which it is useful to distinguish. (1) The most impressive genre is the formal treatise on colonization, of which there were in general two sorts: treatises which, anticipating settlement, theorized from inference or from the example of other nations about the character of the proposed colony; and treatises which drew general conclusions from English experience, once it had begun. The first type is mostly a sixteenth-century product, the second mainly comes from the epoch of the Stuarts. The one is well represented by the admirable expository prose of Gilbert's *Discourse* (1576) and Hakluyt's *Discourse of Western Planting* (1584), both addressed directly to government. The most illustrious example of the later type is probably Bacon's *Of Plantations* (1625). (2) One may associate with the formal treatise the general prefaces or other introductory matter to collections of voyages or even to works dealing with a specific expedition or colony. Of this kind of essay the prefaces to the various volumes of the second edition of the *Principal Navigations* are notable; and the introductory pages of *The Golden Fleece* (1626) and of John Hammond's *Leah and Rachel* (1656) show how perfunctory the form became.

The great bulk of "promotion literature," however, is related to some particular enterprise. Propaganda for such a plantation might begin with a third type of writing, (3) the official request to government for a patent or with the patent itself, both published in order to persuade "adventurers" to invest and settlers to emigrate. Accompanying the official documents or published separately might be (4) the report of the exploratory voyage or voyages, which usually stressed the economic plenitude of the new settlement, the excellence of its climate, the healthiness of its situation, and the gentleness of the natives. Such a report might be merely the log of the voyage, or it might be, as in the classical instance of Hariot's *Virginia* (1588), a formal exposition of the potential benefits of the country as well. Once settlement had begun, the proprietor or the supporting company authorized, directly or indirectly, (5) the circulation of material likely to induce emigration, such as the "Coppie of a letter from Virginia, dated 22d of June, 1607, from the Councell their to the Councell of Virginia here in England," written to

quicken those good spirritts wch haue alreadie bestowed themselues heere, and to put life into such dead understandings or beleefs that muste firste see and feele the wombe of o^r labour and this land before they will entertaine anie good hope of vs or of the land. . . .

Such letters had at once an official sanction and a personal tang. Pamphlets like Robert Johnson's *Nova Britannia,* dedicated to Sir Thomas Smith of the Council for Virginia, were printed at least at the instigation of the company, and one like *A Trve Declaration of the estate of the Colonie in Virginia* (1610) was a direct official utterance intended, as the title page indicates, to be a "confutation of such scandalous reports as haue tended to the disgrace of so worthy an enterprise." Among publications directly emanating from authority must also be reckoned (6) the official laws and the regulations concerning the acquirement of land, both being intended to assure the settler of the morality and good order of the enterprise. Perhaps, however, the best known form of company-inspired propaganda was (7) the official sermon, such as Robert Gray or William Crashaw preached for the Virginia company. The occasion of these was some such event as "the said Lord Generall His leaue taking of England his Natiue Countrey, and departure for Virginia." Such discourses appealed to the serious middle class, and by the atmosphere of religious respectability which they threw over colonization helped to combat wild talk in the taverns and the evil tales of returning seamen. Sometimes the official origins of a particular sermon or pamphlet were disguised, as in the case of *A Relation of The successefull beginnings of the Lord Baltemore's Plantation in Mary-Land* (1634), which, purporting to be compounded from "certaine Letters written from thence, by some of the Aduenturers to their friends in *England*," failed to reveal that it was put together by Cecilius Calvert, Lord Baltimore, from correspondence sent him by Leonard and George Calvert.

Emanating neither directly from the company or the proprietor nor from any other official source, another variety of "promotion literature" is what may be called (8) the personal report by an interested observer. The writer may or may not have been a colonist, just as he may or may not have had a financial stake in the welfare of the plantation but, because he reports as an individual, the note of personal experience gives special force to his narrative. Thus the fascinating *A true reportory of the wracke, and redemption of Sir Thomas Gates Knight; upon, and from the Ilands of the Bermudas; his comming to Virginia, and the estate of that Colonie then, and after, under the government of the Lord La Warre* by William Strachey contains much material which a company might conceivably have wished to suppress, though the general drift of the narrative favors a strong colonial establishment. Edward Winslow's *Good News from New England: or a true Relation of things very remarkable at the Plantation of Plymouth* . . . (1624) is both a personal narrative and a contribution to the general theory of colonization, written "to discourage such as, with too great lightness," desire to emigrate. And of course many of the writings of Captain John Smith fall into this general category.

Although the style and manner of "promotion literature" vary from document to document and decade to decade, certain general observations can be made regarding its literary quality. It is at once a literature of action and a literature of persuasion directed to a non-literary audience, and, being such, it was cut off from the vagaries of Euphuism or the tortuousness of Jacobean experimental prose. Its style usually remains within the central tradition of English prose, the intent being to tell a plain tale simply or to present argument in its clearest form. Being a literature of action, it is also in the main removed from the introspective and brooding quality of certain Elizabethan and Jacobean traditions. However impressive the appeal to morality, religion, patriotism, or profit, the documents exhibit no curiosity about individual psychology. Even in New England one finds no subjective Hamlets, and in Virginia the weak complainings of Edward Maria Wingfield startle one because of the contrast between his sick and lonely vanity and the rugged strength of his companions. For this is a masculine literature. No woman recorded her impressions of the hardships of the sea, the beauty and horror of the woods, the "civilitie" of the Indians or the hardships of building a colonial home at Roanoke or Jamestown. It is not until deep into the seventeenth century that feminine comment on American topics begins to appear. "Promotion literature" likewise mirrors a world without childhood. And finally, except for the allure of land and riches which it holds out to all comers, it is a literature which one would search in vain to find out what the indentured servant thought and felt. "Promotion literature" seldom or never falls below the level of the middle class, to which it was in the main addressed. This audience conditioned the quality of its stylistic appeal.

2. THE APPEAL TO VIRTU

What are the chief themes of "promotion literature"? If it be true, in Williamson's words, that the first thirty years of the seventeenth century represent "an outburst of colonizing energy which renders the Elizabethan achievements insignificant in comparison," an Elizabethan atmosphere envelopes the dawn of American settlement-making. It is therefore to be expected that among the principal appeals made to the nobility and the gentry is the appeal to Renaissance *virtù*—to that combination of a well-rounded activity with the promise of immortal fame which is in part heroic and in part polite. The heroic note was early sounded, the promise of fame was early given. Explorers and colonizers sometimes wrote (or were written about) as if they were eternizing their own courage. Confronted by the perils of the Northwest Passage, Frobisher, according to George Best,

> determined and resolved with himselfe to go make full proofe thereof, and to accomplish or bring true certificate of the truth, or els never to returne againe, knowing this to be the only thing of the world that was left yet undone, whereby a notable minde might be made famous and fortunate.

To discover the Northwest Passage, wrote Ramusius in his account of Sebastian Cabot,

> would be the most glorious, and of most importance of all other that can be imagined to make his name great, and fame immortall, to all ages to come, farre more then can be done by any of all these great troubles and warres which dayly are used in Europe among the miserable Christian people.

Only he could succeed as a colonial leader, wrote Edward Hayes, whose "motives be derived from a vertuous & heroycall minde," and like many another commentator Hayes attributed the many failures to unworthy ideals—colonizing is "an action doubtlesse not to be intermedled with base purposes." . . .

These were general observations, but the aura of Renaissance greatness settled around particular individuals as well. The earliest such case is perhaps that of Sir Humphrey Gilbert who, before Drake, was *par excellence* the model of colonial "magnanimity." Of him George Gascoigne wrote that one must

> highly prayse the noble minde and courage of the Author [i. e., Gilbert], who more respectinge the publique profit that might ensue by this *Discoverie*, then the delicate life of a Courtier, well countenanced and favoured both by his Prince and all the Nobilitie, had prepared his owne bodie to abide the malice of the windes and waves, and was even ready to have perfourmed the voyage in proper person, if he had not beene by her Majestie otherwise commanded. . . .

This compliment was accompanied by a "prophetical sonnet":

> Men praise *Columbus* for the passing skil
> Which he declared, in *Cosmographie*,
> And nam'd him first (as yet we cal him stil)
> The 2. *Neptune*, dubd by dignity.
> *Americus Vesputius*, for his paine,
> *Neptune* the 3. ful worthely was named,
> And *Magellanus*, by good right did gaine,
> *Neptune* the 4. ful fitly to be famed.
> But al those three, and al the world beside,
> Discovered not, a thing of more emprice,
> Then in this booke, is learnedly describe.
> By vertue of my worthie friendes device.
> Yf such successe, to him (as them) then fall,
> *Neptune* the 5. we justly may him call.

. . . Other explorers and colonial leaders were likewise draped in the glory of Renaissance fame. Having reference to the second voyage to Guiana,

Chapman said that Raleigh was one of

> you patrician spirits that refine
> Your flesh to fire, and issue like a flame
> On brave endeavours, knowing that in them
> The tract of heaven in morn-like glory opens.

A pamphlet declared that Hawkins

> returned home the second time, laden with as much wealth and honor, as euer any
> had done before him, and to this braue heroicall scale of Discouery, had now added
> diuers noble and spacious Stayres . . . you may see how euen from the infancy of our
> English trauell, euery man hath had a noble ambition, and most probable assurances
> of good hope to attaine a height of honour and wealth, which yet rests vnattained. . . .
> [What is fitter for a king than] the very toppe and Garland of All Heroyicall actions?

Such men, said Michael Drayton, are "our Argonauts," whose "great Mindes"
descry "farre Regions," and in the nineteenth song of the endless *Poly-Olbion*
he rhymed the immortality of Frobisher, Davis, Gilbert, Drake, Raleigh, Amadas,
Barlow, Grenville, and others. . . . Thus the literary men praised "the famous
ranke of our Sea-searching men."

Classical examples were to be emulated, or were surpassed:

> These and the like Heroicall intents and attempts of our Princes, our Nobilitie, our
> Clergie, & our Chivalry, I have in the first place exposed and set foorth to the view of
> this age, with the same intention that the old Romans set up in wax in their palaces
> the Statuas or images of their worthy ancestors. . . . Not that the sayd wax or por-
> traiture had any . . . force at all in it selfe, but that by the remembring of their woorthy
> actes, that flame was kindled in their noble breasts, and could never be quenched,
> untill such time as their owne valure had equalled the fame and glory of their
> progenitors.

So wrote the great historian of the English voyages. Sir Humphrey Gilbert was
but one among many who held up the "experience of Alexander the great,
in the time of his conquest of India" for emulation. In 1609 Robert Johnson
concluded his *Nova Britannia* by saying:

> . . . it would be my griefe and sorrow, to be exempted from the company of so many
> honourable minded men, and from this enterprise, tending to so many good endes,
> and then which, I truely thinke this day, there is not a worke of more excellent hope
> vnder the Sun, and farre excelling (all circumstances wayed) those Noble deedes of
> *Alexander, Hercules,* and those heathen Monarks, for which they were deemed Gods
> among their posterity.

And when in 1612 Englishmen seemed to be failing in their support of Virginia, Johnson reminded them of

> that worthie Ramane [*sic*] Scipio, preserver of his Countrie, which when all the Romanes in that sudden feare of Hannibals approach threw off their arms to take themselves to flight, drew out his sword and staied their running out, and ruine of the citie.

... Let the English imitate the Romans and send out colonies. Crashaw implored his audience to remember, from the example of the companions of Romulus and Remus, that "a harder course of life, wanting pleasures," "a strict forme of gouernement," and "seuere discipline" were essential to the creation of a new nation. ...

To the sanction of classical history was added the sanction of religious fame. "Whole Decads," wrote Sir Robert Gordon, "are filled with discoveries there, and volumes with their actions of plantation"; and of the "renowned *Drake*," the "memorable *Candisch*," Raleigh, Amadas, White, Grenville and others he prophesied that "all [Christian] after-ages" would "eternize" their courage as a "shining brightnesse." The preacher Robert Gray said in 1609 that

> The name, memorie and actions of those men doe only liue in the records of eternitie, which haue emploied their best endeuours in such vertuous and honourable enterprises, as haue aduanced the glorie of God, and inlarged the glorie and wealth of their countrie;

wherefore the fame of the Virginia Company must last "so long as the Sunne and Moone endureth."

Such language is not mere rhetorical ornamentation. Captain John Smith, to be sure, lamented the presence of incompetent "gentlemen" at Jamestown, but it is easy to become bemused by this famous passage, and in truth, if the colonies were to have leaders, it was felt that they must come from the nobility and the gentry. As Ralph Lane wrote Walsingham in 1585, the colony

> has undertaken with a good company to remain there, resolute rather to lose their lives "than to defer possession" of so noble a kingdom to the Queen, their country, and their noble patron Sir Walter Ralegh. ...

and this concept of *noblesse oblige* demanded men who could understand the force of Smith's appeal to leadership:

> Such actions haue ever since the worlds beginning beene subject to such accidents, and every thing of worth is found full of difficulties: but nothing so difficult as to establish a common wealth so farre remote from men and meanes; and where mens mindes are so vntoward as neither do well themselues, nor suffer others.

Only the patriotic magnanimity of the nobles of Rome and Athens, or of the Goths and Vandals, thought "Orpheus Junior," had created colonies in the past, for these leaders

> forsooke their owne habitations, to accompany the meaner sort of people, and to lead them into forraigne Countries, who without their personall presence, would haue staied at home like Drones. . . .

. . . Smith himself well knew the need of securing capable leaders from the upper classes. Lords and gentlemen, he says,

> haue imployed great paines and large expence in laying the foundation of this State, wherein much hath beene buried vnder ground, yet some thing hath sprung vp, and giuen you a taste of your adventures. Let no difficulties alter your noble intentions . . . [and let] valiant and generous spirits, personall posessors of these new-found Territories . . . banish . . . Cowardise, covetousnes, iealousies, and idlenes.

He could utter propaganda about their usefulness, saying that "30 or 40 of such voluntary Gentlemen would doe more in a day then 100 of the rest that must bee prest to it by compulsion," and he could pen a paragraph designed to appeal to Renaissance "magnanimity":

> Who can desire more content, that hath small meanes; or but only his merit to advance his fortune [i. e., younger sons], then to tread and plant that ground hee hath purchased by the hazard of his life? If he haue but the taste of virtue and magnanimitie, what to such a minde can bee more pleasant, then planting and building a foundation for his Posteritie, gotte from the rude earth, by Gods blessing and his owne industrie, without preiudice to any? If hee haue any graine of faith or zeale in Religion, what can he doee less hurtfull to any: or more agreeable to God, then to seeke to conuert those poore Saluages to know Christ, and humanitie, whose labors with discretion will triple requite thy charge and paines? What so truely sutes with honour and honestie, as discouering things vnknowne? erecting Townes, peopling Countries, informing the ignorant, reforming things vniust, teaching virtue; and gaine to our Natiue mother-countrie a kingdom to attend her: finde imployment for those that are idle, because they know not what to doe: so farre from wronging any, as to cause Posteritie to remember thee; and remembring thee, euer honour that remembrance with praise? . . .

3. THE RIGHT TO EMPIRE

By the time Jamestown was founded there were probably very few Englishmen who did not understand that, if England was to survive, Spain must be met and matched in the New World. The literature of colonizing, like the literature of Elizabethan England, is filled with examples of the cruelty of the Spaniards towards the English, their ill-treatment of the Indians, their greed, their treachery, and, what amounted to the same thing from the English point of view, their Catholicism. Arguments directed towards the larger strategy of statesmanship, however, were presumably directed mainly to government or to influential leaders—great lords, captains, entrepreneurs, the wealthy, prominent clergymen, and the like. It seems appropriate therefore to turn to the political motives for colonization. Hatred and distrust of Spain, however powerful as emotional forces, did not constitute a policy. How to use colonization as a check on the most powerful country in the world was the problem set before promotion literature.

The theory that an English colonial empire could be built up to balance the empires of other European powers radically altered the whole concept of plantations. In the earlier literature the idea of a settlement meant the seizure of a river-mouth or other excellent harbor as a fortified trading post. The problem of over-running the interior was held in abeyance. Thus the directions furnished by Richard Hakluyt of the Middle Temple for Frobisher's expedition advise a "first Seate" on the seacoast with a view to protecting his vessels, creating a naval base and controlling trade with the interior. An interesting corollary of this theory is the insistence upon cordial relations with the Indians in order that trade may go forward. Earlier attempts at settlement—for example, at Newfoundland—were sometimes intended only to control fishing. By the time of issuing letters patent to Sir Thomas Gates (and others) for Jamestown, however, settlers are instructed to move inland a hundred miles, if they can, and emphasis is laid upon exploring a wide interior area, as the work of John Smith and others demonstrates. Moreover, the necessity of thinking of colonies in political terms meant that the notion of a plantation as a private enterprise had to be modified, so that in the minds of some theorists, it became the business of the state rather than that of "adventurers," to support the colony.

The example of other nations, and notably of Spain, had its profound effect, as a variety of passages shows. The Spanish and Portuguese empires, wrote Peckham, should

> minister just cause of incouragement to our Countreymen, not to account it so hard and difficult a thing for the subjects of this noble realme of England, to discover, people, plant and possesse the like goodly lands and rich countreys not farre from us . . . [and] not a little animate and encourage us to looke out and adventure abroad, understanding what large Countreys and Islands the Portugals with their small number have within these few yeeres discovered, peopled and planted. . . .

Portugal, he thought, was not bigger than "three shires of England," Spain was no more populous than the realm of Elizabeth. Hakluyt argued that "our true and syncere relligion" ought to spread at least as readily as Iberian Catholicism, and was fearful lest the Spaniards or the French "seize and fortify" before the English got around to it. . . . If the English suffered disasters, the fact that the Spaniards had overcome similar disasters was turned into an expansionist argument. In sum, for "inlarging their bounds, in truth their [the Spaniards'] praise is duly given, and well deserved," wrote Johnson, "and it may justly serve to stirre us up by all our means to put off . . . reproachfull censures." But the only way to rival Spain was to cease thinking of colonies as mere trading posts and to begin thinking about them in terms of empire. Thus it was that the imperial spirit was born.

Despite occasional "little England" arguments, an expansionist note was sounded in promotion literature while the economic struggle with Spain fused with the political conflict. If Columbus and Cortes had in their time been laughing stocks, they could now (1583), wrote Peckham, be considered "neither . . . fantasticke nor vainely imagined." . . . The queen's grant of Virginia to Raleigh was "for uniting in more perfect league and amitie, of such Countryes, landes, and territories so to be possessed and inhabited as aforesayd with our Realmes of England and Ireland," and other colonial patents ran to the same effect. Promotion literature is filled with the casuistry of imperialism: perhaps Johnson's *Nova Britannia* is as characteristic as any. Directed against the "blind diffidence of our English natures, which laugh to scorne the name of *Virginia*," it argues that "diuine testimonies" require the English to fulfill a manifest destiny. . . . Thus to increase British territory seemed to Sir Robert Gordon of Lochinvar a participation in the "mysticall bodie politicke," demanding those "constant resolutions," that "incomparable honour" which the Spanish and Portuguese had displayed.

The vigor with which English writers from Thorne downward denied the right of Spain to the North American continent is equalled only by their insistence upon the prior right of English discovery. "The landes, countries, and territories of this parte of America which we call ours, and by the name of Virginia, or Nova Britannia," wrote Strachey, "being carefully laid out (of purpose) to avoid offence unto certaine boundes, and regions" cannot interfere with Spain. But more characteristic was the argument of Gilbert, Hakluyt, and Strachey himself that British discoverers, beginning with Madoc, had first set foot on the mainland, from which, by their own logic, the Spaniards were to be excluded. Edward Hayes held that God, not permitting the Spanish or the French to colonize North America, had preserved it for the realm of England, Hayes' countrymen being

> now arrived into the time by God prescribed of their vocation, if ever their calling unto the knowledge of God may be expected.

Even the Indians, by receiving the English kindly, recognized the providential quality of English imperialism. . . .

But it was not alone by the conquest of North American soil that Spain was to be checked. The Spanish navy had to be beaten, and Spanish trade with both the Indies had to be reduced or centered on England. For both these purposes a far-flung colonial establishment seemed necessary. Because, as Johnson wrote, "Experience hath lately taught vs by some of our neighbour Prouinces, how exceedingly it mounts the State of a Commonwealth, to put forth Nauigation . . . into all parts and corners of the world," almost all the writers agreed that the New World was an inexhaustible source of naval supplies. One citation will do as well as twenty:

> And if an Iland needs woodden Wals to secure it against others, to enrich it from others, Virginia offers her service herein, and will looke so much more cheerefully on you, how much more you shall disburthen her in this kind: yea, as England hath wooed and visited Virginia, so herein Virginia will be glad and rejoyce to visit England, in her there-built ships, and to dwell here with us in thence-brought Timbers, and esteeme her selfe advanced to adorne our Townes, and take view of our Pomps and Spectacles.

Every part of the New World, from the Straits of Magellan to Labrador, had its eager advocates, who alleged that a favorite region offered the safest base for a conquering navy.

> . . . this Countrey lyeth so neere the course which the Spanish ships, that come from *Mexico, Hauona,* and other places of the *West-Indies,* hold in their returne from thence, that they often saile within 190. leagues from the South part thereof,

wrote Whitbourne, arguing that an English plantation on Newfoundland would protect the route from the British Isles to New England, Virginia, and the Bermudas. Others advocated the seizure of naval bases in the West Indies, and some held Jamestown to be the proper center, provided only it was sufficiently well fortified. All agreed, however, on the intimate relation of plantations and an imperial naval policy:

> [Supplies] shall be made within those her Majesty's own dominions, by her own subjects, and brought hither through the ocean, free from the restraint of any other prince: whereby the customs and charges bestowed by our merchants (to the enriching of foreign estates) shall be lessened, and turned to the benefit of her Highness and her deputies in those parts; which also shall deliver our merchants from many troubles and molestations which they now unwillingly endure in our East trades; and shall make us the less to doubt the malice of those States which now we may not offend, lest we should be intercepted of the same provisions, to the weakening of our navy, the most royal defence of this noble realm.

Thus runs a typical paragraph in the Brereton-Hayes *Briefe and True Relation* of 1602, the second edition of which also quoted the "inducements to the liking of the Voyage intended towards Virginia," by "M. Richard Hakluyt the elder," among which one may read:

> By this ordinary trade we may annoy the enemies to Ireland, and succor the Queen's Majesty's friends there and in time we may from Virginia yield them whatsoever commodity they now receive from the Spaniard: and so the Spaniards shall want the ordinary victual that heretofore they received yearly from thence, and so they shall not continue trade, nor fall so aptly in practice against this government as now by their trade thither they may.

Inasmuch as fear of the terrors of the deep interfered with colonization, one can explain the printing of the account of seafights against the Spanish cheek by jowl with arguments for emigration only by noting the powerful place which anti-Spanish sentiments had in the nation as a whole. Such battles, if successful, showed that God was aiding the English navy against Spain. Thus Purchas described a fight between two Spanish men-of-war and a single English merchant vessel as being providentially directed:

> [The English ship was but] one poore Merchant and Passenger, being but a hundred and sixtie tunnes, having eight Iron Peeces and one Falcon, over-loaden with Stuffe and Wares, encombred with Passengers, toyled with a storme, tyred with a long Voyage, affrighted with wants, and every way insufficient to answere any such enemie: but as it is in the Scripture, it is all one to thee, O God, whether there be few or many, and Gedeons three hundred shall slay many thousands of the Midianites: as for deliverances, the people of Israell shall passe through the Red Sea dry foot: Jonas shall bee cast safe on shoare out of the Whales belly: and Paul shall escape shipwracke, saving his life with all his Passengers in the Iland of Malta.
>
> For to conclude with the purpose in hand, there is one thing most remarkable as an inducement to this our deliverance, that Captaine Chester embraced Doctor Bohune beeing mortally wounded, and thus recomforted him, saying O Doctor Bohune what a disaster is this; the Noble Doctor no whit exanimated replyed: Fight it out brave man, the cause is good, and Lord receive my soule.

The putting down of piracy and the long search for a Northwest Passage, which seems so incomprehensible to the modern man, were alike associated with the desire to vanquish Spain. Sir Humphrey Gilbert's whole discourse, for example, is a persuasion to hunt for the elusive strait, the reasons being, among others, that "the wealth of all the East parts" is "infinite," that the English "should be able to sell all maner of merchandize, brought from thence, farre better cheape then either the Portugall or Spaniard," that "great abundance of golde, silver, precious stones, cloth of gold, silkes, all maner of spices, grocery wares, and other kinds of merchandize of an inestimable price" will become an English monopoly to the detriment of Iberian trade, and that "we shall increase both our ships and mariners, without burthening of the state." . . . In sum, hatred of Spain merged easily into that romance of geography which dazzled the imagination of Marlowe and gave Hakluyt one of his most splendid passages:

> ... it can not be denied, but as in all former ages, [Englishmen] have bene men full of activity, stirrers abroad, and searchers of the remote parts of the world, so in this most famous and peerlesse governement of her most excellent Majesty, her subjects through the speciall assistance, and blessing of God, in searching the most opposite corners and quarters of the world, and to speake plainly, in compassing the vaste globe of the earth more then once, have excelled all the nations and people of the earth. For, which of the kings of this land before her Majesty, had theyr banners ever seene in the Caspian sea? which of them hath ever dealt with the Emperor of Persia, as her Majesty hath done, and obteined for her merchants large & loving privileges? who ever saw before this regiment, an English Ligier in the stately porch of the Grand Signor at Constantinople? who ever found English Consuls & Agents at Tripolis in Syria, at Aleppo, at Babylon, at Balsara, and which is more, who ever heard of English-men at Goa before now? what English shippes did heeretofore ever anker in the mighty river of Plate? passe and repasse the unpassable (in former opinion) straight of Magel-lan, range along the coast of Chili, Peru, and all the backside of Nova Hispania, further then any Christian ever passed, travers the mighty bredth of the South sea, land upon the Luzones in despight of the enemy, enter into alliance, amity, and traffike with the princes of the Moluccaes, & the Isle of Java, double the famous Cape of Bona Speranza, arive at the Isle of Santa Helena, & last of al returne home most richly laden with the commodities of China, as the subjects of this now flourishing monarchy have done?

To sail into distant seas, create a navy, promote trade, plant colonies, and defeat Spain became one and the same thing.

4. THE POPULATION PROBLEM AND THE COMMON MAN

That England was actually suffering from a glut of population at the end of the sixteenth century may be doubted, but that scores of writers thought England was over-populated is undeniable. Alarm over social dislocation is one of the commonest notes in Tudor literature. If the impact of the enclosure movement upon mediaeval agrarian economy has been exaggerated, "to sup-pose" Tawney writes "that contemporaries were mistaken as to the general nature of the movement is to accuse them of an imbecility which is really incredible." Throughout the century a significant fraction of the population silently moved out of its customary place in the mediaeval manor and drifted into the towns (to the alarm of the gilds) where they became an Elizabethan proletariat, or wandered the highways as sturdy beggars, dispossessed and homeless. "The sixteenth century lived in terror of the tramp." The tramp was a new social phenomenon with whom Tudor political science was scarcely equipped to deal—an able-bodied worker who, finding no employment, had been thrust outside the framework of society. . . . Contemporaries were acutely conscious of the social discord resulting from the upsets in the old national economy. "Radical social changes were in progress . . . they bore with especial hardness on the lower classes of the people, and left a deep impress on the literature of the time."

Against this background of social change a considerable part of the promotion literature must be read, if its meaning is to be understood. What may be called the sociological appeal of colonization plays its important part, the appeal being in some degree to all classes but principally to the socially dispossessed and those under the threat of being uprooted. All social ranks were apparently invited to ponder the threat and significance of over-population, which, from the beginning, looms large in the literature and for which plantations in the New World were confidently held to be a sovereign remedy. Thus Gilbert, among the eight numbered reasons of "commodities" which "would ensue," once the Northwest Passage was discovered, declares:

> Also we might inhabite some part of those countryes, and settle there such needy people of our countrey, which now trouble the common wealth, and through want here at home are inforced to commit outragious offences, whereby they are dayly consumed with the gallowes.

Our prisons, wrote Hakluyt in the *Divers Voyages,* are "pestered and filled with able men to serue their Countrie, which for small roberies are dayly hanged vp in great numbers"—"twentie at a clappe" at Rochester—and we English ought to send them to the colonies. ". . . yf this voyadge were put in execution," he wrote elsewhere,

> these pety theves mighte be condempned for certen yeres in the westerne partes, especially in Newefounde lande, in sawinge and fellinge of tymber for mastes of shippes, and deale boordes,

and in the south, they could be employed in mining, pearl-fishing, the growing of sugar cane, silkworms, cotton, various grains, grapes, and other "commodities." Our idle soldiers, he wrote again, go

> up and downe in swarms for lack of honest intertainment, I see no fitter place to employ some part of the better sort of them trained up thus long in service, then in the inward partes of the firme of Virginia against such stubborne Savages as shal refuse obedience to her Majestie.

Ministers of the gospel were equally concerned that colonization should prove a cure for over-population. The English, said Robert Gray in 1609, are as "the thousand of *Manasses,* and as the ten thousands of *Ephraim;*" they are entitled to exclaim, with the children of Israel, "we are a great people, and the lande is too narrow for ys," and, somewhat oddly, the good clergy-man compared James I to Joshua.

> . . . although the honour of the king be in the multitude of people . . . yet when this multitude of people increaseth to ouer great a number, the commonwealth stands subiect to many perillous inconueniences. . . .

"Look seriously into the land," preached William Symonds, "and see whether there be not just cause, if not a necessity, to seek abroad. The people, blessed be God, do swarm in the land, as young bees in a hive," and like a swarm of bees they must seek out a new home. Colonization, thought John Donne,

> shall redeeme many a wretch from the Lawes of death, from the hands of the Execu-tioner, vpon whom, perchance a small fault, or perchance a first fault, or perchance a fault heartily and sincerely repented, perchance no fault, but malice, had otherwise cast a present and ignominious death. It shall sweepe your streets, and wash your doores, from idle persons, and the children of idle persons, and imploy them: and truely, if the whole Countrey were but such a *Bridewell*, to force idle persons to work, it had a good vse . . . alreadie the imployment breedes Marriners; alreadie the place giues Essayes, nay, Fraights of Marchantable Commodities. . . .

But the transitional qualities of the Tudor period are nowhere more patent than in the contradictory attitude shown in the promotion literature towards the common man. On the one hand, he was promised easy riches, the pos-session of land in his own right, and the opportunity to stabilize his family. On the other hand, the promotion literature is filled with complaints about the unruliness, the lack of discipline, the insubordination and the want of practical sense exhibited by the Tudor commoner during the period of explora-tion and first settlement. According to Raleigh, the chief cause of the failure of his second voyage to Guiana was that, some forty gentlemen excepted, his forces were composed of "the very scum of the world, drunkards, blasphemers, and such others as their fathers, brothers, and friends thought it an exceeding good gain to be discharged of." Sir Ferdinando Gorges complained of the "idle proceedinges" of his colony which "have mutch prejudcialld the publique good, devidinge themselves into factions, each disgracing the other, even to the Savages, the on[e] emulatinge the others reputation amongst those brutish people." Conspiracies among the commoners brought both the original James-town plantation and the shipwrecked "supply" of Sir Thomas Gates to the verge of ruin. Some deserted and, returning to England, spread scandal; and on those who remained Captain John Smith poured his scorn. English fisher-men on the Maine coast were "worse than the very Savages, impudently and openly lying with their Women, teaching their Men to drinke drunke, to sweare and blaspheme the name of *GOD*, and in their drunken humour to fall together by the eares. . . ." And Edward Winslow makes a similar complaint of Weston's colony, listing among the three causes of the "overthrow and bane" of plantations the carelessness of those that send over men too often "endued with bestial, yea, diabolical affections." Only gradually in a given colony did an "honest and vertuous" minority emerge out of the confusion, as John Hammond noted of Virginia, which had become, he thought, "a modell on which industry may as much improve itself in, as in any habitable part of the World."

. . . The writer of promotion literature was inevitably caught between the contradictory claims of authority and liberty. On the one hand, except by creating a small, quasi-feudal military garrison and trading post supported by communal enterprise, the Tudor mind could find no way to assure to the individual colonist adequate protection from enemies and initial sustenance; on the other hand, since each settler looked forward to making his private fortune on *laissez-faire* principles, he chafed against the restrictions of communal enterprise, which were eventually abandoned. The contradiction lay deep in Tudor life; it appears in the colonial literature from the beginning; and it was never logically resolved. . . .

5. THE APPEAL OF TRADE

A plantation, however, was not merely a place for the display of *virtù*, a pawn in international diplomacy, or a safety valve for surplus commoners, it was also—perhaps primarily—a trading post. Beside the gentleman, the statesman, and the commoner stood the merchant,

> he whose travaile ought
> Commodiously, to doe his countrie good,
> And by his toyle, the same for to enriche,

as George Gascoigne wrote in *The Steele Glas*. A passage in John Wheeler's *A Treatise of Commerce* (1601), though it describes the entry of Philip into Antwerp in 1549, gives us some sense of the power and importance of the Tudor merchant:

Maister John Sturgeon, at that tyme Gouuernour of the Companie, was at the receyuing in of the said Prince accompanied with thirtie Merchantes of the Companie on horse-back all in a liuerie of Purple veluit in grain coates, and paneld hose embrodered full of siluer waues like the waues of the sea; their Dublettes and drawinge out of their hose purple sattin, their Hattes of purple veluit with golde bandes, faire brouches, and white feathers; and each of them a chain of golde about his neck of great valew; buskins of purple velvitt; their Rapiers, Daggers, Spurres, Stirropps and Bridles all gilt; the furniture of their horses was of purple veluit, Sadles and Trappinges, etc., embrodered with golde, and greene silke and white, and green feathers on their horse heades: they were attended with three skore Lackies, apparailed in white veluitt ierkins cutt, embrodered with siluer twist, green sattin dublettes, with hose and buskins of the same, purple veluitt Cappes, and green Feathers: behinde them roade the abouesaid Gouernour vpon a white English gelding, in a longe purple veluitt gowne, lyned with purple sattin, a black velvitt coat, and cappe with a fair brouche therein, and a chain of golde about his neck: his Dublett and Hose, with the trappinges of his Horse, were as the other of his Companie wore; he was attended on by six Lackies on foot, and three Pages on horseback apparailed as aforesaid. In which their doeing they shewed themselues for the honour of their Prince and Cuntrye nothing inferiour to the Merchantes of other nations. . . .

If one is to avoid the common error of thinking about the Tudor merchant as if he were a Victorian shopkeeper, one must keep steadily in mind the implications of the last sentence: "in which their doeing they shewed themselues for the honour of their Prince and Cuntrye nothing inferiour to the Merchantes of other nations." The Tudor investor wanted good returns on his money, but he was also susceptible to the appeal of patriotism and glory.

Perhaps the commonest element in the promotion literature is the allure of economic plenitude. The sober prose of the discoverer became as gorgeous as the verse of Spenser in enumerating the endless commodities of the New World, and the catalogues of the vegetable, animal, and mineral kingdoms are as encyclopaedic as the *Polyolbion*. Out of a hundred instances two or three must suffice. Thus concerning Newfoundland Anthony Parkhurst could write:

As touching the kindes of Fish beside Cod, there are Herrings, Salmons, Thornebacke, Plase, or rather wee should call them Flounders, Dog fish, and another most excellent of taste called of us a Cat, Oisters, and Muskles, in which I have found pearles above 40. in one Muskle, and generally all have some, great or small. . . . There are also other kinds of Shel-fish, as limpets, cockles, wilkes, lobsters, and crabs: also a fish like a Smelt which commeth on shore, and another that hath the like propertie, called a Squid: these be the fishes, which (when I please to bee merie with my old companions) I say, doe come on shore when I commaund them in the name of the 5. ports, and conjure them by such like words: These also bee the fishes which I may sweepe with broomes on a heape, and never wet my foote, onely pronouncing two or three wordes whatsoever they be appoynted by any man, so they heare my voyce: the vertue of the words be small, but the nature of the fish great and strange. . . . Smelt you may take up with a shove-net as plentifully as you do Wheate in a shovell, sufficient in three or foure houres for a whole Citie.

The good Parkhurst tells with a twinkle in his eye about "trees that bare Oisters," but, letting "these merrie tales passe," he urges trading and settlement upon Hakluyt, to whom he is writing. Of the "North Part of Virginia" the Brereton-Hayes narrative lists innumerable birds, animals, and fish;

remarks upon fish, whale, seal oils, soap ashes and soap, tar and pitch, rosin and turpentine, masts, timber and boards of cedars, firs and pines, hemp, flax, cables and ropes, sail cloths, grapes, raisins, wines, corn, rape-seed and oils, hides, skins, furs, dyes and colors for painting, pearls, metals and other minerals as marketable products "after that we have planted our people skilful and industrious." In fact, the account prophesies a shift in the balance of world trade since "northern Virginia" will produce commodities

for the which all nations that have been accustomed to repair unto the Newfoundland for the commodity of fish and oils alone, will henceforward forsake the Newfoundland, and trade with us, when once we have planted people in those parts. . . . Then will the Spaniards and Portugals bring unto us in exchange . . . wines, sweet oils, fruits, spices, sugars, silks, gold and silver, or whatsoever that Europe yieldeth to supply our necessities and to increase our delights.

Enumerating twenty-five "arguments of particular comodities and commodiousnesse," the author of *Virginias Verger*, said in his odd style that

the Lands and seas contend by fresh Rivers and Armes of the Sea so to diversifie the soyle as if in luxuriant wantonnesse they were always engendring manifold Twinnes of Commoditie and Commodiousnesse, Profit and Pleasure, Hunting and Fishing, Fruits and Merchandizing, Marinership and Husbandry, Opus and Usus, Meate and Drinke, Wares and Portage, Defending and Offending, Getting and Keeping, Mountaines and Valleyes, Plaines and Hillocks, Rivers Navigable and shallower Foords, Ilands and Land-iles (or Peninsulae), Woods and Marishes, Vegetatives and living creatures marvellously diversified,

in sum a land productive of trees for timber, diversified crops, silk, wines, drugs, iron, naval stores, cattle—an indefinite list. . . . Small wonder that the satirical authors of *Eastward Ho* (1605) put into the mouth of the rascally Seagull such language as this:

I tell thee, gold is more plentiful there than copper is with us; and for as much red copper as I can bring, I'll have it thrice the weight in gold. Why, man all their dripping-pans, and their chamber-pots are pure gold; and all the chains with which they chain up their streets are massy gold; all the prisoners they take, are fettered in gold; and for rubies and diamonds, they go forth on holidays and gather them by the seashore, to hang on their children's coats, and stick in their caps, as commonly as our children wear saffron guilt Brooches and groates with holes in them.

The economic motivation varied little during the decades of the promotion literature. Because the mercantilist theory of political economy laid stress upon the possession of gold and silver as the incarnation of wealth rather than as a means to wealth, the phantom of mineral treasures hung ever on the horizon. Frobisher loaded his ships with "such stone or supposed gold min-erall" as he could find in the frozen north; Ralph Lane sought for a mine in Roanoke, "for that the discovery of a good Mine, by the goodnesse of God, or a passage to the South-sea, or some way to it, and nothing els can bring this Countrey in request to be inhabited by our nation"; Raleigh turned *The Discovery of Guiana* into a golden poem; the letters patent issued to all the explorers stipulated the search for precious metals as foremost among the aims of the crown; the waste of energy at Jamestown caused by the futile search for gold is well known; and even as late as 1628 the Privy Council was considering petitions for the formation of a company to work gold and silver mines in the West Indies. And when no gold turned up in Virginia, apologists were hard put to it to get over the difficulty, which they explained on moral grounds.

The mercantile theory also implied the monopoly of trade by the mother country, the cutting off of trade between the plantations and foreign powers, and the substituting of colonial commerce for foreign commerce on the part of the mother country, as we have seen. This trade meant traffic in fish, marine stores, furs and similar goods; it meant also, as has been hinted, the creation of a trading post and the "civilizing" of the natives so that they would desire to buy English manufactures. . . .

6. THE MORAL SANCTION

But was it lawful to intrude upon the harmless savages? To claim sovereignty over lands that conceivably belonged to the Emperor of China or at least the Emperor Powhatan? Casuistical writers went presently to work, some in the field of ethics, some in the field of religion, to find moral sanctions for the making of plantations.

For one thing, it was obviously God's Providence that had reserved North America for the English. "As is to be conjectured by infallible arguments of the world's end approaching," wrote Edward Hayes, the English are

now arrived unto the time by God prescribed of their vocation, if ever their calling unto the knowledge of God may be expected. Which is also very probable by the revolution and course of Gods word and religion, which from the beginning hath moved from the East, towards, & at last unto the West, where it is like to end, unlesse the same begin againe where it did in the East, which were to expect a like world againe.

"In my private opinion," said Sir George Peckham, "I do verily thinke that God did create land, to the end that it should by culture and husbandry yeeld things necessary for mans life." . . . "Their land," says Robert Cushman, "is spacious and void"; the Indians "do but run over the grass, as do also the foxes and wild beasts"; wherefore "As the ancient Patriarchs therefore removed from straiter places into more roomthy . . . so it is lawful now to take a land, which none useth; and make use of it." The rule of nature, thought John Donne, permitted the English to occupy, since the natives had failed to use their land. God, argued John Winthrop, gave the earth to man; "why then should we stand starving here for places of habitation?" . . .

But the law of nature and the workings of Providence were reenforced by arguments from the Christian, and specifically from the Protestant, point of view. The English were the successors of the Chosen People, for whom a new Canaan had been appointed; this they were to possess peacefully, if they could—by force, if they must. Had not the ancient Jews slain the idolator? Had they not acted at the direct command of the Almighty? *"The land which we haue searched out,"* Robert Johnson solemnly wrote, following Joshua, *"is a very good land, if the Lord loue vs, he will bring our people to it, and will giue it vs for a possession."* "Wee goe to liue peacablie," argued Robert Gray, "not to supplant" the Indians; yet Christian rulers may, if necessary, conquer the heathen by force of arms. . . .

But the ethical sanction laid on the English was not merely the Old Testament command to increase and multiply; it was also the New Testament command to preach the gospel to all peoples—a theme which appears in travel literature from the beginning and which, because it accompanies, or is accompanied by, the profit motive, illustrates the complexity of the Tudor mind. To the Elizabethan or Jacobean Englishman there was no disharmony between the argument for gain and the argument for religious glory. God was to prosper His faithful, but their faithfulness could be shown only by obedience to His command; to deny this patent truth was to do the work of the devil:

> . . . such is the malice of wicked men the devils instruments in this our age, that they cannot suffer any thing (or at least few) to proceed and prosper that tendeth to the setting forth of Gods glory, and the amplifying of the Christian faith, wherein hitherto princes have not bene so diligent as their calling required. Alas, the labourers as yet are few, the harvest great. I trust God hath made you an instrument to increase the number, and to moove men of power, to redeeme the people of Newfoundland and those parts from out of the captivitie of that spirituall Pharao, the devill.

This was not the utterance of a Puritan preacher, but of a secular Elizabethan. . . .

So long as the Indians did not resist conquest the ethical problem was simple, and invasion could even be justified as protection of gentle people against more bloodthirsty foes. But it soon appeared that the Indians would "steale any thing comes neare them; yea, are so practized in this art, that, lookeing in our face, they would with their foot, betweene their toes, convey a chizell, knife, percer, or any indifferent light thing," from which it was natural to argue that "they are naturally given to trechery"; their "assaults and Ambuscadoes" were as characteristic as those of the wild Irish; and the necessity of explaining the natural disinclination of the natives to surrender their country to the newcomers led to some interesting exercises in ethical casuistry. One viable explanation was obvious: the Indians were the children of the devil, a being whose jealousy had been excited by the coming of the Christians—to slaughter them was therefore but to defeat Satan: "Remember the end of this voiage," exclaimed the Rev. W. Crashaw, "is the destruction of the diuels kingdome," and the devil was no passive adversary. . . . But if the Indians lived under the law of nature, if they enjoyed civil government, then it was lawful to enforce treaties made with them:

> What injury can yt be to people of any nation for Christians to come unto their ports, havens, or territoryes, when the lawe of nations (which is the lawe of God and man) doth priviledge all men to doe soe, which admitts yt lawfull to trade with any manner of people, in so much as no man is to take upon him (that knoweth any thing) the defence of the salvadges in this point, since the salvadges themselves may not impugne or forbid the same, in respect of common fellowship and community betwixt man and man. . . .

The Virginia Council therefore dwelt with ethical pride upon the fact that they had entered into lawful treaty with "Paspehay" for the purchase of land, and argued it was not unlawful to snatch the sword out of the hands of a madman (i.e., take even more land),

> So that if just offences shalt arise, it can bee no more iniustice to warre against infidells, than it is when vpon iust occasions wee warre against Christians. And therefore I cannot see, but that these truths, will fanne away all those chaffie imputations, which anie Romish boasters (that challenge a monopolie of all conuersions) will cast vpon it, or any scrupulous conscience can impute vnto it.

And the New England mind dwelt with equal complacency upon the fact that Massasoit, "the imperial Governor," acknowledged the supremacy of King James and by "a joint consent, hath promised and appointed us to live at peace, where we will, in all his dominions. . . ." Besides, the land was "a vast and empty chaos." We English must do as we have been done by; and if the ancient Romans converted the ancient Britons to "*ciuilitie*," let the English here repay the debt, especially since the papists were misrepresenting the situation—"I would not one, seasoned with the least taint of that leauen, to be setled in our plantation, nor in any part of that country," as Robert Johnson exclaimed. And as a curious footnote to these ethical sanctions for invading the lands of another people, one may watch Sir William Alexander turning the marriage of Pocahontas and John Rolfe into a justification for the white man's treatment of the red:

Lawfull allyances thus by admitting equalitie remoue contempt, and giue a promiscuous off-spring extinguishing the distinction of persons, which if that People become Christians, were in some sort tolerable, for it is the onely cause that vniting minds, free from jealousies, can first make strangers confide in a new friendship, which by communicating their bloud with mutuall assurance is left hereditary to their posteritie.

Following this interesting passage, he discusses the Indian massacres at Jamestown! But perhaps it remained for a more cynical age to see the inconsistencies of the Tudor mind in this regard; for the most part the contemporaries of Smith, Myles Standish, and Lord Baltimore were content with the conclusion of John White in *The Planters Plea*:

> ... if in the Worlds infancy, men out of an ambitious humour, or at present for private advantages and expectation of gaine, thrust themselves out from their owne dwellings into parts farre remote from their native soyle; why should not we conceive, that if they doe this for a corruptible crowne; that the desire and expectation of an incorruptible ... may as strongly allure such as by patient continuance in well-doing, seeke immortalitie & life?

Even a Thomas Morton was susceptible to promotional enthusiasm; and as this study began with an appeal to Renaissance *virtù*, it may well conclude with the unexpected tribute by a genial son of this world to the glamor of the Promised Land:

> If art and industry should doe as much
> As Nature hath for Canaan, not such
> Another place, for benefit and rest,
> In all the universe can be possest.
> The more we proove it by discovery,
> The more delight each object to the eye
> Procures; as if the elements had here
> Bin reconcil'd, and pleas'd it should appeare
> Like a faire virgin, longing to be sped
> And meete her lover in a Nuptiall bed,
> Deck'd in rich ornaments t'advaunce her state
> And excellence, being most fortunate
> When most enjoy'd: so would our Canaan be
> If well imploy'd by art and industry;
> Whose offspring now, shewes that her fruitfull wombe,
> Not being enjoy'd, is like a glorious tombe,
> Admired things producing which there dye,
> And ly fast bound in darck obscurity;
> The worth of which, in each particuler,
> Who list to know, this abstract will declare.

THE USES OF LEGEND

The modern discoverer of North America was John Cabot, a Venetian, who made two voyages out of Bristol to Labrador and Nova Scotia under the auspices of King Henry VII in the years 1497 and 1498. Cabot's discoveries were almost forgotten in England, but his son, Sebastian, who as a boy of twelve accompanied his father on the voyage of 1497, never completely forgot them. In 1509, he himself undertook a voyage to North America, where he sailed along the coast, discovering a vast strait which he ever afterwards maintained was the passage to India. An expert cartographer, he incorporated this concept into his maps, which greatly influenced the thinking of his age.

After 1512, Sebastian Cabot left England and settled in Seville in the service of the King of Spain, where he became the chief maritime authority and piloto mayor of the Spanish fleet. In 1526 he sailed to Brazil, and in 1536 he made another voyage to North America. As time wore on, he appears to have sought to increase his reputation by confusing his considerable voyage of 1509 with the basic discoveries made by his father in 1497. To virtually everyone who would listen, he passed on a garbled account of "his" voyage in "1496." Since there were a number of Bristol men living in Seville, Cabot's story reached England very quickly and helped to renew interest in voyaging to the New World.

The account presented here was given by Cabot to the Pope's legate in Spain, and in 1600 was published in Richard Hakluyt's The Principal Voyages, Traffiques and Discoveries of the English Nation Made by Sea or Over-land to the Remote and Fartherest Distant Quarters of the Earth at any time within the compass of these 1600 Yeeres. Hakluyt's work, which came out in various forms beginning in 1583, culminating in his masterpiece of three volumes and some 1,700,000 words, was a massive compendium of all available original and hearsay accounts of travel and exploration. It was a masterful historical compilation, an incomparable geographical reference, and a great epic story designed to emphasize above all the feats of English sailors, explorers, and men of commerce. Since Hakluyt was directly interested financially in English expansion and served as close adviser to all colonial planners and gentlemen adventurers, his work was an extremely functional part of British imperialism in the Age of Discovery and Colonization. It was evident

*that the Cabot stories served an important purpose in his writing: they legit-
imatized, by right of discovery, all British claims to North America and the
Northwest Passage, if it should ever be found.*

A DISCOURSE OF SEBASTIAN CABOT

*A discourse of Sebastian Cabot touching his discovery of part of the West
India out of England in the time of king Henry the seventh, used to Galeacius
Butrigarius the Popes Legate in Spaine, and reported by the sayd Legate in
this sort*

Doe you not understand sayd he (speaking to certaine Gentlemen of Venice)
how to passe to India toward the Northwest, as did of late a citizen of Venice,
so valiant a man, and so well practised in all things pertaining to navigations,
and the science of Cosmographie, that at this present he hath not his like in
Spaine, insomuch that for his vertues he is preferred above all other pilots
that saile to the West Indies, who may not passe thither without his license,
and is therefore called Piloto mayor, that is, the grand Pilot. And when we
sayd that we knew him not, he proceeded, saying, that being certaine yeres
in the city of Sivil, and desirous to have some knowledge of the navigations
of the Spanyards, it was tolde him that there was in the city a valiant man, a
Venetian borne named Sebastian Cabot, who had the charge of those things,
being an expert man in that science, and one that coulde make Cardes for the
Sea with his owne hand, and that by this report, seeking his acquaintance,
hee found him a very gentle person, who intertained him friendly, and shewed
him many things, and among other a large Mappe of the world, with certaine
particuler Navigations, as well of the Portugals, as of the Spaniards, and that
he spake further unto him to this effect.

When my father departed from Venice many yeeres since to dwell in England, to follow the trade of marchandises, hee tooke mee with him to the
citie of London, while I was very yong, yet having neverthelesse some knowledge of letters of humanitie, and of the Sphere. And when my father died in
that time when newes were brought that Don Christopher Colonus Genuese
had discovered the coasts of India, whereof was great talke in all the Court
of king Henry the 7. who then raigned, insomuch that all men with great
admiration affirmed it to be a thing more divine then humane, to saile by the

Richard Hakluyt, *The Principal Voyages, Traffiques and Discoveries of the English Nation Made
by Sea or Over-land to the Remote and Fartherest Distant Quarters of the Earth at any time within
the compass of these 1600 Yeeres*, Glasgow Edition, 12 vols. (Glasgow, 1903–1905), VII, pp. 147–
149. Marginal notes from the Glasgow Edition have been eliminated in the present work.

West into the East where spices growe, by a way that was never knowen before, by this fame and report there increased in my heart a great flame of
desire to attempt some notable thing. And understanding by reason of the
Sphere, that if I should saile by way of the Northwest, I should by a shorter
tract come into India, I thereupon caused the King to be advertised of my
devise, who immediately commanded two Carvels to bee furnished with all
things appertayning to the voyage, which was as farre as I remember in the
yeere 1496. in the beginning of Sommer. I began therefore to saile toward the
Northwest, not thinking to finde any other land then that of Cathay, & from
thence to turne toward India, but after certaine dayes I found that the land
ranne towards the North, which was to mee a great displeasure. Neverthelesse,
sayling along by the coast to see if I could finde any gulfe that turned, I found
the lande still continent to the 56. degree under our Pole. And seeing that
there the coast turned toward the East, despairing to finde the passage, I turned
back againe, and sailed downe by the coast of that land toward the Equinoctiall (ever with intent to finde the saide passage to India) and came to that
part of this firme lande which is nowe called Florida, where my victuals failing, I departed from thence and returned into England, where I found great
tumults among the people, and preparation for warres in Scotland: by reason
whereof there was no more consideration had to this voyage.

Whereupon I went into Spaine to the Catholique king, and Queene Elizabeth,
which being advertised what I had done, intertained me, and at their charges
furnished certaine ships, wherewith they caused me to saile to discover the
coastes of Brasile, where I found an exceeding great and large river named
at this present Rio de la plata, that is, the river of silver, into the which
I sailed and followed it into the firme land, more then six score leagues,
finding it every where very faire, and inhabited with infinite people, which
with admiration came running dayly to our ships. Into this River runne so
many other rivers, that it is in maner incredible.

After this I made many other voyages, which I nowe pretermit, and waxing
olde, I give my selfe to rest from such travels, because there are nowe many
yong and lustie Pilots and Mariners of good experience, by whose forward-
nesse I doe rejoyce in the fruit of my labours, and rest with the charge of this
office, as you see.

THE USES OF GEOGRAPHY

This document, written in 1527 by Robert Thorne, one of the Bristol merchants resident in Seville during the period of Sebastian Cabot's ascendancy, is one of the most important works of its time. It presents a nearly complete picture of the world as the most advanced geographers believed it to be in the early sixteenth century, as well as detailed instructions on the use and construction of "cards" or maps. The latter was an art or science known to relatively few men of the time, as were the principles of scientific navigation. Such geographical knowledge and technical skills were closely guarded by both the Spanish and the Portuguese. In sending this letter and map to King Henry VIII via the British ambassador, Robert Thorne was, in effect, smuggling out of Spain a piece of intelligence comparable to the atomic secrets of today. Though it was widely circulated as propaganda among English policy makers, and perhaps influenced the search for a Northwest Passage to India, it was not printed until 1583 when Hakluyt included it in his book Divers Voyages, the forerunner of his great work. Like most of the items in Hakluyt's collection, it was utilized to stimulate expansionist ventures.

ROBERT THORNE'S PICTURE OF THE WORLD

The booke made by the right worshipful M. Robert Thorne in the yeere 1527. in Sivil, to Doctour Ley, Lord ambassadour for king Henry the eight, to Charles the Emperour, being an information of the parts of the world, discovered by him and the king of Portingal: and also of the way to the Moluccaes by the North

Right noble and reverend in &c. I have received your letters, and have procured and sent to know of your servant, who, your Lordship wrote, should be sicke in Merchena. I cannot there or els where heare of him, without he be returned to you, or gone to S. Lucar, and shipt. I cannot judge but that of some contagious sicknesse hee died, so that the owner of the house for defaming his house would bury him secretly, and not be knowen of it. For such things have often times happened in this countrey.

Also to write unto your Lordshippe of the new trade of Spicery of the Emperour, there is no doubt but that the Islands are fertile of Cloves, Nutmegs, Mace, and Cinnamom: and that the said Islands, with other there about, abound with golde, Rubies, Diamondes, Balasses, Granates, Jacincts, and other stones & pearles, as all other lands, that are under and neere the Equinoctiall. For we see, where nature giveth any thing, she is no nigard. For as with us and other, that are aparted from the said Equinoctiall, our mettals be Lead, Tinne, and Iron, so theirs be Gold, Silver, and Copper. And as our fruits and graines bee Apples, Nuts, and Corne, so theirs be Dates, Nutmegs, Pepper, Cloves, and other Spices. And as we have Jeat, Amber, Cristall, Jasper, and other like stones, so have they Rubies, Diamonds, Balasses, Saphyres, Jacincts, and other like. And though some say that of such precious mettals, graines, or kind of spices, and precious stones, the abundance and quantity is nothing so great, as our mettals, fruits or stones above rehearsed: yet if it be well considered how the quantitie of the earth under the Equinoctiall to both the Tropicall lines, (in which space is found the sayd Golde, spices and precious stones) is as much in quantity, as almost all the earth from the Tropickes to both the Poles; it cannot be denied but there is more quantity of the sayd mettals, fruites, spices, and precious stones, then there is of the other mettals and other things before rehearsed. And I see that the preciousnes of these things is measured after the distance that is between us, and the things that we have appetite unto. For in this navigation of the Spicerie was discovered, that these Islands nothing set by golde, but set more by a knife and a nayle of iron, then by his quantitie of Golde: and with reason, as the thing more necessary for mans service. And I doubt not but to them should be as precious our corne and seedes, if they might have them, as to us their spices: & likewise the pieces of glasse that here we have counterfeited are as precious to them, as to us their stones: which by experience is seene daylie by them that have trade thither. This of the riches of those countries is sufficient.

Touching that your Lordship wrote, whether it may bee profitable to the Emperor or no? it may be without doubt of great profite: if, as the king of Portingal doth, he would become a merchant, and provide shippes and their lading, and trade thither alone, and defend the trade of these Islands for himselfe. But other greater businesse withholdeth him from this. But still, as now it is begunne to be occupied, it would come to much. For the shippes comming in safetie, there would thither many every yere, of which to the Emperour is due of all the wares and jewels that come from thence the fift part for his custome cleare without any cost. And besides this hee putteth in every flote a certaine quantitie of money, of which hee enjoyeth of the gaines pound and pounds like as other adventurers doe. In a fleete of three shippes and a Caravel that went from this citie armed by the marchants of it, which departed in Aprill last past, I and my partener have one thousand foure hundred duckets that we

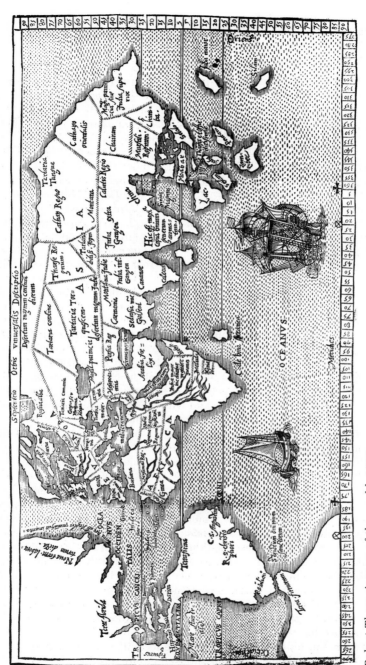

Robert Thorne's map of the world, 1527.

employed in the sayd fleete, principally for that two English men, friends of mine, which are somewhat learned in Cosmographie, should goe in the same shippes, to bring me certaine relation of the situation of the countrey, and to be expert in the navigation of those seas, and there to have informations of many other things, and advise that I desire to knowe especially. Seeing in these quarters are shippes, and mariners of that countrey, and cardes by which they saile, though much unlike ours, that they should procure to have the said cards, and learne how they understand them, and especially to know what navigation they have for those Islands Northwards, and Northeastward.

For if from the sayd Islands the sea did extend, without interposition of land, to saile from the North point to the Northeast poynt one thousand seven hundred or one thousand eight hundred leagues, they should come to the New found Islands that we discovered, and so we should be neerer to the sayd Spicerie by almost two thousand leagues then the Emperour, or the king of Portingal are. And to advise your Lordship whether of these Spiceries of the king of Portingal or the Emperours is neerer, and also of the titles that either of them hath, and howe our New found lands are parted from it, (for that by writing without some demonstration, it were hard to give any declaration of it) I have caused that your Lordship shall receive herewith a little Mappe or Carde of the world: the which, I feare me, shall put your Lordship to more labour to understand, then me to make it, onely for that it is made in so litle roome that it cannot be but obscurely set out, that is desired to be seene in it, and also for that I am in this science little expert: Yet to remedy in part this difficulty, it is necessary to declare to your Lordship my intent, with which I trust you shall perceive in this Card part of your desire, if, for that I cannot expresse mine intent, with my declaration I doe not make it more obscure.

First, your Lordship knoweth that the Cosmographers have divided the earth by 360 degrees in latitude, and as many in longitude, under the which is comprehended all the roundnes of the earth: the latitude being divided into foure quarters, ninetie degrees amount to every quarter, which they measure by the altitude of the Poles, that is the North and South starres, being from the line Equinoctiall till they come right under the North starre the said ninetie degrees: and as much from the sayd line Equinoctiall to the South starre be other ninety degrees. And as much more is also from either of the sayd starres agayne to the Equinoctiall. Which imagined to bee round, is soone perceived thus, 360 degrees of latitude to be consumed in the said foure quarters of ninetie degrees a quarter: so that this latitude is the measure of the worlde from North to South, and from South to North. And the longitude, in which are also counted other 360, is counted from West to East, or from East to West, as in the Card is set.

The sayd latitude your Lordship may see marked and divided in the ende of this Card on the left hand: so that if you would know in what degrees of latitude any region or coast standeth, take a compasse, and set the one foot of the same in the Equinoctial line right against the said region, & apply the other foote of the compasse to the said region or coast, & then set the sayd compasse at the end of the Card, where the degrees are divided. And the one foote of the compasse standing in the line Equinoctial, the other will shew in the scale the degrees of altitude or latitude that the said region is in. Also the longitude of the world I have set out in the nether part of the Card, conteining also 360 degrees: which begin to be counted after Ptoleme and other Cosmographers from an headland called Capo Verde, which is over against a little crosse made in the part Occidental, where the division of the degrees beginneth, and endeth in the same Capo Verde.

Now to know in what longitude any land is, your Lordship must take a ruler or a compasse, and set the one foot of the compasse upon the land or coast whose longitude you would know, and extend the other foot of the compasse to the next part of one of the tranversall lines in the Orientall or Occidental part: which done, set the one foot of the compasse in the said transversal line at the end of the nether scale, the scale of longitude, and the other foot sheweth the degree of longitude that the region is in. And your Lordship must understand that this Card, though little, conteineth the universall whole world betwixt two collaterall lines, the one in the Occidentall part descendeth perpendicular upon the 175 degree, & the other in the Orientall on the 170 degree, whose distance measureth the scale of longitude. And that which is without the two said transversall lines, is onely to shew how the Orientall part is joined with the Occident, and Occident with the Orient. For that that is set without the line in the Orientall part, is the same that is set within the other line in the Occidentall part: and that that is set without the line in the Occidentall part, is the same that is set within the line in the Orientall part, to shew that though this figure of the world in plaine or flatte seemeth to have an end, yet one imagining that this sayd Card were set upon a round thing, where the endes should touch by the lines, it would plainely appeare howe the Orient part joyneth with the Occident, as there without the lines it is described and figured.

And for more declaration of the said Card, your Lordship shall understand, that beginning on the part Occidental within the line, the first land that is set out, is the maine land and Islands of the Indies of the Emperour. Which maine land or coast goeth Northward, and finisheth in the land that we found, which is called here Terra de Labrador. So that it appeareth the sayd land that we found, and the Indies to be all one maine land.

The sayd coast from the sayd Indies Southward, as by the Card your Lordshippe may see, commeth to a certaine straight Sea, called Estrecho de todos Santos: by which straight Sea the Spaniards goe to the Spiceries, as I shall declare more at large: the which straight Sea is right against three hundred

fifteene degrees of longitude, and is of latitude or altitude from the Equi-
noctiall three and fifty degrees. The first land from the sayd beginning of the
Card toward the Orient are certaine Islands of the Canaries, and Islandes of
Capo verde. But the first maine land next to the line Equinoctial is the sayd
Capo verde, and from thence Northward by the straight of this sea of Italie.
And so followeth Spayne, France, Flanders, Almaine, Denmarke, and Nor-
way, which is the highest parte toward the North. And over against Flanders
are our Islands of England and Ireland. Of the landes and coastes within the
streights I have set out onely the Regions, dividing them by lines of their
limits, by which plainely I thinke your Lordship may see, in what situation
everie region is, and of what highnesse, and with what regions it is joyned.
I doe thinke few are left out of all Europe. In the parts of Asia and Affrica I
could not so wel make the sayd divisions: for that they be not so wel knowen,
nor need not so much. This I write because in the said Card be made the said
lines & strikes, that your Lordship should understand wherefore they doe
serve. Also returning to the foresaid Capo verde, the coast goeth Southward
to a Cape called Capo de buona speransa: which is right over against the 60. &
65. degree of longitude. And by this Cape go the Portingals to their Spicerie.
For from this Cape toward the Orient, is the land of Calicut, as your Lordship
may see in the headland over against the 130. degree. From the sayd Cape of
Buona speransa the coast returneth toward the line Equinoctial, and passing
forth entreth the red sea, & returning out, entreth again into the gulfe of Persia,
and returneth toward the Equinoctiall line, till that it commeth to the headland called Calicut aforesayd, and from thence the coast making a gulfe,
where is the river of Ganges, returneth toward the line to a headland called
Malaca, where is the principall Spicerie: & from this Cape returneth and
maketh a great gulfe, and after the coast goeth right toward the Orient, and
over against this last gulfe and coast be many Islands, which be Islandes of
the Spiceries of the Emperour. Upon which the Portingals and he be at variance.

The sayd coast goeth toward the Orient, and endeth right against the 155.
degrees, and after returneth toward the Occident Northward: which coast not
yet plainely knowen, I may joine to the New found lande found by us, that
I spake of before. So that I finish with this briefe declaration of the Card
aforesayd. Well I know I should also have declared how the coasts within
the straights of the Sea of Italie runne. It is playne that passing the streights
on the North side of that Sea after the coast of Granado, and with that which
pertaines to Spaine, is the coast of that which France hath in Italie. And then
followeth in one piece all Italie, which land hath an arme of the Sea, with
a gulfe which is called Mare Adriaticum. And in the bottome of this gulfe
is the citie of Venice. And on the other part of the sayd gulfe is Scla-
vonia, and next Grecia, then the streits of Constantinople, and then the sea
called Euxinus, which is within the sayd streights: and comming out of

the sayd streights, followeth Turcia major (though now on both sides it is called Turcia.) And so the coast runneth Southward to Syria, and over against the sayd Turcia are the Islands of Rhodes, Candie, and Cyprus. And over against Italie are the Islands of Sicilia and Sardinia. And over against Spaine is Majorca and Minorca. In the ende of the gulfe of Syria is Judea. And from thence returneth the coast toward the Occident, till it commeth to the streights where we began, which all is the coast of Affrike and Barbarie. Also your Lordship shall understand that the coastes of the Sea throughout all the world, I have coloured with yellow, for that it may appeare that all that is within the line coloured yellow, is to be imagined to be maine land or Islands: and all without the line so coloured to bee Sea: whereby it is easie and light to know it. Albeit in this little roome any other description would rather have made it obscure then cleere. And the sayd coasts of the Sea are all set justly after the maner and forme as they lie, as the navigation approveth them throughout all the Card, save onely the coastes and Isles of the Spicerie of the Emperour which is from over against the 160. to the 215. degrees of longitude, For these coastes and situations of the Islands, every of the Cosmographers and pilots of Portingal & Spayne do set after their purpose. The Spaniards more towards the Orient, because they should appeare to appertain to the Emperour: & the Portingals more toward the Occident, for that they should fal within their jurisdiction. So that the pilots and navigants thither, which in such cases should declare the truth, by their industrie do set them falsly every one to favour his prince. And for this cause can be no certaine situation of that coast and Islands, till this difference betwixt them be verified. Now to come to the purpose of your Lordships demaund touching the difference between the Emperour and the king of Portingal, to understand it better, I must declare the beginning of this discoverie. Though peradventure your Lordship may say that in that I have written ought of purpose, I fall in the proverbe, A gemino ovo bellum: But your Lordship commanded me to be large, and I take licence to be prolixious, and shalbe peradventure tedious, but your Lordship knoweth that Nihil ignorantia verbosius.

In the yeere 1484 the king of Portingal minded to arme certaine Carvels to discover this Spicerie. Then forasmuch as he feared that being discovered, every other prince woulde sende and trade thither, so that the cost and perill of discovering should be his, and the profite common: wherefore first hee gave knowledge of this his minde to all princes Christened, saying that hee would seeke amongst the infidels newe possessions of regions, and therefore would make a certaine armie: and that if any of them would helpe in the cost of the sayd armie, he should enjoy his part of the profite or honour that should come of it. And as then this discovering was holden for a strange thing and uncertaine. Nowe they say, that all the Princes of Christendome answered, that they would be no part of such an armie, nor yet of the profit that might come of it. After the which he gave knowledge to the Pope of his purpose, and of the answere of all the Princes, desiring him that seeing that none would helpe in the costes, that he would judge all that should bee found and discovered to be of his jurisdiction, and commannd that none other princes should intermeddle therewith. The Pope sayd not as Christ saith, Quis me constituit judicem inter vos? He did not refuse, but making himselfe as Lord and Judge of all, not onely granted that all that should be discovered from Orient to Occident, should be the kings of Portingal, but also, that upon great censures no other Prince should discover but he. And if they did, all to bee the kings of Portingal. So he armed a fleete, and in the yeere 1497 were discovered the Islands of Calicut, from whence is brought all the spice he hath.

After this in the yere 1492 the king of Spaine willing to discover lands toward the Occident without making any such diligence, or taking licence of the king of Portingal, armed certaine Carvels, and then discovered this India Occidentall, especially two Islands of the sayd India, that in this Card I set forth, naming the one la Dominica, and the other Cuba, and brought certaine golde from thence. Of the which when the king of Portingal had knowledge, he sent to the king of Spaine, requiring him to give him the sayd Islands. For that by the sentence of the Pope all that should be discovered was his, and that hee should not proceede further in the discoverie without his licence. And at the same time it seemeth that out of Castil into Portingal had gone for feare of burning infinite number of Jewes that were expelled out of Spaine, for that they would not turne to be Christians, and carried with them infinite number of golde and silver. So that it seemeth that the king of Spaine answered, that it was reason that the king of Portingal asked, and that to be obedient to that which the Pope had decreed, he would give him the sayd Islands of the Indies. Nowe for as much as it was decreed betwixt the sayde kings, that none should receive the others subjects fugitives, nor their goods, therefore the king of Portingal should pay and returne to the king of Spaine a million of golde or more, that the Jewes had caryed out of Spaine to Portingal, & that in so doing, he would give these Islands, and desist from any more discovering. And not fulfilling this, he would not onely not give these Islands, but procure to discover more where him thought best. It seemeth that the king of Portingal would not, or could not with his ease pay this money. And so not paying, that he could not let the king of Spaine to discover: so that he enterprised not toward the Orient where he had begun & found the Spicerie. And consented to the king of Spaine, that touching this discovering they should divide the worlde betweene them two. And that all that should be discovered from Cape Verde, where this Card beginneth to be counted in the degrees of longitude, to 180 of the sayd scale of longitude, which is halfe the world toward the Orient, & finisheth in this Card right over against a litle crosse made at the said 180 degrees, to be the king of Portingals. And all the land from the said

Crosse towarde the Occident, untill it joyneth with the other Crosse in the Orient, which conteineth the other hundreth and eightie degrees, that is the other halfe of the worlde, to be the king of Spaines. So that from the land over against the said hundreth & eighty degrees untill it finish in the three hundred and sixtie on both the ends of the Card, is the jurisdiction of the king of Spaine. So after this maner they divided the world betweene them. . . .

But now touching that your Lordship wrote, whether that which we discovered toucheth any thing the foresayd coastes: once it appeareth plainely, that the Newefound land that we discovered, is all a maine land with the Indies Occidentall, from whence the Emperour hath all the gold and pearles: and so continueth of coast more then 5000 leagues of length, as by this Carde appeareth. For from the said New lands it proceedeth toward the Occident to the Indies, and from the Indies returneth toward the Orient, and after turneth Southward up till it come to the Straits of Todos Santos, which I reckon to be more then 5000 leagues.

So that to the Indias it should seeme that we have some title, at least that for our discovering we might trade thither as other doe. But all this is nothing neere the Spicerie.

Now then if from the sayd New found lands the Sea be navigable, there is no doubt, but sayling Northward and passing the Pole, descending to the Equinoctial line, we shall hit these Islands, and it should be a much shorter way, then either the Spaniards or the Portingals have. . . .

Your servant Robert Thorne, 1527

THE USES OF HISTORY

The following document was written by Captain John Smith, one of the greatest of the English New World colonizers. His incredible feats in early Virginia, thanks to the persistence of the Pocahontas story, need no underscoring here, though any serious student of American history should take the trouble to familiarize himself with the whole range of John Smith's efforts in behalf of English colonization. In this selection, part of his The General Historie of Virginia, New England, and the Summer Isles . . . , *published in 1624, Smith is at great pains to establish through historical precedent the legitimacy of British claims to the New World. Does he appear to have any other aims?*

JOHN SMITH ON ENGLISH EXPLORATION
AND SETTLEMENT IN THE NEW WORLD

For the Stories of *Arthur, Malgo,* and *Brandon,* that say a thousand yeares agoe they were in the North of *America;* or the Fryer of *Linn* that by his blacke Art went to the North pole in the yeare 1360. in that I know them not. Let this suffice.

The Chronicles of *Wales* report, that *Madock,* sonne to *Owen Quineth,* Prince of *Wales* seeing his two brethren at debate who should inherit, prepared certaine Ships, with men and munition, and left his Country to seeke aduentures by Sea: leauing *Ireland* North he sayled west till he came to a Land vnknowne. Returning home and relating what pleasant and fruitfull Countries he had seene without Inhabitants, and for what barren ground his brethren and kindred did murther one another, he provided a number of Ships, and got with him such men and women as were desirous to liue in quietnesse, that arriued with him in this new Land in the yeare 1170: Left many of his people there and returned for more. But where this place was no History can show.

The *Spanyards* say *Hanno* a Prince of *Carthage* was the first: and the next *Christopher Cullumbus,* a Genoesian, whom they sent to discover those vnknowne parts. 1492.

But we finde by Records, *Cullumbus* offered his seruice in the yeare 1488. to King *Henry* the seauenth; and by accident vndertooke it for the *Spanyards.* In the Interim King *Henry* gaue a Commission to *Iohn Cabot,* and his three sonnes, *Sebastian, Lewis,* and *Sautius. Iohn* and *Sebastian* well provided, setting sayle, ranged a great part of this vnknowne world, in the yeare 1497. For though *Cullumbus* had found certaine Iles, it was 1498. ere he saw the Continent, which was a yeare after *Cabot.* Now *Americus* came a long time after, though the whole Continent to this day is called *America* after his name, yet *Sebastian Cabot* discovered much more then them all, for he sayled to about forty degrees Southward of the lyne, and to sixty-seauen towards the North: for which King *Henry* the eight Knighted him and made him grand Pilate of *England.* Being very aged King *Edward* the sixte gaue him a Pention of 166£. 13s. 4d. yearely. By his directions Sir *Hugh Willowby* was sent to finde out the Country of *Russia,* but the next yeare he was found frozen to death in his Ship, and all his Company.

The present selection is from John Smith, *Travels and Works,* Edward Arber, ed. (Edinburgh, 1910), I, pp. 303–310. The basic account of Amadas and Barlow also appears in Hakluyt's *Voyages,* VIII, pp. 297–310. Most of Smith's information in this section appears to have been taken from Hakluyt's work.

Master *Martin Frobisher* was sent in the yeare 1576. by our most gracious Queene *Elizabeth,* to search for the Northwest passage, and *Meta incognita:* for which he was Knighted, honored, and well rewarded.

Sir *Humphrey Gilbert* a worthy Knight attempted a Plantation in some of those parts: and obtained Letters Pattents to his desire: but with this *Proviso,* He should maintaine possession in some of those vast Countries within the tearme of sixe yeares. Yet when he was provided with a Navy able to incounter a Kings power, even here at home they fell in diuisions, and so into confusion, that they gaue over the Designe ere it was begun, notwithstanding all this losse, his vndanted spirit began againe, but his Fleet fell with *New-found land,* and he perished in his returne, as at large you may read in the third Volume of the English Voyages, written by Master *Hackluit* [in 1599–1600].

Vpon all those Relations and inducements, Sir *Walter Raleigh,* a noble Gentleman, and then in great esteeme, vndertooke to send to discover to the Southward. And though his occasions and other imployments were such he could not goe himselfe, yet he procured her Maiesties Letters Pattents, and perswaded many worthy Knights and Gentlemen to adventure with him to finde a place fit for a Plantation. Their Proceedings followeth.

The most famous, renowned, and euer worthy of all memory, for her courage, learning, iudgement, and vertue, Queene *Elizabeth,* granted her Letters Patents to Sir *Walter Raleigh* for the discovering and planting new Lands and Countries, not actually possessed by any Christians. This Patenty got to be his assistants Sir *Richard Grenvell* the valiant, Master *William Sanderson* a great friend to all such noble and worthy actions, and divers other Gentlemen and Marchants, who with all speede prouided two small Barkes well furnished with all necessaries, vnder the command of Captaine *Philip Amidas* and Captaine *Barlow.* The 27. of Aprill [1584] they set sayle from the Thames, the tenth of May passed the *Canaries,* and the tenth of Iune the West Indies: which vnneedfull Southerly course, (but then no better was knowne) occasioned them in that season much sicknesse.

The second of Iuly [1584] they fell with the coast of *Florida* in shoule water, where they felt a most delicate sweete smell, though they saw no land, which ere long they espied, thinking it the Continent: an hundred and twenty myles they sayled not finding any harbor. The first that appeared with much difficulty they entred, and anchored, and after thankes to God they went to view the next Land adioyning to take possession of it for the Queenes most excellent Maiestie: which done, they found their first landing place very sandy and low, but so full of grapes that the very surge of the Sea sometimes over-flowed them: of which they found such plenty in all places, both on the sand, the green soyle and hils, as in the plaines as well on euery little shrub, as also climbing towardes the tops of high Cedars, that they did thinke in the world were not the like abundance.

We passed by the Sea-side towards the tops of the next hills being not high: from whence we might see the Sea on both sides, and found it an Ile of twentie myles in length, and six in breadth, the vallyes replenished with goodly tall Cedars. Discharging our Muskets, such a flocke of Cranes, the most white, arose by vs, with such a cry as if an Army of men had shouted altogether. This Ile hath many goodly Woods, and Deere, Conies, and Foule in incredible abundance, and vsing the Authors owne phrase, the Woods are not such as you finde in *Bohemia, Moscovia,* or *Hercinia,* barren and fruitlesse, but the highest and reddest Cedars of the world, bettering them of the Assores, Indies, or *Libanus:* Pynes, Cypres, Saxefras, the Lentisk that beareth Mastick, and many other of excellent smell and qualitie. Till the third day we saw not any of the people, then in a little Boat three of them appeared, one of them went on shore, to whom wee rowed, and he attended vs without any signe of feare; after he had spoke much though we vnderstood not a word, of his owne accord he came boldly aboord vs, we gaue him a shirt, a hat, wine and meate, which he liked well, and after he had well viewed the barkes and vs, he went away in his owne Boat, and within a quarter of a myle of vs in halfe an houre, had loaden his Boat with fish, with which he came againe to the poynt of land, and there devided it in two parts, poynting one part to the Ship, the other to the Pinnace, and so departed.

The next day came diuers Boats, and in one of them the Kings Brother, with forty or fifty men, proper people, and in their behauiour very ciuill; his name was *Granganameo,* the King is called *Winginia,* the Country *Wingandacoa.* Leauing his Boats a little from our Ships, he came with his trayne to the poynt: where spreading a Matte he sat downe. Though we came to him well armed, he made signes to vs to sit downe without any shew of feare, stroking his head and brest, and also ours, to expresse his loue. After he had made a long speech vnto vs, we presented him with diuers toyes, which he kindly accepted. He was greatly regarded by his people, for none of them did sit, nor speake a word, but foure, on whom we bestowed presents also, but he tooke all from them, making signes all things did belong to him.

The King himselfe in a conflict with a King his next neighbour and mortall enemy, was shot in two places through the body, and the thigh, yet recouered: whereby he lay at his chiefe towne six dayes iourney from thence.

A day or two after shewing them what we had, *Granganameo* taking most liking to a Pewter dish, made a hole in it, hung it about his necke for a brest-plate: for which he gaue vs twenty Deere skins, worth twenty Crownes; and for a Copper Kettell, fiftie skins, worth fiftie Crownes. Much other trucke we had, and after two dayes he came aboord, and did eate and drinke with vs very merrily. Not long after he brought his wife and children, they were but of meane stature, but well fauoured and very bashfull; she had a long coat of Leather, and about her priuities a peece of the same, about her forehead a band of white Corrall, and so had her husband, in her eares were bracelets of pearle, hanging downe to her middle, of the bignesse of great Pease; the rest of the women had Pendants of Copper, and the Noblemen fiue or sixe in an eare; his apparrell as his wiues, onely the women weare their haire long on both sides, and the men but on one; they are of colour yellow, but their hayre is blacke, yet we saw children that had very fayre Chesnut coloured hayre.

After that these women had beene here with vs, there came downe from all parts great store of people, with Leather, Corrall, and diuers kinde of dyes, but when *Granganameo* was present, none durst trade but himselfe, and them that wore red Copper on their heads, as he did. When euer he came, he would signifie by so many fires he came with so many boats, that we might know his strength. Their Boats are but one great tree, which is but burnt in the forme of a trough with gins and fire, till it be as they would haue it. For an armour he would haue ingaged vs a bagge of pearle, but we refused, as not regarding it, that wee might the better learn where it grew. He was very iust of his promise, for oft we trusted him, and he would come within his day to keepe his word. He sent vs commonly euery day a brace of Bucks, Conies, Hares, and fish, sometimes Mellons, Walnuts, Cucumbers, Pease, and diuers rootes. This Author sayth, their corne groweth three times in fiue moneths; in May they sow, in Iuly reape; in Iune they sow, in August reape; in Iuly sow, in August reape. We put some of our Pease in the ground, which in ten dayes were 14. ynches high.

The soyle is most plentifull, sweete, wholesome, and fruitfull of all other, there are about 14. seuerall sorts of sweete smelling tymber trees: the most parts of the vnderwood, Bayes and such like: such Okes as we, but far greater and better.

After this acquaintance, my selfe with seauen more went twenty myle into the Riuer *Occam,* that runneth toward the Cittie *Skicoack,* and the euening following we came to an Ile called *Roanoak,* from the harbour where we entred 7. leagues; at the North end was 9. houses, builded with Cedar, fortified round with sharpe trees, and the entrance like a Turnpik. When we came towards it, the wife of *Granganameo* came running out to meete vs, (her husband was absent) commanding her people to draw our Boat ashore for beating on the billowes, other she appoynted to carry vs on their backes aland, others to bring our Ores into the house for stealing. When we came into the other roome, (for there was fiue in the house) she caused vs to sit downe by a great fire; after tooke off our clothes and washed them, of some our stockings, and some our feete in warme water, and she her selfe tooke much paines to see all things well ordered, and to provide vs victuall.

After we had thus dryed our selues, she brought vs into an Inner roome, where she set on the bord standing a long the house somewhat like frumentie, sodden venison, and rosted fish; in like manner mellons raw, boyled rootes and fruites of diuers kindes. The[i]re drinke is commonly water boyled with Ginger, sometimes with Saxefras, and wholsome herbes, but whilest the Grape lasteth they drinke wine. More loue she could not expresse to entertaine vs; they care but onely to defend themselues from the short winter, and feede on what they finde naturall in sommer. In this feasting house was their Idoll of whom they tould vs vncredible things. When we were at meate two or three of her men came amongst vs with their Bowes and Arrowes, which caused vs to take our armes in hand. She perceiuing our distrust, caused their Bowes and Arrowes to be broken, and they beaten out of the gate: but the euening approaching we returned to our boate, where at she much grieuing brought our supper halfe boyled, pots and all, but when she saw vs but put our boat a little off from the shoar and lye at Anchor, perceiuing our Ielousie, she sent diuers men and 30. women to sit at night on the shoare side against vs, and sent vs fiue Mats to couer vs from the raine, doing all she could to perswade vs to her house. Though there was no cause of doubt, we would not aduenture: for on our safety depended the voyage: but a more kinde louing people cannot be.

Beyond this Ile is the maine land and the great riuer *Occam,* on which standeth a Towne called *Pomeiock,* and six dayes higher, their City *Skicoak:* those people neuer saw it, but say the[i]re fathers affirme it to be aboue two houres iourney about. Into this riuer falleth an other called *Cipo,* where is found many Mustells wherein are Pearles: likewise another Riuer called *Nomapona,* on the one side whereof standeth a great towne called *Chawanock,* the Lord of the Country is not subiect to *Wingandacoa.* Beyond him an other king they cal *Menatonon.* These 3. are in league each with other. Towards the south. 4. dayes iourney is *Sequotan,* the southermost part of *Wingandacoa.*

Adioyning to *Secotan* beginneth the country *Pomouik,* belonging to the King called *Piamacum,* in the Country *Nusiok* vpon the great riuer *Neus.* These haue mortall warres with *Wingina,* King of *Wingandacoa.* Betwixt *Piemacum* and the Lord of *Secotan,* a peace was concluded: notwithstanding there is a mortall malice in the *Secotans,* because this *Piemacum* invited diuers men, and 30. women to a feast, and when they were altogether merry before their Idoll, which is but a meere illusion of the Deuill, they sudainly slew all the men of *Secotan,* and kept the women for their vse. Beyond *Roanoak* are many Isles full of fruits and other Naturall increases, with many Townes a long the side of the Continent. Those Iles lye 200. myles in length, and betweene them and the mayne, a great long sea, in some places. 20. 40. or 50. myles broad, in other more, somewhere lesse. And in this sea are 100. Iles of diuers bignesses, but to get into it, you haue but 3. passages and they very dangerous.

Though this you see for most part be but the relations of Saluages, because it is the first, I thought it not a misse to remember them as they are written by them that returned and ariued in *England* about the middest of *September* [1584] the same yeare.

This discouery was so welcome into *England* that it pleased her Maiestie to call this Country of *Wingandacoa, Virginia,* by which name now you are to vnderstand how it was planted, disolued, renued, and enlarged.

The Performers of this voyage were these following.

Philip Amadas. } Captaines	
Arthur Barlow. }	

William Grenuill. ⎫
Iohn Wood.
Iames Browewich.
Henry Greene.   } Of the
Beniamen Wood.   Companie.
Simon Ferdinando.
Nicholas Peryman.
Iohn Hewes.   ⎭

THE PIRATE AS NATIONAL HERO

In his compilation of English narratives of exploration, Hakluyt included numerous tales of bold sea adventure. This is one reason why his book is still read today. The two greatest heroes of the age were Francis Drake and John Hawkins, favorites of Queen Elizabeth, who raided the Spanish Main and kept England's rivals off balance until 1588, when they helped to deliver the final blow against the Spanish Armada. Hawkins, besides being a hero, was also a pirate and a slave trader who forced his helpless and wretched cargoes upon Spanish colonies in the Caribbean at the point of a sword. It was important at the time to England that men like Hawkins be portrayed as heroes. Why was this so? And what does it tell us about Hakluyt and other promoters of British expansion?

The following selection, written by Hawkins, reveals the weaknesses, strengths, and tactics of England as she fought against the superior power of Spain in the New World.

SIR JOHN HAWKINS IN AFRICA AND THE SPANISH MAIN

The third troublesome voyage made with the Jesus of Lubeck, the Minion, and foure other ships, to the parts of Guinea, and the West Indies, in the yeeres 1567 and 1568 by M. John Hawkins

The ships departed from Plimmouth, the second day of October, Anno 1567 and had reasonable weather untill the seventh day, at which time fortie leagues North from Cape Finister, there arose an extreme storme, which continued foure dayes, in such sort, that the fleete was dispersed, and all our great boats lost, and the Jesus our chiefe shippe, in such case, as not thought able to serve the voyage: whereupon in the same storme we set our course homeward, determining to give over the voyage: but the eleventh day of the same moneth, the winde changed with faire weather, whereby we were animated to followe our enterprise, and so did, directing our course with the Ilands of the Canaries, where according to an order before prescribed, all our shippes before dispersed, met at one of those Ilands, called Gomera, where we tooke water, and departed from thence the fourth day of November, towards the coast of Guinea, and arrived at Cape Verde, the eighteenth of November: where we landed 150 men, hoping to obtaine some Negros, where we got but fewe, and those with great hurt and damage to our men, which chiefly proceeded of their envenomed arrowes: and although in the beginning they seemed to be but small hurts, yet there hardly escaped any that had blood drawen of them, but died in strange sort, with their mouthes shut some tenne dayes before they died, and after their wounds were whole; where I my selfe had one of the greatest woundes, yet thankes be to God, escaped. From thence we past the time upon the coast of Guinea, searching with all diligence the rivers from Rio Grande, unto Sierra Leona, till the twelfth of Januarie, in which time we had not gotten together a hundreth and fiftie Negros: yet notwithstanding the sicknesse of our men, and the late time of the yeere commanded us away: and thus having nothing wherewith to seeke the coast of the West Indias, I was with the rest of our company in consultation to goe to the coast of the Mine, hoping there to have obtained some golde for our wares, and thereby to have defraied our charge. But even in that present instant, there came to us a Negro, sent from a king, oppressed by other Kings his neighbours, desiring our aide, with promise that as many Negros as by these warres might be obtained, aswell of his part as of ours, should be at our pleasure: whereupon we concluded to give aide, and sent 120 of our men, which the 15 of Januarie, assaulted a towne of the Negros of our Allies adversaries, which had in it 8000 Inhabitants, being very strongly impaled and

Hakluyt's *Voyages*, X, pp. 64–74.

fenced after their manner, but it was so well defended, that our men prevailed not, but lost sixe men and fortie hurt: so that our men sent forthwith to me for more helpe: whereupon considering that the good successe of this enterprise might highly further the commoditie of our voyage, I went my selfe, and with the helpe of the king of our side, assaulted the towne, both by land and sea, and very hardly with fire (their houses being covered with dry Palme leaves) obtained the towne, put the Inhabitants to flight, where we tooke 250 persons, men, women, & children, and by our friend the king of our side, there were taken 600 prisoners, whereof we hoped to have had our choise: but the Negro (in which nation is seldome or never found truth) meant nothing lesse: for that night he remooved his campe and prisoners, so that we were faine to content us with those few which we had gotten our selves.

Now had we obtained between foure and five hundred Negros, wherwith we thought it somewhat reasonable to seeke the coast of the West Indies, and there, for our Negros, and other our merchandize, we hoped to obtaine, whereof to countervaile our charges with some gaines, wherunto we proceeded with all diligence, furnished our watering, tooke fuell, and departed the coast of Guinea the third of Februarie, continuing at the sea with a passage more hard, then before hath bene accustomed till the 27 day of March, which day we had sight of an Iland, called Dominica, upon the coast of the West Indies, in fourteene degrees: from thence we coasted from place to place, making our traffike with the Spaniards as we might, somewhat hardly, because the king had straightly commanded all his Governors in those parts, by no meanes to suffer any trade to be made with us: notwithstanding we had reasonable trade, and courteous entertainement, from the Ile of Margarita unto Cartagena, without any thing greatly worth the noting, saving at Capo de la Vela, in a towne called Rio de la Hacha (from whence come all the pearles) the treasurer who had the charge there, would by no meanes agree to any trade, or suffer us to take water, he had fortified his towne with divers bulwarkes in all places where it might be entered, and furnished himselfe with an hundred Hargabuziers, so that he thought by famine to have inforced us to have put a land our Negros: of which purpose he had not greatly failed, unlesse we had by force entred the towne: which (after we could by no meanes obtaine his favour) we were enforced to doe, and so with two hundred men brake in upon their bulwarkes, and entred the towne with the losse onely of two men of our partes, and no hurt done to the Spaniards because after their voley of shot discharged, they all fled.

Thus having the town with some circumstance, as partly by the Spaniards desire of Negros, and partly by friendship of the Treasurer, we obtained a secret trade: whereupon the Spaniards resorted to us by night, and bought of us to the number of 200 Negros: in all other places where we traded the Spaniards inhabitants were glad of us and traded willingly.

At Cartagena the last towne we thought to have seene on the coast, we could by no meanes obtaine to deale with any Spaniard, the governour was so straight, and because our trade was so neere finished we thought not good either to adventure any landing, or to detract further time, but in peace departed from thence the 24 of July, hoping to have escaped the time of their stormes which then soone after began to reigne, the which they call Furicanos, but passing by the West end of Cuba, towards the coast of Florida there happened to us the 12 day of August an extreme storme which continued by the space of foure dayes, which so beat the Jesus, that we cut downe all her higher buildings, her rudder also was sore shaken, and withall was in so extreme a leake that we were rather upon the point to leave her then to keepe her any longer, yet hoping to bring all to good passe, we sought the coast of Florida, where we found no place nor Haven for our ships, because of the shalownesse of the coast: thus being in greater dispaire, and taken with a newe storme which continued other 3 dayes, we were inforced to take for our succour the Port which serveth the citie of Mexico called Saint John de Ullua, which standeth in 19 degrees: in seeking of which Port we tooke in our way 3 ships which carried passengers to the number of an hundred, which passengers we hoped should be a meane to us the better to obtaine victuals for our money, & a quiet place for the repairing of our fleete. Shortly after this the 16 of September we entered the Port of Saint John de Ullua and in our entrie the Spaniardes thinking us to be the fleete of Spaine, the chiefe officers of the Countrey came aboord us, which being deceived of their expectation were greatly dismayed: but immediatly when they sawe our demand was nothing but victuals, were recomforted. I found also in the same Port twelve ships which had in them by report two hundred thousand pound in gold & silver, all which (being in my possession, with the kings Iland as also the passengers before in my way thitherward stayed) I set at libertie, without the taking from them the waight of a groat: onely because I would not be delayed of my dispatch, I stayed two men of estimation and sent post immediatly to Mexico, which was two hundred miles from us, to the Presidentes and Councell there, shewing them of our arrivall there by the force of weather, and the necessitie of the repaire of our shippes and victuals, which wantes we required as friends to king Philip to be furnished of for our money: and that the Presidents and Councell there should with all convenient speede take order, that at the arrivall of the Spanish fleete, which was dayly looked for, there might no cause of quarrell rise betweene us and them, but for the better maintenance of amitie, their commandement might be had in that behalfe. This message being sent away the sixteenth day of September at night, being the very day of our arrivall, in the next morning which was the seventeenth day of the same moneth, we sawe open of the Haven thirteene great shippes, and understanding them to bee the fleete of Spaine, I sent immediatly to advertise the Generall of the fleete of my being there, doing him to understand, that before I would suffer them to enter the Port, these should some order of conditions passe betweene us for our safe being there, and maintenance of peace. Now it is to be understood that this Port is made by a little Iland of stones not three foote above the water in the highest place, and but a bow-shoot of length any way, this Iland standeth from the maine land two bow shootes or more, also it is to be understood that there is not in all this coast any other place for ships to arrive in safety, because the North winde hath there such violence, that unlesse the shippes be very safely mored with their ankers fastened upon this Iland, there is no remedie for these North windes but death: also the place of the Haven was so little, that of necessitie the shippes must ride one aboord the other, so that we could not give place to them, nor they to us: and here I beganne to bewaile that which after followed, for now, said I, I am in two dangers, and forced to receive the one of them. That was, either I must have kept out the fleete from entring the Port, the which with Gods helpe I was very well able to doe, or else suffer them to enter in with their accustomed treason, which they never faile to execute, where they may have opportunitie, to compasse it by any meanes: if I had kept them out, then had there bene present shipwracke of all the fleete which amounted in value to sixe Millions, which was in value of our money 1800000. li. which I considered I was not able to answere, fearing the Queenes Majesties indignation in so waightie a matter. Thus with my selfe revolving the doubts, I thought rather better to abide the Jutt of the uncertainty, then the certaintie. The uncertaine doubt I account was their treason which by good policie I hoped might be prevented, and therefore as chusing the least mischiefe I proceeded to conditions. Now was our first messenger come and returned from the fleete with report of the arrivall of a Viceroy, so that hee had authoritie, both in all this Province of Mexico (otherwise called Nueva Espanna) and in the sea, who sent us word that we should send our conditions, which of his part should (for the better maintenance of amitie betweene the Princes) be both favourably granted, and faithfully performed, with many faire wordes how passing the coast of the Indies he had understood of our honest behaviour towardes the inhabitants where we had to doe, aswell elsewhere as in the same Port, the which I let passe: thus following our demand, we required victuals for our money, and licence to sell as much ware as might furnish our wants, and that there might be of either part twelve gentlemen as hostages for the maintenance of peace: and that the Iland for our better safetie might be in our owne possession, during our abode there, and such ordinance as was planted in the same Iland which were eleven peeces of brasse: and that no Spaniard might land in the Iland with any kind of weapon: these conditions at the first he somewhat misliked, chiefly the guard of the Iland to be in our owne keeping, which if they had had, we had soone knowen our fare: for with the first North winde they had cut our cables and our ships had gone ashore: but in the ende he concluded to our request, bringing the twelve hostages to ten, which with all speede of either part were received, with a writing from the Viceroy signed with his hande and sealed with his seale of all the conditions concluded, & forthwith a trumpet blowen with commandement that none of either part should be meane to violate the peace upon paine of death: and further it was concluded that the two Generals of the fleetes should meete, and give faith ech to other for the performance of the premisses which was so done. Thus at the end of 3 dayes all was concluded & the fleete entered the Port, saluting one another as the maner of the sea doth require. Thus as I said before, thursday we entred the Port, Friday we saw the fleete, and on munday at night they entered the Port: then we laboured 2. daies placing the English ships by themselves & the Spanish ships by themselves, the captaines of ech part & inferiour men of their parts promising great amity of al sides: which even as with all fidelitie it was ment on our part, so the Spaniards ment nothing lesse on their parts, but from the maine land had furnished themselves with a supply of men to the number of 1000, and ment the next thursday being the 23 of September at dinner time to set upon us on all sides. The same Thursday in the morning the treason being at hand, some appearance shewed, as shifting of weapon from ship to ship, planting and bending of ordinance from the ships to the Iland where our men warded, passing too and fro of companies of men more then required for their necessary busines, & many other ill likelihoods, which caused us to have a vehement suspition, and therewithall sent to the Viceroy to enquire what was ment by it, which sent immediatly straight commandement to unplant all things suspicious, and also sent word that he in the faith of a Viceroy would be our defence from all villanies. Yet we being not satisfied with this answere, because we suspected a great number of men to be hid in a great ship of 900 tunnes, which was mored next unto the Minion, sent againe to the Viceroy the master of the Jesus which had the Spanish tongue, and required to be satisfied if any such thing were or not. The Viceroy now seeing that the treason must be discovered, foorthwith stayed our master, blew the Trumpet, and of all sides set upon us: our men which warded a shore being stricken with sudden feare, gave place, fled, and sought to recover succour of the ships; the Spainardes being before provided for the purpose landed in all places in multitudes from their ships which they might easily doe without boates, and slewe all our men a shore without mercie, a fewe of them escaped aboord the Jesus. The great ship which had by the estimation three hundred men placed in her secretly, immediatly fell aboord the Minion, but by Gods appointment, in the time of the suspicion we had, which was onely one halfe houre, the Minion was made readie to avoide, and so leesing her hedfasts, and hayling away by the sternefastes she was gotten out: thus with Gods helpe she defended the violence of the first brunt of these three hundred men. The Minion being past out, they came aboord the Jesus, which also with very much a doe and the losse of manie of our men were defended and kept out. Then there were also two other ships that assaulted the Jesus at the same instant, so that she had hard getting loose, but yet with some time we had cut our headfastes and gotten out by the sterne-fastes. Nowe when the Jesus and the Minion were gotten about two shippes length from the Spanish fleete, the fight beganne so hotte on all sides that within one houre the Admirall of the Spaniards was supposed to be sunke, their Viceadmirall burned and one other of their principall ships supposed to be sunke, so that the shippes were little able to annoy us.

Then it is to be understood, that all the Ordinance upon the Ilande was in the Spaniardes handes, which did us so great annoyance, that it cut all the mastes and yardes of the Jesus, in such sort that there was no hope to carrie her away: also it sunke our small shippes, wereupon we determined to place the Jesus on that side of the Minion, that she might abide all the batterie from the land, and so be a defence for the Minion till night, and then to take such reliefe of victuall and other necessaries from the Jesus, as the time would suffer us, and to leave her. As we were thus determining, and had placed the Minion from the shot of the land, suddenly the Spaniards had fired two great shippes which were comming directly with us, and having no meanes to avoide the fire, it bredde among our men a marvellous feare, so that some sayd, let us depart with the Minion, other said, let us see whither the winde will carrie the fire from us. But to be short, the Minions men which had alwayes their sayles in a readinesse, thought to make sure worke, and so with-out either consent of the Captaine or Master cut their saile, so that very hardly I was received into the Minion.

The most part of the men that were left alive in the Jesus, made shift and followed the Minion in a small boat, the rest which the little boate was not able to receive, were inforced to abide the mercie of the Spaniards (which I doubt was very little) so with the Minion only and the Judith (a small barke of 50 tunne) we escaped, which barke the same night forsooke us in our great miserie: we were now remooved with the Minion from the Spanish ships two bow-shootes, and there rode all that night: the next morning we recovered an Iland a mile from the Spaniards, where there tooke us a North winde, and being left onely with two ankers and two cables (for in this conflict we lost three cables and two ankers) we thought alwayes upon death which ever was present, but God preserved us to a longer time.

The weather waxed reasonable, and the Saturday we set saile, and having a great number of men and little victuals our hope of life waxed lesse and lesse: some desired to yeeld to the Spaniards, some rather desired to obtaine a place where they might give themselves to the Infidels, and some had rather abide with a little pittance the mercie of God at Sea: so thus with many sorow-ful hearts we wandred in an unknowen Sea by the space of 14 dayes, till hunger inforced us to seek the land, for hides were thought very good meat, rats, cats, mice and dogs, none escaped that might be gotten, parrats and monkeyes that were had in great price, were thought there very profitable if they was borne out as it might be, but in the end although there were none of our men suffered to goe a land, yet by accesse of the Spaniards, our feeblenesse was knowen to them. Whereupon they ceased not to seeke by all meanes to betray us, but with all speede possible we departed to Vigo, where we had some helpe of certaine English ships and twelve fresh men, wherewith we repaired our wants as we might, and departing the 20 day of January 1568 arrived in Mounts bay in Cornewall the 25 of the same moneth, praised be God therefore.

If all the miseries and troublesome affaires of this sorrowfull voyage should be perfectly and throughly written, there should neede a painefull man with his pen, and as great a time as he had that wrote the lives and deathes of the Martyrs.

John Hawkins

IN SEARCH OF EL DORADO

Perhaps the most tragic figure of the age, as well as one of its grandest symbols, Sir Walter Raleigh was the ideal courtier described in the article by Professor Jones at the beginning of this section. He had been instrumental in launching the ill-fated colony at Roanoke under a patent from the Queen. He had also failed by ever so little, in his opinion, to locate the fabulous kingdom of El Dorado in northern South America in the year 1595. Later, fallen from favor, Raleigh sat imprisoned in the Tower of London, writing his History of the World and dreaming of another Incan empire buried deep in the mountains and jungles of South America. In 1617 he was given one last chance to make his fabulous discovery of wealth. He set out with a great fleet for Guiana with high hopes and wild dreams.

The selection that follows is part of a piece entitled "Newes of Sir Walter Rauleigh." It is a report on his progress, probably dictated by him. As such, it clearly reflects one of the major objectives of English exploration—instant wealth and plunder in imitation of the Spaniards. It reveals that, as late as 1617, the Spanish model of imperialism still persisted in the minds of some Englishmen.

Unfortunately, Raleigh failed to find El Dorado, producing only the rich imagery of his own promotional literature. The Crown was disappointed, while the Spanish were worried that further expeditions might locate the desired riches. Thus, at the urging of the Spanish ambassador, and to keep an uneasy peace with Spain, the gallant but quixotic Raleigh was beheaded in the courtyard of the Tower of London by his own people.

RALEIGH'S VOYAGE TO GUIANA IN 1617

Newes of Sir Walter Rauleigh

By these orders and Commandements, you may see to what Coast wee are bound, and namely to the South parts of *America,* and no doubt to the onely best part therof: For as all the Springs and Riuers in the world haue but one head, namely, the Sea: so it is thought all the wealthy Mynes in the world haue but one Soueraigne, which is an Empire placed in these parts, and that is the great Empire of *Guiana,* ruled by the great Emperour *Inga:* of the great wealth and riches whereof *Francisco Lopez* and others thus report; That all the vessels of the Emperours house, Tables, and Kitchen were of Siluer and Gold, and the very meanest of all of Siluer and Copper, for the strength and hardnesse of the mettall: That in his Wardrobe were hollow Statues of gold, which seemed gyants, and Figures in proportion and bigness of all the Beasts, Birds, Trees, and Hearbs, that the earth bringeth forth in pure Gold also, and of all the Fishes that the Sea and waters of that Empyre breedeth. Also there was Ropes, Budgets, Chests, and Troughs of Gold and Siluer; great heaps of Billets of Gold, which seemed wood marked out to burne; nay, that there was nothing in all that Empire (the most flourishing of the whole world) whereof there was not a counterfeit in pure Gold.

Besides, there was seene in a certaine Iland neare the Emperours Court, a Garden of pleasure, in which was all kinde of Garden-hearbs, flowers and trees, of Gold and Siluer. As also in other places diuers great infinits of Gold

Peter Force, *Tracts and Other Papers, Relating Principally to The Origin, Settlement, and Progress of the Colonies In North America, From The Discovery of The Country To The Year 1776,* 4 vols. (New York, Peter Smith, repr., 1947), III, Part 4.

and siluer vnwrought, as in one place to the value of fifty two thousand Markes of pure Siluer, and one Million and three hundred twenty and sixe thousand and fiue hundred *Pesoes* in Gold.

Now it is to be vnderstood that all this wealth belonged but to one Emperour: for the custome of the Country is, that whosoeuer dyeth hath all his Treasure buryed with him, so that euen from the first Ruler to the Emperour now liuing, it is thought no lesse Treasure will be found in euery Monument; which how vnspeakable it is, I leaue to iudgement. . . .

Thus you may see this *El Dorado*, or golden seate, hath beene sought by many worthy Spanyards, one Noble Englishman, and diuers Frenchmen, yet none so successefull as the English, which makes me Prophetiquely suppose, that the glory of the action is reserued for vs only, and the Kingdome such a Paragon and rich stone as shall adorne no crowne but the crowne of King *Iames*.

The rest I leaue to their iudgement which shall reade what hath beene formerly written of it, or else these few protestations which doe follow.

First, Sir *Walter Rauleigh* himself protesteth from his owne sight and knowledge, that vpon this maine Riuer in which he sailed, whose branches doe runne and diuide into diuers Nations and Countries, aboue two thousand miles to the East and West, and eight hundred miles South and North, a man may see as many seuerall Kingdomes and Prouinces as may satisfie any industrious iudgement whatsoeuer; and of them, the most, eyther rich in Gold or in other. Merchandise: that in this place the Souldier may fight for Gold, and pay himselfe in stead of pence with plates of gold a foot broad: that the Commanders which shoot at honor and abundance, may finde there more beautifull Cities, more Temples adorned with Golden Images, more Sepulchers filled with Treasure, then eyther was found in *Mexico* or *Peru*: and that the shining glory of this Conquest would eclypse all the beames of the Spanish Nation.

Also hee saith, there is no Country which yeeldeth more pleasure to the Inhabitants, for the delights of Hunting, Hawking, Fishing, Fowling, and the rest, then these Lands which hee saw did. They haue also so many Plaines, cleare Riuers, abundance of Pheasants, Partridges, Quailes, Rayles, Cranes, Herons, and all other Fowle: Deere of all sorts, Porkes, Hares, Lyons, Tygers, Leopards, and diuers other sorts of Beasts eyther for chase or foode, that no Nation of the world can exceede them.

And to conclude, hee saith, that both for health, good Ayre, pleasure and riches, it is not to be equald by any Region eyther in the East or West: and that there is in it great store of Brasillwood, and diuers Berryes which dye a most perfect Crimson and Carnation; and for painting, not all France, Italy, nor the East-Indies yeeld any such, for the more the skinne is washed, the fairer the colour appeareth.

Also there is great store of Cotton, of Silke, of Balsamum, and of those kindes most excellent, and neuer knowne in *Europe*. There are all sorts of Gummes, of Indian Pepper, besides what the Country may afford inwardly, which hee had not leasure to search, is yet vnknowne. Also the Soyle is so excellent and so full of Riuers, that it will beare Sugar, Ginger, and all commodities that the West Indies hath.

Now for the easinesse of the Nauigation, hee saith it may be sayled in sixe weekes thither, and in sixe weekes backe againe: and by the way neyther be shoare, enemies coast, rockes, nor sands; all which other Voyages are subiect vnto.

Also hee saith, the best time to sayle from England thither, is in Iuly, because the Summer in *Guyana* is in October, Nouember, December, Ianuary, February, and March, and so shipping may returne from thence in Aprill, and arriue at home in England, in Iune; and by that means neuer be subiect to winter weather, eyther comming, going, or staying, which no doubt is an excellent comfort to all men that shall vndertake the Action.

And thus much touching his worthy and noble Relation, who being an eyewitnesse, would not for his honour and vertues sake abuse his Soueraigne with vntruths.

Now let vs see what the Spanyards say of this rich Kingdome. First, *Alonso*, a chiefe Gouernour in the *Grand Canaria*, saith; that there was a Land newly discouered, called *Nueuo Dorado*, in which was abundance of Gold, and wonderfull riches aboue imagination: that the course to fall with it, was fifty leagues to the windeward to the *Marguarita*.

Againe hee saith in another affirmation, that in *Nueuo Dorado* lately found out there was gold in that abundance, as the like hath neuer formerly been heard of, nor was any part of the world to be compared with it; and the like affirmeth *Domingo de Vera* who was Campe Maister and Generall for *Anthony Bereo* in this Discouery, and no lesse saith *Rodrigo de Caranoa* Register for the Sea, and many others: So that to conclude your trouble and the tediousnes of my weary discourse, this Empire is that rich *Magazany* which yet hath her Maidenhead neuer sackt, turn'd, nor wrought, the face of the earth hath not beene turnd nor the vertue and salt of the soyle spent by manurance, The graues haue not been opened for Gold, the Mines not broken with the sledge or pickaxe, nor their Images puld downe out of their Temples. It hath neuer beene entred by any army of strength, and neuer conquered or possessed by any Christian Prince: Besides by the report of all former Discouerers, especially our Generall, it is so defensible and easie to bee kept from the assaults of any inuaders, that if two Forts bee builded in one of the Prouinces which he beheld and tooke especiall note of; the flood setteth in so neere the banke where the channell also lyeth that no Ship can passe vp, but within a pikes length, of the artillery, first of the one, and afterwards of the other, which two

Forts he supposeth will bee sufficient guard, both to the Empire of *Inga*, and to one hundred other seuerall Kingdomes, all lying within the great Riuer of *Orenoque*, euen to the Citty of *Quito* in *Peru*.

Of this Empire if it shall please God to make the King our Maister Soueraigne, what honor and reward it will bring him and his Subiects may easily bee coniectured by what is before written; and since it is or may bee vndertaken by his owne vassaile, and one who is bound in extraordinary bonde more then euery common Subiect, to spend the vttermost of his life in the same, no doubt but hee will effect it with that wisedome, diligence, and care which shall bee sutable to the greatnes of the action, and the trust reposed, being thus far forth further encouraged by *Anthonio Bereo* the Spaniard, who in great earnestnes, and vpon his Soules health protested, that hee had seene amongst diuers most antient Prophesies in *Peru* (at such time as that Empire was reduced to the Spanish obedience) one that affirmed, that from *Inglatierra* (which is to say, England) those *Ingas* should bee againe in time to come restored and deliuered from the seruitude of the former Conquerors, and this hee auowed to haue seene in diuers of their most principall and chiefest Temples, preserued with great reuerence and care, and till this day beleeued of all the Indians: Now an entrance in former yeares our Generall did make, as you haue read, with that successe that not any before or since hath euer equalled & displanted the first garrisons, if then now he succeed and haue fortune answerable to his rare wisedome, industry and direction, whether it bee in this or any other to himselfe onely concealed, there is no doubt but (God assisting) hee will with such honor and high thoughts, passe and go thorow the same, that his nation shall haue praise, his friendes comfort, and himselfe the true aduancement of his merits.

But to giue you a little tast of what hath succeeded in our present Iourney, you shall vnderstand that we departed from *Plimouth* to *Corke* in Ireland, where after some refreshment wee set saile out of the riuer of *Corke*, and thence sailed more than three Moneths before we came to the Coast of *Guiana*, which albeit generally it bee euer run in seauen or eight weekes, yet were the windes so strangely crosse vnto vs, (a thing seldome seene in that passage) that in lesse time we could not effect our purpose: So that vpon the seauenth day of Nouember last past, 1 6 1 7. wee discouered the Coast of *Guiana*, during which time of our being at Sea, we had a great visitation of Sicknesse, so that many were sick, and some are dead, amongst which, the most eminent persons that dyed were these. Captaine *Iohn Pygot* our Lieftenant Generall, worthy Captaine *Hastings*, my Lord of *Huntingtons* brother, a Gentleman of so much foreward hope, and goodnes, that that he was couered with many teares, and much mourning; also there died Maister *Talbot* Scholler, which hath been long imployed by our Generall; M. *Newball*, the maister Chirurgeon of our Generalls Ship, and others, with which I will not trouble your eares.

Vpon the discouering of the Coast, we came into the faire Riuer of *Caliana*, being (as it appeareth to me) a branch of *Oerenoque*, where my Lord, our Generall cast Anchor, and doth purpose to refresh his sick men, and to take in fresh water and other necessary prouisions, of which that Coast aboundeth, and so to proceed in his enterprise which God in his mercy prosper, for our hopes euery day grow stronger and stronger. This part of *Guiana* in which we now are, is to me a very Paradise, and so excellent in all perfections and beauties, that Nature seemes only here to haue her Temple; we haue euen now (being the Month of Nouember) a much more delicate Sommer, then is in England at Mid-sommer, the Sun and Ayre so wholesome & pleasant without offence or scorching, the trees & ground so brauely flourishing, and euery thing in Generall so absolute and full of fruitfull promise, that more cannot be by man desired: for mine own part I dare assure you, that in my life time I neuer saw or tasted more strange, more delicate, & more pleasant fruits, then heere we may continually gather in most infinite aboundance, being besides so wondrous wholsome and vnoffensiue, that I haue not heard any complaine either of surfet, or other accidentall sickness, as wormes, fluxes & such like, which commonly follow the much eating of sweet and pleasant fruit. To enter into a Description of the beautifull prospect of this Country which wee now see, although it be but the out-borders and skirts of the Empire, so neare a neighbour to the maine Ocean, that in reason it should promise the least fertilitie; yet I say again, to describe the goodlinesse thereof, the brauery of the Hils, and comlinesse of the vallies, both shadowed and adorned with goodly tall green trees; the pleasantnesse and coolnesse of the Riuers which runne and mixe themselues in the most conuenientest places, plentifully stored with fish of seuerall natures; the variety of rare coloured Birds which flie vp and down in euery place about vs, no colour almost vnder the Sun but being reuealed in their feathers: were to draw a Landskip of that excellent perfection, which no Art could better, hardly imitate. For truely hitherto to mine eye this Country hath appeared a very earthly Paradise, and therefore doubtlesse is full of strong promises, that our attemptings cannot returne without much honour and reward, a rent hopefully due to euery such noble action. But since it yet resteth in hope, I will leaue it to the will and direction of the great G O D of Heauen: To whose protection I refer you, with this assurance, that as our successe shall happen, and the action either decrease or diminish, so you shall by writing more amply vnderstand thereof.

From the Riuer of *Caliana* on the Coast of *Guiana*, this seauenteenth of *Nouember*, 1617.   R. M.

THE FIRST SCIENTIFIC VIEW OF VIRGINIA

In 1585 Raleigh launched another expedition of seven ships to Virginia under the command of Sir Richard Grenville. This expedition established the unfortunate lost colony at Roanoke Island. It also produced the first on-the-spot pictorial representations of the new land, made by the artist John White. Equally important, it produced the first scientific description of the country, written by Thomas Heriot, the foremost mathematician in England, who went along on the voyage. His is a sober, practical account which contrasts sharply with the kind of description that might have been written by Raleigh himself had he been present. This is a forerunner of many such geographical descriptions by British naturalists of exotic parts of the globe. They defined, in the long run, the main current of scientific activity in an age increasingly devoted to the empirical study of nature.

THOMAS HERIOT'S REPORT

The Observations of Master Thomas Heriot in this Voyage

FOR MARCHANDIZE AND VICTUALLS

What before is writ, is also confirmed by that learned *Mathematician* Master *Thomas Heriot*, with them in the Country, whose particular Relation of all the Beasts, Birds, Fishes, Foules, Fruites, and Rootes, and how they may be vsefull; because I haue writ it before for the most part in the Discourse[s] of Captaine *Amidas*, and Captaine *Layne*, except Silk grasse, Worme silke, Flax like Hempe, Allum, Wapeith or *Terra sigillata*, Tar, Rosen, and Turpentine, Civet-cats, Iron ore, Copper that held Silver, Coprose and Pearle: Let those briefes suffice, because I would not trouble you with one thing twice.

DYES

For Dyes, *Showmack*, the herbe *Wasebur*, little rootes called *Chapacor*, and the barke of a tree called by the Inhabitants *Tangomockonominge*, which are for divers sorts of Reds.

John Smith, *Travels and Works*, I, pp. 319–325. This report also appears in Hakluyt's *Voyages*, VIII, pp. 348–373.

What more then is related is an herbe in Dutch called *Melden*, described like an Orange, growing foure foote high; the seede will make good broth, and the stalke burnt to ashes makes a kinde of Salt: other Salt they know not, and we vsed of it for Pot-herbs. Of their *Tobacco* we found plenty, which they esteeme their chiefe Physicke.

Ground nuts, *Tiswaw* we call *China* roots; they grow in clusters, and bring forth a bryer stalke, but the leafe is far vnlike, which will climbe vp to the top of the highest tree: the vse knowne is to cut it in small peeces, then stampe and straine it with water, and boyled makes a gelly good to eate. *Cassavia* growes in Marishes, which the *Indians* oft vse for bread and broth. *Habascon* is like a Parsnip, naught of it selfe, except compounded: and their Leekes like those in *England*.

Sequenummener, a kinde of Berry like Capers, and three kinde of Berries like Acornes, called *Sagatamenor, Osamenor,* and *Pummuckoner.*

Saquenuckot and *Maquowoc*, two kinde of beasts, greater then Conies, and very good meate; in some places such plenty of gray Conies, like hayres, that all the people make them mantels of their skins. I haue the names of 28. severall sorts that are dispersed in the Country: of which 12. kindes we haue discouered and good to eate; but the Salvages sometimes kill a Lyon and eate him.

There is plentie of Sturgeon in February, March, Aprill, and May; all Herings in abundance; some such as ours, but the most part of 18. 20. or 24. ynches long, and more. Trouts, Porpisses, Rayes, Mullets, Old-wiues, Plaice, Tortoises both by Sea and Land: Crabs, Oysters, Mussels, Scalops, Periwinckles, Crevises, Secanank: we haue the Pictures of 12. sorts more, but their names we know not.

Turkyes, Stockdoues, Partridges, Cranes, Hernes, Swans, Geese, Parrots, Faulcons, Merlins. I haue the names in their language of 86. severall sorts.

Their woods are such as ours in *England* for the most part, except *Rakeock*, a great sweet tree, whereof they make their Canowes: and *Ascopo*, a kinde of tree like Lowrell, and Saxefras.

THEIR NATURES AND MANNERS

Their Clothing, Townes, Houses, Warres, Arts, Tooles, handy crafts, and educations, are much like them in that part of *Virginia* we now [1607–1624] inhabite: which at large you may reade in the Description thereof. But the relation of their Religion is strange, as this Author reporteth.

Some Religion they haue, which although it be farre from the truth, yet being as it is, there is hope it may be the easier reformed. They beleeue there are many gods which they call *Mantoac*, but of different sorts and degrees. Also that there is one chiefe God that hath beene from all eternitie, who as they say when he purposed first to make the world, made first other gods of a principall order, to be as instruments to be vsed in the Creation and government to follow: And after the Sunne, Moone, and Starres, as pettie gods; and the instruments of the other order more principall. First (they say) were made waters, out of which by the gods were made all diversitie of creatures that are visible or invisible.

For mankinde they say a Woman was made first, which by the working of one of the gods conceiued and brought forth children; and so they had their beginning, but how many yeares or ages since they know not; having no Records but onely Tradition from Father to sonne.

They thinke that all the gods are of humane shape, and therefore represent them by Images in the formes of men; which they call *Kewasowok*: one alone is called *Kewasa*; them they place in their Temples, where they worship, pray, sing, and make many offerings. The common sort thinke them also gods.

They beleeue the immortalitie of the Soule, when life departing from the body, according to the good or bad workes it hath done, it is carried vp to the Tabernacles of the gods, to perpetuall happinesse, or to *Popogusso*, a great pit: which they thinke to be at the furthest parts of the world, where the Sunne sets, and there burne continually.

To confirme this they told me of two men that had beene lately dead, and revived againe; the one hapned but few yeares before our comming into the country; of a bad man, which being dead and buried, the next day the earth over him being seene to moue, was taken vp, who told them his soule was very neare entering into *Popogusso*, had not one of the gods saued him and gaue him leaue to returne againe, to teach his friends what they should doe to avoyd such torment. The other hapned the same yeare we were there, but sixtie myles from vs, which they told me for news, that one being dead, buried, and taken vp as the first, shewed, that although his body had layne dead in the graue, yet his soule liued, and had travailed far in a long broad way, on both sides whereof grew more sweet, fayre, and delicate trees and fruits, then ever he had seene before; at length he came to most braue and fayre houses, neare which he met his Father, that was dead long agoe, who gaue him charge to goe backe, to shew his friends what good there was to doe, to inioy the pleasures of that place; which when hee had done hee should come againe.

What subtiltie so ever be in the Weroances, and Priests: this opinion worketh so much in the common sort, that they haue great respect to their Governours: and as great care to avoyde torment after death, and to enioy blisse. Yet they haue divers sorts of punishments according to the offence, according to the greatnesse of the fact. And this is the sum of their Religion, which I learned by having speciall familiaritie with their Priests, wherein they were not so sure grounded, nor gaue such credit but through conversing with vs, they were brought into great doubts of their owne, and no small admiration of ours: of which many desired to learne more then we had meanes for want of vtterance in their Language to expresse.

Figure drawings by John White: Pictish men and woman (top), and a Weroans, or chieftain, of Virginia (bottom). These drawings suggest that White's view of the Indian was conditioned by his artistic training in England.

Most things they saw with vs as Mathematicall Instruments, Sea-Compasses; the vertue of the Loadstone, Perspectiue Glasses, burning Glasses: Clocks to goe of themselues; Bookes, writing, Guns, and such like; so far exceeded their capacities, that they thought they were rather the workes of gods then men; or at least the gods had taught vs how to make them, which loued vs so much better then them; and caused many of them [to] giue credit to what we spake concerning our God. In all places where I came, I did my best to make his immortall glory knowne. And I told them, although the Bible I shewed them, contained all; yet of it selfe, it was not of any such vertue as I thought they did conceiue. Notwithstanding many would be glad to touch it, to kisse, and imbrace it, to hold it to their breasts and heads, and stroke all their body over with it.

The King *Wingina* where we dwelt, would oft be with vs at Prayer. Twice he was exceeding sicke and like to dye. And doubting of any helpe from his Priests, thinking he was in such danger for offending vs and our God, sent for some of vs to pray, and be a meanes to our God, he might liue with him after death. And so did many other in the like case.

One other strange Accident (leauing others) will I mention before I end, which mooued the whole Country that either knew or heard of vs, to haue vs in wonderfull admiration.

There was no Towne where they had practised any villany against vs (we leauing it vnpunished, because we sought by all possible meanes to winne them by gentlenes) but within a few dayes after our departure, they began to dye; in some Townes twenty, in some forty, in some sixty, and in one an hundred and twenty, which was very many in respect of their numbers. And this hapned in no place (we could learn) where we had bin, but where they had vsed some practise to betray vs. And this disease was so strange, they neither knew what it was, nor how to cure it; nor had they knowne the like time out of minde; a thing specially observed by vs, as also by themselues, in so much that some of them who were our friends, especially *Wingina*, had observed such effects in foure or fiue Townes, that they were perswaded it was the worke of God through our meanes: and that we by him might kill and slay whom we would, without weapons, and not come neare them. And therevpon, when they had any vnderstanding, that any of their enemies abused vs in our Iourneyes, they would intreat vs, we would be a meanes to our God, that they, as the others that had dealt ill with vs, might dye in like sort: although we shewed them their requests were vngodly; and that our God would not subiect himselfe to any such requests of men, but all things as he pleased came to passe: and that we to shew our selues his true servants, ought rather to pray for the contrary: yet because the effect fell out so suddenly after, according to their desires, they thought it came to passe by our meanes, and would come giue vs thankes in their manner, that though we satisfied them not in words, yet in deeds we had fulfilled their desires.

This marueilous Accident in all the Country wrought so strange opinions of vs, that they could not tell whether to thinke vs gods or men. And the rather that all the space of their sicknesse, there was no man of ours knowne to die, or much sicke. They noted also we had no women, nor cared for any of theirs: some therefore thought we were not borne of women, and therefore not mortall, but that we were men of an old generation many yeares past, and risen againe from immortalitie. Some would Prophesie there were more of our generation yet to come, to kill theirs and take their places. Those that were to come after vs they imagined to be in the ayre, yet invisible and without bodies: and that they by our intreaties, for loue of vs, did make the people die as they did, by shooting invisible bullets into them.

To confirme this, their Physicians to excuse their Ignorance in curing the disease, would make the simple people beleeue, that the strings of bloud they sucked out of the sicke bodies, were the strings wherein the invisible bullets were tyed, and cast. Some thought we shot them our selues from the place where we dwelt, and killed the people that had offended vs, as we listed, how farre distant soever. And others said it was the speciall worke of God for our sakes, as we had cause in some sort to thinke no lesse, whatsoever some doe, or may imagine to the contrary; especially some *Astrologers* by the eclipse of the Sunne we saw that yeare [1584] before our Voyage, and by a *Comet* which began to appeare but a few dayes before the sicknesse began: but to exclude them from being the speciall causes of so speciall an Accident, there are farther reasons then I thinke fit to present or alledge.

These their opinions I haue set downe, that you may see there is hope to imbrace the truth, and honor, obey, feare and loue vs, by good dealing and government: though some of our company towards the latter end, before we came away with Sir *Francis Drake* shewed themselues too furious, in slaying some of the people in some Townes, vpon causes that on our part might haue bin borne with more mildnesse; notwithstanding they iustly had deserued it. The best nevertheless in this, as in all actions besides, is to be indevoured and hoped; and of the worst that may happen, notice to be taken with consideration; and as much as may be eschewed; the better to allure them hereafter to Civilitie and Christianitie.

Thus you may see, *How*

Nature her selfe delights her selfe in sundry Instruments,
That sundry things be done to decke the earth with Ornaments;
Nor suffers she her servants all should runne one race,
But wills the walke of every one frame in a divers pace;
That divers wayes and divers workes, the world might better grace.

Written by *Thomas Heriot*, one of the Voyage.

AMERICAN ABUNDANCE

This optimistic report by Captain John Smith is clearly intended to encourage emigration from England to Virginia, and stresses the New World's advantages in a rather concise statement. Note the "emulative" or "other-directed" assessment that Smith makes of Virginia's economic potential.

JOHN SMITH ON VIRGINIA

The Commodities in Virginia, or that may be had by Industrie

The mildnesse of the ayre, the fertilitie of the soyle, and situation of the rivers are so propitious to the nature and vse of man, as no place is more convenient for pleasure, profit, and mans sustenance, vnder that latitude or climat. Here will liue any beasts, as horses, goats, sheepe, asses, hens, &c. as appeared by them that were carried thether. The waters, Isles, and shoales, are full of safe harbours for ships of warre or marchandize, for boats of all sorts, for transportation or fishing, &c.

The Bay and rivers haue much marchantable fish, and places fit for Salt coats, building of ships, making of Iron, &c.

Muscovia and *Polonia* doe yearely receiue many thousands, for pitch, tarre, sopeashes, Rosen, Flax, Cordage, Sturgeon, Masts, Yards, Wainscot, Firres, Glasse, and such like; also *Swethland* for Iron and Copper. *France* in like manner, for Wine, Canvas, and Salt. *Spaine* asmuch for Iron, Steele, Figges, Reasons, and Sackes. *Italy* with Silkes and Velvets consumes our chiefe Commodities. *Holland* maintaines it selfe by fishing and trading at our owne doores. All these temporize [traffic] with other for necessities, but all as vncertaine as peace or warres. Besides the charge, travell, and danger in transporting them, by seas, lands, stormes, and Pyrats. Then how much hath *Virginia* the prerogatiue of all those flourishing Kingdomes, for the benefit of our Land, when as within one hundred myles all those are to be had, either ready provided by nature, or else to be prepared, were there but industrious men to labour. Onely of Copper we may doubt is wanting, but there is good probabilitie that both Copper and better Minerals are there to be had for their labour. Other Countries haue it. So then here is a place, a nurse for souldiers, a practise for mariners, a trade for marchants, a reward for the good, and that which is most of all, a businesse (most acceptable to God) to bring such poore Infidels to the knowledge of God and his holy Gospell.

John Smith, *Travels and Works*, I, pp. 359–360.

VIRGINIA'S DARKER SIDE

Other early settlers did not share John Smith's sanguine outlook. One of these was his bitter rival, George Percy, whose account of the horrors of the first months at Jamestown in 1607 is reprinted below. This selection is from Percy's "A Discourse of the Plantation of the Southern Colony in Virginia by the English" in a book, Purchas His Pilgrims, published by Samuel Purchas, a follower and imitator of Hakluyt.

THE AWFUL TRIALS OF
THE HONOURABLE GEORGE PERCY IN VIRGINIA

The fifteenth of Iune [1607], we had built and finished our Fort, which was triangle wise: hauing three Bulwarkes, [one] at euery corner, like a halfe Moone, and foure or fiue pieces of Artillerie mounted in them; [thus] we had made our selues sufficiently strong for these Sauages. We had also sowne most of our Corne on two Mountaines. It sprang [had sprung] a mans height from the ground. This Countrey is a fruitfull soile, bearing many goodly and fruit-full Trees, as Mulberries, Cherries, Walnuts, Cedars, Cypresse, Sassafras, and Vines in great abundance.

Munday the two and twentieth of June [1607], in the morning, Captaine *Newport* in the Admirall departed from *Iames* Port for *England.*

Captaine *Newport* being gone from *England,* leauing vs (one hundred and foure persons) verie bare and scantie of victualls; furthermore, in warres and in danger of the Sauages. We hoped after a supply, which Captaine *Newport* promised within twentie weekes. But if the beginners of this action doe care-fully further vs, the Country being so fruitfull, it would be as great a profit to the Realme of *England,* as the *Indies* to the King of *Spaine.* If this Riuer which wee haue found had beene discouered in the time of warre with *Spaine,* it would haue beene a commoditie to our Realme, and a great annoyance to our enemies.

The seuen and twentieth of Iuly, the King of *Rapahanna* demanded a Canoa, which was restored. [He] lifted vp his hand to the Sunne (which they worship as their God), besides he laid his hand on his heart, that he would be our speciall friend. It is a generall rule of these people; when they swere by their

John Smith, *Travels and Works,* I, pp. lxx–lxxiii.

God which is the Sunne, no Christian will keep their Oath better vpon this promise. These people haue a great reuerence to the Sunne aboue all other things: at the rising and the setting of the same, they sit downe lifting vp their hands and eyes to the Sunne, making a round Circle on the ground with dried Tobacco; then they began to pray, making many Deuillish gestures, with a Hellish noise, foming at the mouth, staring with their eyes, wagging their heads and hands in such a fashion and deformitie as it was monstrous to behold.

The sixt of August [1607], there died *Iohn Asbie*, of the bloudie Flixe.

The ninth day, died *George Flowre*, of the swelling.

The tenth day, died *William Bruster* Gentleman, of a wound giuen by the Sauages, and was buried the eleuenth day.

The fourteenth day, *Ierome Alikock*, Ancient, died of a wound. The same day, *Francis Midwinter*, [and] *Edward Moris* Corporall died suddenly.

The fifteenth day, their died *Edward Browne* and *Stephen Galthorpe*.

The sixteenth day, their died *Thomas Gower* Gentleman.

The seuenteenth day, their died *Thomas Mounslic*.

The eighteenth day, there died *Robert Pennington*, and *Iohn Martine* Gentlemen.

The nineteenth day, died *Drue Piggase* Gentleman.

The two and twentieth day of August [1607], there died Captaine *Bartholomew Gosnold*, one of our Councell: he was honourably buried, hauing all the Ordnance in the Fort shot off, with many vollies of small shot.

After Captaine *Gosnol[d]s* death, the Councell could hardly agree by the dissention of Captaine *Kendall*; which [who] afterwards was committed about hainous matters which was proued against him.

The foure and twentieth day, died *Edward Harington* and *George Walker*; and were buried the same day.

The sixe and twentieth day, died *Kenelme Throgmortine*.

The seuen and twentieth day, died *William Roods*.

The eight and twentieth day, died *Thomas Stoodie*, Cape Merchant.

The fourth day of September [1607], died *Thomas Iacob* Sergeant.

The fift day, there died *Beniamin Beast*.

Our men were destroyed with cruell diseases, as Swellings, Flixes, Burning Feuers, and by warres; and some departed suddenly: but for the most part, they died of meere famine.

There were neuer *Englishmen* left in a forreigne Countrey in such miserie as wee were in this new discouered *Virginia*. Wee watched euery three nights, lying on the bare cold ground, what weather soeuer came; [and] warded all the next day: which brought our men to bee most feeble wretches. Our food was but a small Can of Barlie sod[den] in water, to fiue men a day. Our drinke, cold water taken out of the Riuer; which was, at a floud, verie salt; at a low tide, full of slime and filth: which was the destruction of many of our men.

Thus we liued for the space of fiue months [August 1607 to January 8, 1608] in this miserable distresse, not hauing fiue able men to man our Bulwarkes vpon any occasion. If it had not pleased God to haue put a terrour in the Sauages hearts, we had all perished by those vild and cruell Pagans, being in that weake estate as we were; our men night and day groaning in euery corner of the Fort most pittifull to heare. If there were any conscience in men, it would make their harts to bleed to heare the pitifull murmurings and out-cries of our sick men without reliefe, euery night and day, for the space of sixe weekes [August 8 (?) to September 19, 1607]: some departing out of the World, many times three or foure in a night; in the morning, their bodies [being] trailed out of their Cabines like Dogges, to be buried. In this sort, did I see the mortalitie of diuers of our people.

It pleased God, after a while, to send those people which were our mortall enemies, to releeue vs with victuals, as Bread, Corne, Fish, and Flesh in great plentie; which was the setting vp of our feeble men: otherwise wee had all perished. Also we were frequented by diuers Kings in the Countrie, bringing vs store of prouision to our great comfort.

The eleuenth day [of September, 1607], there was certaine *Articles* laid against Master *Wingfield* which was then President: thereupon he was not only displaced out of his President ship, but also from being of the Councell. Afterwards Captain *Iohn Ratcliffe* was chosen President.

The eighteenth day [of September], died one *Ellis Kinistone,* which was starued [frozen] to death with cold. The same day at night, died one *Richard Simmons.*

The nineteenth day [of September], there died one *Thomas Mouton.*

William White (hauing liued with the Natiues) reported to vs of their customes. In the morning, by breake of day, before they eate or drinke, both men, women, and children (that be aboue tenne yeares of age), runnes into the water; there washes themselues a good while till the Sunne riseth: then offer Sacrifice to it, strewing Tobacco on the water or Land, honouring the Sunne as their God. Likewise they doe at the setting of the Sunne.

JOHN SMITH ON NEW ENGLAND

In 1614, Captain John Smith also journeyed to New England, picking Massachusetts Bay as an ideal spot for a future settlement. His report on that country indicates something of what the English had learned even during their few brief years as New World colonists. Instead of advising imitation of the gold-oriented Spanish model, as most of his peers were doing, Smith holds up the practical and versatile Dutch as most worthy of emulation by prospective New England settlers.

FROM THE SPANISH TO THE DUTCH MODEL

The maine Staple, from hence to bee extracted for the present to produce the rest, is fish; which howeuer it may seeme a mean and a base commoditie: yet who will but truely take the pains and consider the sequell, I thinke will allow it well worth the labour. It is strange to see what great aduentures the hopes of setting forth men of war [privateers] to rob the industrious innocent, would procure; or such massie promises in grosse: though more are choked then well fedde with such hastie hopes. But who doth not know that the poore Hollanders, chiefly by fishing, at a great charge and labour in all weathers in the open Sea, are made a people so hardy and industrious? and by the venting this poore commodity to the Easterlings for as meane, which is Wood, Flax, Pitch, Tarre, Rosin, Cordage, and such like (which they exchange againe, to the French, Spaniards, Portugales, and English, &c., for what they want) are made so mighty, strong and rich, as no State but Venice, of twice their magnitude, is so well furnished with so many faire Cities, goodly Townes, strong Fortresses, and that aboundance of shipping and all sorts of marchandize, as well of Golde, Siluer, Pearles, Diamonds, Pretious stones, Silkes, Veluets, and Cloth of golde; as Fish, Pitch, Wood, or such grosse commodities? What Voyages and Discoueries, East and West, North and South, yea about the world, make they? What an Army by Sea and Land, haue they long maintained in despite of one of the greatest Princes of the world? And neuer could the Spaniard with all his Mynes of golde and Siluer pay his debts, his friends, and army, halfe so truly, as the Hollanders stil haue done by this contemptible trade of fish. Diuers (I know) may alledge, many other assistances. But this is their Myne; and the Sea the source of those siluered streames of all their vertue; which hath made them now the very miracle of industrie, the pattern

---

John Smith, *Travels and Works*, I, pp. 194–196.

of perfection for these affaires: and the benefit of fishing is that *Primum mobile* that turnes all their *Spheres* to this height of plentie, strength, honour and admiration.

Herring, Cod, and Ling, is that triplicitie that makes their wealth and shippings multiplicities, such as it is, and from which (few would thinke it) they yearly draw at least one million and a halfe of pounds starling; yet it is most certaine (if records be true): and in this faculty they are so naturalized, and of their vents [sales] so certainely acquainted, as there is no likelihood they will euer be paralleld, hauing 2 or 3000 Busses, Flat bottomes, Sword pinks, To[a]des, and such like, that breedes them Saylers, Mariners, Souldiers and Marchants, neuer to be wrought out of that trade, and fit for any other. I will not deny but others may gaine as well as they, that will vse it: though not so certainely, nor so much in quantity; for want of experience. And this Herring they take vpon the Coast of *Scotland* and *England*; their Cod and Ling, vpon the Coast of *Izeland* and in the North Seas.

Hamborough and the *East Countries*, for Sturgion and Cauiare, gets many thousands of pounds from *England*, and the *Straites: Portugale*, the *Biskaines*, and the *Spaniards*, make 40 or 50 Saile yearely to *Cape-blank*, to hooke for Porgos, Mullet, and [to] make *Puttardo*: and *New found Land*, doth yearely fraught neere 800 sayle of Ships with a sillie leane skinny Poore-Iohn, and Corfish; which at least yearely amounts to 3 or 400000 pound.

If from all those parts such paines is taken for this poore gaines of fish, and by them [that] hath neither meate, drinke, nor clothes; wood, iron nor steele; pitch, tarre, nets, leades, salt, hookes, nor lines; for shipping, fishing, nor prouision, but at the second, third, fourth, or fift hand, drawne from so many seuerall parts of the world ere they come together to be vsed in this voyage. If these I say can gaine, and the Saylers liue going for shares, [on] lesse then the third part of their labours, and yet spend as much time in going and comming as in staying there, so short is the season of fishing: why should wee more doubt then *Holland, Portugale, Spaniard, French,* or other, but to doe much better then they, where there is victuall to feede vs, wood of all sorts to build Boats, Ships, or Barks; the fish at our doores; pitch, tarre, masts, yards, and most of other necessaries onely for making? And here are no hard Landlords to racke vs with high rents, or extorted fines to consume vs; no tedious pleas in law to consume vs with their many years disputations for Iustice; no multitudes to occasion such impediments to good orders, as in popular States. So freely hath God and his Maiesty bestowed those blessings on them that will attempt to obtaine them, as here euery man may be master and owner of his owne labour and land; or the greatest part in a small time. If hee haue nothing but his hands, he may set vp this trade; and by industrie quickly grow rich; spending but halfe that time wel, which in *England* we abuse in idlenes, worse or as ill.

2 / VIRGINIA: FROM COMPANY
TO COLONY TO EMPIRE

INTRODUCTION

The case study of colony building in seventeenth-century Virginia affords the historian an opportunity for analyzing the basic economic, social, and political problems involved in attempting to exploit an underdeveloped area far removed from the mother country. By viewing the whole century, moreover, it is possible to observe not only the problems, but also some of the consequences that resulted from the colonists' and the mother country's attempts to solve the problems. One of the most useful ways of gaining insight into these problems, their solutions, and their consequences is to focus on significant institutions or established patterns of regular behavior. If one wishes to clarify and highlight the unique features of these forms of institutionalized behavior, it is also useful to compare them to those of other cultures in similar situations, allowing for the fact that two historical situations are rarely exactly alike. This is the technique employed by Professor Herbert Klein in his focal article on Virginia. He compares the Spanish experience in Cuba with that of the English in Virginia—two plantation economies far removed from the home culture and highly dependent on shipping and world commerce. By focusing on institutions and comparing them over a relatively long time span, he is able to make some broad and widely applicable generalizations about the whole period.

The student will note that Professor Klein's interest in the Virginia experience is somewhat different from that expressed in the general introduction to this book. Once again, however, the various source materials selected for this section are intended to test, and hopefully support, the interpretations offered in the introduction and in Professor Klein's focal article. By concentrating on economic, political, and social institutions and excluding intellectual history, it is possible to narrow down the range of sources that must be considered relevant by the historian in forming his picture of early Virginia. This selection device greatly simplifies research in the source materials, since the student is able to concentrate on records relating to these three kinds of institutions and most of these records are official documents preserved in government archives. However, this procedure by no means reduces the complexity of the problems to be analyzed. The student still has to consider the numerous variables and combinations of variables made possible by the shifting relationships through time of the three central sets of institutions. Nevertheless, certain kinds of sources stand out more prominently than others for the institutional historian. These include charters, minutes of assemblies, resolutions, reports to the Company, instructions to the governors and other officials, letters describing or revealing institutional relationships, and more or less formal surveys of economic, social, and political conditions. Statistics, too, are extremely useful, though reliable data for this period are relatively scarce.

The student should note that, throughout this sequence of documents, an attempt has been made to follow up the legal or official records with materials revealing something of the consequences in human terms of these official acts. At the end of this reading it should be possible to form a picture of the Virginia society as it gradually evolved out of necessary adjustment to New World conditions, and to compare meaningfully this picture of the evolving Virginia experience with that presented in the general introduction.

INTERPRETATION

Professor Herbert S. Klein, the author of the focal article which follows, is a historian of Latin America at the University of Chicago. He is primarily interested in the institution of slavery in the New World, and the selection included here is a chapter from his book Slavery in the Americas: a Comparative Study of Virginia and Cuba. *The chapter reprinted here deals with the general institutional history of Virginia, making contrasts, where appropriate, to the experience of the Spanish in Cuba.*

HERBERT S. KLEIN, *Virginia's Institutions*

In the development of the English colonization of Virginia, the lack of royal direction and control stands out in sharpest contrast to the Cuban experience. It was largely with indifference that the newly enthroned House of Stuart saw the first successful plantation established in America. It was an indifference that allowed the early Stuarts to surrender royal authority over the New World colony at almost every point at which it was challenged. Nor would the crown allow any other political authority to exercise a unified control in its place, and for almost half a century was successful in denying Parliament any jurisdiction over colonial affairs. The establishment of Parliamentary authority would later bring an attempt to subordinate the empire to central direction, but by then the colonials had so thoroughly established their claim to self-government that even when certain of their rights were successfully whittled away by the metropolis, their control over essential domestic institutions was left entirely alone, as traditionally belonging to the colonial regimes themselves. Thus, for the most formative period of growth, the Virginia colonials would find themselves unchallenged in their drive to create their own institutions and entrench their authority.

Any analysis of the Cuban conquest and colonization had of necessity to focus on the crown and its actions. In the case of Virginia, however, the starting place must be with the commercial classes of Great Britain. For it was the

Herbert S. Klein, *Slavery in the Americas: a Comparative Study of Virginia and Cuba* (Chicago, University of Chicago Press, 1967), pp. 22–36. Reprinted without footnotes by permission of the University of Chicago Press.

mercantile interests and not the monarchs who would undertake the financing and organization of the expansion of England into the New World.

It was the late sixteenth century that not only saw the rise of the famed British naval power, but also the great expansion of English commerce, which was soon to rule the world's markets, even penetrating behind the very barriers of the Spanish Empire. By the beginning of the sixteenth century, the English commercial classes had achieved control over their own commerce with the outside world, first from the Venetians and then from the Hanse Towns. With this overthrow of the foreign merchants had come the rise of London as a commercial center and the organization of the first overseas trading adventurers into regulated companies. Such companies, especially the Merchant Adventurers, were soon challenging the Hanse towns for leadership on the continent. The first of the great joint-stock corporations, arising out of these more primitive, individualistic, "regulated companies," was the Muscovy Company chartered in 1555. This first corporate company was soon followed by a host of other such commercial ventures in all the major areas of the world. The joint-stock companies early provided the vehicles for England's leadership in world trade, for they were able to organize large amounts of capital savings for purposes of foreign trade and colonization, and with their free issuance of stock, limited liability, concentrated management, and many other unique features, enabled England to outdistance its rivals in the Western world's carrying trade.

Through the activities of these companies, England soon found itself in possession of a large merchant fleet, a strong navy, and surplus capital. So vigorous were these developments that with the fall of Portugal to Spain in 1580, England was able to undertake successfully the establishment of British intervention in the fabled Far East; in 1588 to challenge successfully the mightiest naval power of the time; and by the end of that century to challenge Spain in her New World empire.

The economic theories that rose with the mercantile classes of England held that colonization and expansion were necessary for commercial survival. This theory of mercantilism and the obvious benefits being conferred upon Spain by her wealthy empire convinced English leaders that their nation's prosperity lay in establishing permanent colonies overseas, and especially in disputing Spain's exclusive control over the entire Western Hemisphere. The late sixteenth century was a most propitious time for England to lay down this challenge, for Castilian energy had finally dissipated itself in the conquest, and the crown of Castile, after successfully rebuffing French interference in the early part of the century, contented itself with merely holding the strategically vital Florida peninsula while relinquishing all physical control over the territory to the north. Stressing these considerations, and especially emphasizing England's position as a rising commercial state needing new outlets for capital as well as new markets and sources of raw materials, such vigorous publicists as the Hakluyts were able to convince England's commercial leaders that expansion had become a necessity.

The first attempts at New World colonization were carried out by individual adventurers, much in the style of the conquistadores. In the last quarter of the sixteenth century, Gilbert had tried and Raleigh had temporarily succeeded in planting a colony along the Carolina coast, but both eventually failed. For unlike the Spanish Indies whose wealth quickly supplied the means for support and further colonization, the North American coasts proved barren of precious metals, or of such established Indian agricultural communities as encountered by Spain. Such a colonial area to be economically successful had to create goods and/or services needed in European markets. The failure of Roanoke Island proved that individuals alone could not supply the capital necessary to sustain such overseas colonies until this kind of commercial crop or product could be found to take the place of Indian labor or precious metals.

This inability of individual enterprise constantly to supply a colony with the necessary resources until it could find the means to sustain itself, and the long period before it would even begin to show a profit, early led to the question of royal support. But English colonization encountered an extremely parsimonious crown, to an extent unmatched even by the often debt-ridden and hard pressed Castilian monarchs. The English crown, as early as Elizabeth, offered moral support and sanction to colonization, but refused entirely to supply the needed capital. Not only did this limit the size of the colonizing effort to the amount of private capital that could be drawn into such a highly speculative investment as overseas settlement, but it would ultimately mean that the crown would capitulate its authority over the entire colonization movement to the English mercantile classes.

At the beginning of the seventeenth century, a group of London merchants who had longstanding interests in colonization and were also involved in the great joint-stock companies of their time, decided to pool their resources in a joint-stock adventure and make another try at colonization. In the first charter (1606) granted to this group of merchants and financeers known as the London Company, the crown attempted to retain direct control over the colony, however it refused to commit itself financially to its development or support. Under this charter a royal council was established in England that was granted full administrative authority over the entire New World region from Cape Fear to Ste. Croix. The company was to appoint all members of a resident colonial council, which was allowed to control local affairs. But all political and administrative authority was vested in the so-called Royal or Superior Council, all of whose members were crown appointees; whereas to the company was left only direction over the actual business of settlement,

Courtesy of Stefan Lorant.

Map of Virginia by John White.

maintenance, and trade. In effect, this Royal Council was the English crown's first step to the creation of something akin to the Council of the Indies and was the forerunner of later attempts at centralized imperial control.

The crown also maintained that the newly discovered territory was to be considered as its own possession, much in the manner of the Castilian throne's relation to its empire. But although it was initially successful in maintaining its rights as opposed to Parliament in this area, it was forced to abandon its direct administrative and political control over the Virginia colony to the London merchants. For such assertions of extensive royal control deterred private capital from investment, and in the charter of 1609 the Royal Council was eliminated entirely, and the crown relinquished all active control over Virginia to the London Company.

The charter of 1609 was to establish a pattern that the crown would follow, not only in the Virginia charter of 1612, but in all the subsequent individual and company colonial grants. Bitterly involved in a desperate struggle for power at home and on the continent, unwilling to supply any capital for overseas settlement whatsoever, the crown gave up any cohesive control over its burgeoning empire. Every colonizing enterprise was given complete freedom over its undertaking, with little or no interference from the crown and its administrative organization. In the grants and charters following that of 1609, all immediate control over the colony was given to the proprietor, whether an individual or corporation, and he became virtually the sole connecting link between the colonists and the metropolis, his only challenge to undivided authority being the provincial legislature that might develop.

Like the crown who had been forced to concede authority because of its financial position, the London Company itself did not prove immune to the problems involved in financing a long colonization and was early forced to provide liberal grants to stimulate investment and immigration. In the joint-stock issue of 1609, the principle of equality between planter in Virginia and adventurer in London was established when the majority of emigrating colonists were given coequal shares in the enterprise (shares that were to be retired in 1616). In the years that followed, the company was reduced to offering patents or charters to groups of adventurers for the setting up of private plantations or colonies, usually known as hundreds, within the territory covered by the company charter. In these grants the subsocieties usually received extensive control over their plantations, to the detriment of the over-all power of the company itself.

In the charter of 1612, there occurred within the company a shift in power from a select council to a general assembly of the stockholders. For the colonists—coequal shareholders—this democratization of the company organization would ultimately mean the shift of power over Virginia from London to Jamestown. With the maturation of the stock issue of 1609, the emigration of many London stockholders, and the coming of peace and prosperity to the colony, this step was taken by the leaders of the company; and in 1618 they proposed setting up a governmental organization in the colony along the lines of the general assembly of the London Company. In the Great Charter of 1618, the London Company provided for the creation of a colonial general assembly with representation in the lower house for all the boroughs, hundreds, and private plantations. The culmination in this extraordinary reorganization came in 1621 in the Ordinances and Constitutions issued by the London Company, which provided that "no orders shall bind the colony unless they be ratified in the Virginia general assembly."

Even the form of Virginia colonization, like the control over government, was determined by the will of the colonials. For while the township organization had been envisioned by the company as the soundest and most secure means of organization, it was abandoned by the colonials once the company control had been relaxed. Under the authoritarian rule of the first company governors, the settlement had been confined to fortified areas with communal arrangements for planting, harvesting, and selling the various crops produced. In their long-range plans the company leaders had hopefully divided the colony into boroughs. Once the first communal organizations had been dissolved, however, and the power of the Indians finally broken, the colonists dispersed over a vast area, their plantations racing along the rivers (James, York, Rappahonic, and Potomac) toward the falls. As each of these rivers was navigable as far as the falls and much of the area was heavily forested, the majority of plantations were connected to the outside world directly through their own docks. In such a situation, urban development proved impossible, especially as the economy became almost totally absorbed in one commercial crop and therefore provided few possibilities for intra-colonial trade. It was not until after the close of the seventeenth century, when the line of settlement had passed the falls, that urban communities began to develop, and even then only on a very modest scale.

The Virginia General Assembly, taking cognizance of this dispersal of settlement, abandoned the borough system and in 1634 organized the colony into eight counties. By so doing, the Assembly provided a form amenable to the economic realities of the dispersed community, and by 1644 the colony had added nine more counties. The administrative center of this county organization was the powerful county court, which was both an executive and judicial organ.

The county court was in many ways similar to the Cuban cabildo both in the extent of its powers, and in its representation of the power of the prop-ertied classes. Organized and put into operation as early as 1619, the powers of the county court were steadily augmented over the years. Besides having legal jurisdiction over innumerable civil and criminal problems, it was charged with the execution of all government ordinances, and for these purposes it was provided with an assortment of minor officials. Its authority extended to all local economic matters, including the regulation and control of tobacco, maintenance of standard weights and measures, regulation of the price of local commodities, and the upkeep of lines of communication such as ferry services and highways. The county court was also a court of records, and with its clerk were filed licenses, deeds, certificates, contracts, wills, and most important of all, land titles. In short, it was the prime keeper of the vital statistics of the county. Nor was its jurisdiction in legal affairs confined, for by separate acts of the Assembly it was granted the powers of a probate and equity court in 1645, and in 1658 those of admiralty court.

As the court came to symbolize local power, it tended to merge all local authority in its hands. Although the militia system had been created as a separate organization in all counties, in actual fact its personnel became members of the court, and to the court itself fell all the responsibility for the maintenance of the troops and for the selection of the men. The same held true for the vestry, which was composed of the same men and in reality proved a complementary institution in the realms of ecclesiastical and welfare matters on the county level.

Membership in the county court was based on appointment by the governor, and candidates were chosen from among the most powerful and respected planters of the community. Although the eight to ten magistrates appointed were placed in office supposedly for short terms, the very nature of the select group from which they were chosen created a strong tendency for prolonged membership on the court. It was this same select class of wealthy and dominant planters who formed the membership of both the Council and the House of Burgesses, and the same individual often held a position in one of these two houses of the General Assembly and on his local county court as well. Thus colonial leadership fell to the most prominent planters of the community, who entrenched themselves, especially after 1624, in all of the major political and administrative offices of the colony, bringing surprising political concentration for such an economically and geographically decentralized colony.

The fall of the London Company in no way threatened this entrenched power; rather it insured the final triumph of the colonial leadership over imperial England. It was largely because of political differences in England between the leaders of the company and the Royal Councillors that the crown pressed for, and succeeded in gaining, repudiation of the London Company's charter in 1624. Yet despite this reworking of Virginia into a royal province, the crown was as unwilling as ever to contribute its funds to colonial development, and for a time thought to revert back to the scheme of 1606 with a royal council and a subordinate company of adventurers. When this fell through there was even serious consideration given to rechartering the old company.

Nor did the end of the London Company in any significant way alter over-all colonial policy, for the old types of proprietary patents were still being issued to the numerous companies that followed, including that extraordinary grant to the Massachusetts Bay Company in 1629. From year to year the crown vacillated about the type of centralized administration it should create to control the affairs of Virginia, and in the meantime it created nothing of permanence. To replace the company's centralized directorship, various sub-committees of the Privy Council and special commissions were set up. None of these, however, lasted more than a short time, and no separate administrative machinery such as Castile's Council of the Indies and Casa de Contratación —which existed apart from the administrative agencies already in existence for home affairs—was even contemplated at this time. Anything of importance that was accomplished by the first two Stuarts in the direction of imperial centralization was wiped out by the chaotic years of civil war. Imperial control would eventually come to England's New World empire, but this would not begin until after the Restoration, and then it would not fall under the influence of the crown so much as under that of the potent merchants of London who had a vital interest in Virginia's economic development.

The only issues that truly shocked the English crown out of its acquiescence to planter leadership in Virginia were issues in which its revenue was threatened. As early as 1636, the royal customs on one shipload of tobacco from Virginia yielded an impressive £3,334, and although the early Stuarts voiced pious wishes to see diversified agriculture come to Virginia and discoursed on the evils of tobacco, they did nothing seriously to suppress its production. In that same year of 1636 it was estimated that the total royal revenue from tobacco should have been £20,000, if it had been properly collected. Thus the crown—even before the first Parliamentary Navigation Acts of 1651— decided to do all in its power to discourage the foreign trade of the colony because of the loss it entailed for the royal revenues.

The constant years of overproduction in Virginia brought depression prices in the decades of the 1650's and 1660's, and in 1662 the colonials petitioned the crown for one year's total cessation of production—only to be bitterly rebuked by the Privy Council for even petitioning for such a thing. A similar petition in 1664 was again vetoed by the crown despite the economic privations of the colony. As the crown was averaging £100,000 annually by the '80's a third such petition for crop restriction, presented in 1681, was heartily disapproved, for no matter how extreme the fluctuation in price for Virginia leaf, the crown received a fixed return and the greater the production, the greater its own revenues.

This reasoning held true in regard to the crown's interests in the African slave trade, from which it derived extensive revenue. Among the few acts of the Virginia General Assembly ever repealed by the English crown were those of 1723 and 1727, which attempted to place tariffs on imported African slaves—tariffs which in spite of colonial statements to the contrary, seemed to the crown to be prohibitive in intent.

Yet on truly essential matters that had no direct relationship to the royal customs monopolies, the crown was either indifferent or indecisive. Given this royal attitude, the colonials were not slow to assert their "rights" and demand the fullest measure of support for their self-governing institutions. Thus from 1624 until 1639, the General Assembly continued meeting despite nonrecognition until, in the end, the crown gave it its sanction. Eventually, for want of a more positive conception of imperial government, the crown decided to accept what had been established in the colony by custom and usage. The crown gave powerful sanction to the county court system—despite its extensive powers unknown to the local English judiciary—and in 1642 it declared that permanent sites be established in every county for the local court, thus insuring its continued maintenance.

With no centralized agency appearing in the British Isles before the Protectorate to take control over colonial affairs the situation in Virginia showed itself equally unsubordinated to royal direction. Although, with the dissolution of the London Company, the task of appointing the governor and the council now fell to the crown, this did not insure acquiescence to royal authority, nor destroy the independence of colonial leadership. The council, even though it consisted of royal appointees, was in fact chosen almost exclusively from the pool of planter leadership. For the crown habitually confirmed without question the nominations of the governor, and the latter was forced to accept the colonial leaders in his council if anything like an effective administration was to be maintained. At the same time, the crown, ever desirous to spend as little as possible, fostered the use of colonial planters in other public offices of importance so that their salaries might be of the most minimal nature, for the honorific reward would be considered sufficient inducement. Thus of the seven royal officials created in the colony prior to 1700—aside from the governor and his council—almost all were filled by native Virginians. In an attempt to insure the native quality of the colonial leadership, the General Assembly in 1676, with the approval of the crown, provided that at least three years residence in the colony was required for office-holding. There is no doubt that the English crown in Virginia was saved the vast sums that were required to keep the Cuban administrative machinery going, but at the price of its own authority.

The crown did have one representative sensitive to its interests, however, in the person of the governor, whose term of office and actions were directly dependent upon royal sanction. In the majority of cases the holder of this office was chosen from the ruling classes of the home government rather than from the Virginian leadership, and he was personally provided with a salary that removed him from the threats of an opposition General Assembly. Although the positions of governor in Cuba and Virginia proved uniquely advantageous for royal suppression of local autonomy, the Virginia executive was faced by an opposition far more powerfully armed than the Cuban colonials with their cabildos ever were. For key rights of the governor, such as the appointive, military, and other executive functions, were shared by the very powerful and often hostile council, whereas control over initiation of legislation was in the hands of a strong General Assembly.

Because of the crown's crucial refusal to provide adequate funds for colonial administration, it was forced to concede to the General Assembly not only the rights of petition and legislation, but those of taxation and control of finance as well. It was the House of Burgesses' almost absolute control over colonial finances that enabled it to withstand repeated assaults by autocratic governors and also to participate in the executive functions. The first royal treasurer did not arrive in the colony until 1639, and even then the crown was unable to collect the quitrents that had belonged to the London Company, and finally in 1691 the office itself came under the direction of the House of Burgesses, which chose its own treasurer.

Another area in which the royal authority was equally ineffective was in the creation of an imperial judiciary. Whereas Cuba had been subordinated to a tight judicial hierarchy, its history encumbered by countless litigation battles fought at all levels and especially at the Council of the Indies in Spain, an imperial judiciary in England was a long time in the making, not coming until the end of the century and then by the devious route of admiralty courts. During the seventeenth century few cases were carried from the colony to England, and Massachusetts even challenged the appellate jurisdiction of the Privy Council for disputes concerning colonial affairs.

As far as defense was concerned, Virginia largely provided for the maintenance of its own harbor and frontier fortifications, as it had under the company, and as Virginia was isolated both from the main areas of imperial conflict and from the regions of major piratical raidings, no permanent military organization was established in the colony by England. For all invasions, Indian wars, and insurrections, the colony relied upon its own militia, and this militia formed an important branch of colonial self-government, giving essential police powers to the planter leadership.

Although the Anglican church, or Church of England, was made the established church of the colony from the beginning of company rule, no resident bishop would ever be sent to the colony, nor to any of the other continental colonies in which the church was established. It was not even decided to which metropolitan bishopric these colonies pertained until after the Restoration. Only then was the Bishop of London selected, but his representative did not arrive in the colony until 1689. During this period of complete neglect, both on the part of the Anglican hierarchy in England and the crown—the official protector and head of the church—the Virginians were able to reconstruct the high church structure of Anglicanism into a vestry-dominated congregational type of organization completely unknown to the mother church in England. So profound were the changes in structure and control, that the Virginia church became anathema to the majority of English-trained clergy. And although the Church of England did construct a missionary society after the close of the seventeenth century, the S.P.G., as it was called, never sent missionaries to Virginia.

For the most crucial period of its development, Virginia was thus unencumbered by a numerous non-native bureaucracy and was largely ignored by such institutions as a national church and an imperial monarchy. Because of the financial difficulties involved in its colonization, as well as strong royal indifference, the colony had early been granted the most liberal concessions of self-government, and its institutions, once created, were successfully strengthened and fortified against all opposition by the rising planter leadership. Virginia was thus allowed to grow in the light of its own immediate needs, and was able to ignore to a large extent such external forces and institutions with which Cuba had to contend from the beginning of its settlement.

THE VIRGINIA CHARTER OF 1609

The first charter of Virginia was issued to the Virginia Company of London in 1606 by King James I. After three years this charter was revised and the Charter of 1609 became the primary legal basis of Virginia's company government. In 1612, another charter added Bermuda to the Virginia domain. The Charter of 1609 shifted the government of Virginia to a company rather than a royal council. It separated Massachusetts Bay from Virginia, leaving a vast no-man's-land in between. It excluded Catholics and others who would not acknowledge the supremacy of the Church of England and, most important, it granted colonists the same rights as subjects living in England. This was a point that later figured prominently in the arguments of American revolutionists such as Thomas Jefferson.

JAMES, by the Grace of God, King of *England, Scotland, France,* and *Ireland,* Defender of the Faith, *&c.* To all, to whom these Presents shall come, Greeting. Whereas, at the humble Suit and Request of sundry our loving and well-disposed Subjects, intending to deduce a Colony, and to make Habitation and Plantation of sundry our People in that Part of America, commonly called Virginia, and other Parts and Territories in America, either appertaining unto Us, or which are not actually possessed of any *Christian* Prince or People, within certain Bounds and Regions, We have formerly, by our Letters-patents, bearing Date the tenth Day of *April,* in the fourth Year of our Reign of *England, France,* and *Ireland,* and of *Scotland* the nine and thirtieth, Granted to Sir *Thomas Gates,* Sir *George Somers,* and others, for the more speedy Accomplishment of the said Plantation and Habitation, that they should divide themselves into two Colonies (the one consisting of divers Knights, Gentlemen, Merchants, and others, of our City of *London,* called the First Colony; And the other consisting of divers Knights, Gentlemen, and others, of our Cities of *Bristol, Exeter,* and Town of *Plimouth,* and other Places, called the Second Colony). And have yielded and granted many and sundry Privileges and Liberties to each Colony, for their quiet settling and good Government therein, as by the said Letters-patents more at large appeareth.

Ben Perley Poore, ed., *The Federal and State Constitutions, Colonial Charters, and other Organic Laws of the United States,* Part II (Washington, D.C., Government Printing Office, 1878), pp. 1893–1902.

Now, forasmuch as divers and sundry of our loving Subjects, as well Adventurers, as Planters, of the said first Colony, . . . have of late been humble Suitors unto Us, that . . . We would be pleased to grant them a further Enlargement and Explanation of the said Grant, Privileges, and Liberties, and that such Counsellors, and other Officers, may be appointed amongst them, to manage and direct their Affairs, as are willing and ready to adventure with them, as also whose Dwellings are not so far remote from the City of *London*, but they may, at convenient Times, be ready at Hand, to give their Advice and Assistance, upon all Occasions requisite.

We greatly affecting the effectual Prosecution and happy success of the said Company of Dyers, the Company of Brewers, [etc.,] . . . and to such and so many as they do, or shall hereafter admit to be joined with them, in the form hereafter in these presents expressed, whether they go in their Persons to be Planters there in the said Plantation, or whether they go not, but adventure their monies, goods, or Chattles, [declare] that they shall be one Body or Commonalty perpetual, and shall have perpetual Succession and one common Seal to serve for the said Body or Commonalty, and that they and their Successors shall be known, called, and incorporated by the Name of *The Treasurer and Company of Adventurers and Planters of the City of London, for the first Colony in Virginia*. . . . And we do also . . . give, grant and confirm, unto the said Treasurer and Company, and their Successors, under the Reservations, Limitations, and Declarations hereafter expressed, all those Lands, Countries, and Territories, situate, lying, and being in that Part of *America*, called *Virginia*, from the Point of Land, called Cape or *Point Comfort*, all along the Sea Coast to the Northward, two hundred miles, and from the said Point of *Cape Comfort*, all along the Sea Coast to the Southward, two hundred Miles, and all that Space and Circuit of Land, lying from the Sea Coast of the Precinct aforesaid, up into the Land throughout from Sea to Sea, West and Northwest; And also all the Islands lying within one hundred Miles along the Coast of both Seas of the Precinct aforesaid; Together with all the Soils, Grounds, Havens, and Ports, Mines, as well Royal Mines of Gold and Silver, as other Minerals, Pearls, and precious Stones, Quarries, Woods, Rivers, Waters, Fishings, Commodities, Jurisdictions, Royalties, Privileges, Franchises, and Preheminences within the said Territories, and the Precincts thereof, . . . both by Sea and Land, being, or in any sort belonging or appertaining, and which We, by our Letters Patents, may or can grant, . . . Yielding and paying therefore, to Us, our Heirs and Successors, the fifth Part only of all Ore of Gold and Silver, that from Time to Time, and at all Times hereafter, shall be there gotten, had, or obtained, for all Manner of Services. . . . And forasmuch as the good and prosperous Success of the said Plantation, cannot but chiefly depend next under the Blessing of God, and the Support of our Royal Authority, upon the provident and good Direction of the whole Enterprise, by a careful and understanding Council, and that it is not convenient, that all the Adventurers shall be so often drawn to meet and assemble, as shall be requisite for them to have Meetings and Conference about the Affairs thereof; Therefore we do ordain, establish and confirm, that there shall be perpetually one Council here resident, according to the Tenour of our former Letters-Patents. . . .

And further, . . . we do . . . Give and Grant full Power and Authority to our said Council here resident . . . to nominate, make, constitute, ordain and confirm, by such Name or Names, Stile or Stiles, as to them shall seem good, And likewise to revoke, discharge, change, and alter, as well all and singular Governors, Officers, and Ministers, which already have been made, as also which hereafter shall be by them thought fit and needful to be made or used for the Government of the said Colony and Plantation: And also to make, ordain, and establish all Manner of Orders, Laws, Directions, Instructions, Forms and Ceremonies of Government and Magistracy, fit and necessary for and concerning the Government of the said Colony and Plantation; And the same, at all Times hereafter, to abrogate, revoke, or change, not only within the Precincts of the said Colony, but also upon the Seas, in going and coming to and from the said Colony, as they in their good Discretion, shall think to be fittest for the Good of the Adventurers and inhabitants there. . . . And we do further . . . Ordain and establish, that the said Treasurer and Council here resident, and their successors or any four of them being assembled (the Treasurer being one) shall from time to time have full Power and Authority to admit and receive any other Person into their Company, Corporation, and Freedom; And further in a General Assembly of Adventurers, with the consent of the greater part upon good Cause, to disfranchise and put out any Person or Persons out of the said Freedom or Company. And we do also Grant and confirm for Us, our Heirs and Successors, that it shall be lawful for the said Treasurer and Company and their Successors by direction of the Governors there, to dig and to search for all manner of Mines of Gold, silver, Copper, Iron, Lead, Tin, and all sorts of Minerals, as well within the precinct aforesaid, as within and part of the main land not formerly granted to any other; And to have and enjoy the Gold, Silver, Copper, Iron, Lead, and Tin, and all other Minerals to be gotten thereby, to the use and behoof of the said company of Planters and Adventurers; Yielding thereof, and paying Yearly unto Us, our Heirs and Successors as aforesaid. And . . . we do . . . Yield and Grant to and with the said Treasurer and Company, and their Successors, and every of them, their Factors and Assigns, that they and every of them shall be free of all Subsidies and Customs in *Virginia*, for the space of one and twenty Years, and from all Taxes and Impositions for ever upon any Goods or Merchandizes at any Time or Times hereafter, either upon Importation thither, or Exportation from thence into our Realm of *England*, or into any other of our Realms or Dominions, by the said Treasurer and Company, and their Successors, and their Deputies, Factors, or Assigns, or any of them: Except only the five Pounds *per Cent.* due for Custom upon all such Goods and Merchandizes as shall be brought or Imported into our Realm of *England,* or any other of these our Dominions according to the antient Trade of Merchants; . . . Also we do . . . declare . . . that all and every the Persons being our Subjects, which shall go and inhabit within the said Colony and Plantation, and every their Children and Posterity, which shall happen to be born within any of the Limits thereof, shall have and enjoy all Liberties, Franchizes, and Immunities of Free Denizens and natural Subjects within any of our other Dominions to all Intents and Purposes, as if they had been abiding and born within this our Realm of *England.* . . . And forasmuch as it shall be necessary for all such our loving Subjects as shall inhabit within the said Precincts of *Virginia* aforesaid, to determine to live together in the Fear and true Worship of Almighty God, Christian Peace and Civil Quietness each with other, whereby every one may with more Safety, Pleasure and Profit enjoy that whereunto they shall attain with great Pain and Peril; We for Us, our Heires, and Successors are likewise pleased and contented, and by these Presents do give and grant unto the said Treasurer and Company, and their Successors, and to such Governors, Officers, and Ministers, as shall be by our said Council constituted and appointed . . . that they shall and may from Time to Time, for ever hereafter, within the said Precincts of *Virginia,* or in the way by Sea thither and from thence, have full and absolute Power and Authority to correct, punish, pardon, govern, and rule all such the Subjects of Us . . . as shall from Time to Time adventure themselves in any Voyage thither, or that shall at any Time hereafter, inhabit in the Precincts and Territories of the said Colony. . . . And further, our Will and Pleasure is, that in all Questions and Doubts that shall arise upon any difficulty of Construction or Interpretation of any Thing contained either in this, or in our said former Letters-patents, the same shall be taken and interpreted in most ample and beneficial Manner for the said Treasurer and Company. . . . And lastly, because the principal Effect which we can desire or expect of this Action, is the Conversion and Reduction of the People in those Parts unto the true Worship of God and Christian Religion, in which Respect we should be loath that any Person should be permitted to pass that we suspected to affect the Superstitions of the Church of *Rome,* we do hereby declare, that it is our Will and Pleasure that none be permitted to pass in any Voyage from Time to Time to be made into the said Country, but such as first shall have taken the Oath of Supremacy. . . .

STARVING TIME IN VIRGINIA

A True Declaration of Virginia was a pamphlet written as a defense of the first colonists by members of the Virginia Company. While defending the Jamestown venture, it also indicates something of the range of difficulties and horrors faced by the gentlemen colonists in their attempt to master the environment.

A TRUE DECLARATION OF VIRGINIA

If any man shall accuse these reports of partiall falshood, supposing them to be but Vtopian, and legendarie fables, because he cannot conceiue, that plentie and famine, a temperate climate, and distempered bodies, felicities, and miseries can be reconciled together, let him now reade with judgement, but let him not judge before he hath read.

The ground of all those miseries, was the permissiue prouidence of God, who, in the fore-mentioned violent storme, seperated the head from the bodie, all the vitall powers of regiment being exiled with *Sir Thomas Gates* in those infortunate (yet fortunate) Ilands. The broken remainder of those supplies made a greater shipwrack in the continent of *Virginia*, by the tempest of dissention: euery man ouervaluing his own worth, would be a Commander: euery man vnderprising an others value, denied to be commanded. The emulation of *Cæsar* and *Pompey*, watered the plains of *Pharsaly* with bloud, and distracted the sinewes of the Romane *Monarchy*. The dissentions of the three besieged Captains betraied the Citie of *Hierusalem* to *Vespasian:* how much more easily might ambitious discord teare in peeces an infant Colony, where no eminent and respected magistrats had authoritie to punish presumptuous disobedience. *Tacitus* hath obserued, that when *Nero* sent his old trained souldiers to *Tarantum* and *Autium*, (but without their Captains and Centurians) that they rather made a number, then a Colony: euery souldier secretly glided into some neighbour Prouince, and forsooke their appointed places: which hatched this consequent mischiefe; the Cities were vninhabited, and the emperour was frustrated: when therefore licence, sedition, and furie, are the fruits of a headie, daring, and vnruly multitude, it is no wonder that so many in our colony perished: it is a wonder, that all were not deuoured.

Force's *Tracts*, III, pp. 14–18.

Omnis inordinatus animus sibi ipsi fit pœna, euery inordinate soule becomes his owne punishment.

The next fountaine of woes was secure negligence, and improuidence, when euery man sharked for his present bootie, but was altogether carelesse of succeeding penurie. Now, I demand whether *Sicilia,* or *Sardinia* (sometimes the barnes of *Rome*) could hope for increase without manuring? A Colony is therefore denominated, because they should be *Coloni,* the tillers of the earth, and stewards of fertilitie: our mutinous loiterers would not sow with proui-dence, and therefore they reaped the fruits of too deare-bought repentance. An incredible example of their idlenes, is the report of *Sir Thomas Gates,* who affirmeth, that after his first comming thither, he hath seen some of them eat their fish raw, rather than they would go a stones cast to fetch wood and dresse it. *Dij laboribus omnia vendunt,* God sels vs all things for our labour, when *Adam* himselfe might not liue in paridice without dressing the garden.

Vnto idlenesse, you may ioyne treasons, wrought by those vnhallowed creatures that forsooke the Colony, and exposed their desolate brethren to extreame miserie. You shall know that 28. or 30. of the companie, were appointed (in the Ship called the Swallow) to truck for Corne with the *Indians,* and hauing obtained a great quantitie by trading, the most seditious of them, conspired together, persuaded some, & enforced others, to this barbarous proiect. They stole away the Ship, they made a league amongst themselues to be professed pirates, with dreames of mountaines of gold, and happy robberies; thus at one instant, they wronged the hopes, and subuerted the cares of the Colony, who depending vpon their returne, fore-slowed to looke out for further prouision: they created the *Indians* our implacable enemies by some violence they had offered: they carried away the best Ship (which should haue been a refuge, in extremities:) they weakned our forces, by substraction of their armes, and succours. These are that scum of men that fayling in their piracy, that beeing pinched with famine and penurie, after their wilde rouing vpon the Sea, when all their lawlesse hopes failed, some remained with other pirates, they met vpon the Sea, the others resolued to return for England, bound themselues by mutuall oath, to agree all in one report, to discredit the land, to deplore the famyne, and to protest that this their comming awaie, proceeded from desperate necessitie: These are they, that roared out the tragicall historie of the man eating of his dead wife in *Virginia;* when the master of this Ship willingly confessed before 40 witnesses, that at their comming awaie, they left three moneths victuals, and all the cattell liuing in the Fort: sometimes they reported that they saw this horrible action, some-times that *Captain Dauies* sayd so, sometimes that one *Beadle* the Lieutenant of *Captaine Dauies* did relate it, varying this report into diuersitie of false colours, which hold no likenesse and proportion: But to cleare all doubts, *Sir Thomas Gates* thus relateth the tragedie.

There was one of the companie who mortally hated his wife, and therefore secretly killed her, then cut her in pieces and hid her in diuers parts of his house: when the woman was missing, the man suspected, his house searched, and parts of her mangled body were discouered, to excuse himselfe he said that his wife died, that he hid her to satisfie his hunger, and that he fed daily vpon her. Vpon this, his house was againe searched, where they found a good quantitie of meale, oatemeale, beanes and pease. Hee therevpon was araigned, confessed the murder, and was burned for his horrible villany.

Now shall the scandalous reports of a viperous generation, preponderate the testimonies of so worthie leaders? shall their venemous tongues, blast the reputation of an auncient & worthy Peere, who vpon the ocular certainty of future blessings, hath protested in his Letters, that he will sacrifice himselfe for his Countrie in this seruice, if he may be seconded; and if the company doe giue it ouer he will yet lay all his fortunes vpon the prosecution of the plantation? shall sworne lyes, and combined oathes, so far priuiledge trechery, and piracy as to rob vs of our hopes, & to quell our noble resolutions? God forbid: *Qui in mendacio confidit, cito diffidit,* a lyers confidence, is but a blazing diffidence.

Vnto Treasons, you may ioyne couetousnesse in the Mariners, who for their priuate lucre partly imbezled the prouisions, partly preuented our trade with the *Indians,* making the matches in the night, and forestalling our market in the day: whereby the Virginians were glutted with our trifles, and inhaunced the prices of their Corne and Victuall. That Copper which before would haue prouided a bushell, would not now obtaine so much as a pottle: *Non habet euentus sordida præda bonos,* the consequent of sordid gaine is vntimely wretchednesse.

Ioyne vnto these an other euill: there is great store of Fish in the riuer, especially of Sturgeon; but our men prouided no more of them, then for present necessitie, not barrelling vp any store against that season the Sturgeon returned to the sea. And not to dissemble their folly, they suffered fourteene nets (which was all they had) to rot and spoile, which by orderly drying and mending might haue been preserued: but being lost, all help of fishing perished. *Quanto maiora timentur dispendia, tanto promptior debet esse cautela,* fundamentall losses that cannot be repealed, ought with the greatest caution to be preuented.

The state of the Colony, by these accidents began to find a sensible declyning: which *Powhatan* (as a greedy Vulture) obseruing, and boyling with desire of reuenge, he inuited *Captaine Ratclife,* and about thirty others to trade for Corne, and under the colour of fairest friendship, he brought them within the compasse of his ambush, whereby they were cruelly murthered, and massacred. For vpon confidence of his fidelitie, they went one and one into seuerall houses, which caused their seuerall destructions, when if but any sixe had remained together, they would haue been a bulwarke for the generall preseruation. After this, *Powhatan* in the night cut off some of our boats, he draue away all the Deere into the farther part of the Countrie, hee and his people destroyed our Hogs, (to the number of about sixe hundred) he sent none of his *Indians* to trade with vs, but laied secret ambushes in the woods, that if one or two dropped out of the fort alone, they were indaungered.

Cast vp this reckoning together: want of gouernment, store of idlenesse, their expectations frustrated by the Traitors, their market spoyled by the Mariners, our nets broken, the deere chased, our boats lost, our hogs killed, our trade with the *Indians* forbidden, some of our men fled, some murthered, and most by drinking of the brackish water of *Iames* fort weakened, and indaungered, famyne and sicknesse by all these meanes increased, here at home the monies came in so slowly that the *Lo. Laware* could not be dispatched, till the Colony was worne and spent with difficulties: Aboue all, hauing neither Ruler, nor Preacher, they neither feared God nor man, which prouoked the wrath of the Lord of Hosts, and pulled downe his judgements vpon them. *Discite iustitiam moniti.* Now, (whether it were that God in mercie to vs would weede out these ranke hemlockes; or whether in iudgement to them he would scourge their impieties; or whether in wisedome he would trie our patience, *Vt magna magnè desideremus,* that wee may beg great blessings earnestly) our hope is that our Sunne shall not set in a cloude, since this violent storme is dispersed, since all necessarie things are prouided, an absolute and powerful gouernment is setled. . . .

FREEHOLDING AND FREE ENTERPRISE

Realizing that the only way to attract qualified, hard-working settlers to Virginia was to grant them free land, in 1612 the Company Council issued the following instructions. After this date over 4000 settlers poured into Virginia. Only individualism and the desire for private gain—which brought with it a chance for upward social mobility—could have been the stimulus. Company-communalism had failed in the face of New World conditions.

THE VIRGINIA COMPANY'S LAND POLICY

And because our intent is to Ease all the Inhabitants of Virginia forever of all taxes and public burthens as much as may be and to take away all occasion of oppression and corruption we have thought fit to begin (according to the laudable Example of the most famous Common Wealthes both past and present) to alot and lay out A Convenient portion of public lands for the maintenance and support as well of Magistracy and officers as of other public charges both here and there from time to time arising. We therefore the said treasurer and Company upon a solemn treaty and resolution and with the advice consent and assent of his Majesties Council here of Virginia being Assembled in A great and general Court of the Council and Company of Adventurers for Virginia require you the said Governor and Council of Estate to put in Execution with all convenient Speed a former order of Our Courts (which had been commended also to Captain Argal at his making Deputy Governor) for the laying and seting out by bounds and metes of three thousand Acres of land in the best and most convenient place of the territory of James town in Virginia and next adjoining to the said town to be the seat and land of the Governor of Virginia for the time being and his Successors and to be called by the name of the Governors Land which Governors Land shall be of the freed grounds by the common labor of the people sent thither at the Companies Charges And of the Lands formerly conquer'd or purchased of the Paspeheies and of other grounds next adjoining it. In like sort we require you to set and lay out by bounds and Metes other three thousand Acres of good land within the territory of James town which shall be convenient and in such place or places as in your discretions you shall find meet which latter three thousand Acres shall be and so called the Companies Land And we require you Captain Yeardley that immediately upon your arrival you take unto you the Guard assigned to Captain Argal at his going Deputy Governor or sithence by him assumed to be of your guard [for the better defence] of your Government and that as well the said guard as also fifty other persons now sent and transported with you you place as tennants on the said Governors land and that all other persons heretofore transported at the Common Charge of the Company since the coming away of Sr Thomas Dale Knight late Deputy Governor be placed as Tennants on the said Companies Lands And we will and ordain that all the said Tennants on the Governors and Companies Lands shall occupy the same to the half part of the profits of the said Lands so as the one half to be and belong to the said Tennants themselves and the other half respectively to the

---

S. M. Kingsbury, ed., *The Records of the Virginia Company of London* (Washington, D.C., Government Printing Office, 1900–1935), III, pp. 99–101.

said Governor and to us the said Treasurer and Company and our Successors. . . .
And that for all such Planters as were brought thither at the Companies
Charge to inhabit there before the coming away of the said Sr Thomas Dale
after the time of their Service to the Company on the common Land agreed
shall be expired there be set out One hundred Acres of Land for each of their
personal Adventurers to be held by them their heirs and Assigns for ever.
paying for every fifty Acres the yearly free Rent of one Shilling to the said
treasurer and Company and their Successors at one Entire payment on the
feast day of St Michael the archangel for ever And in regard that by the singular
industry and virtue of the said Sr Thomas Dale the former difficulties and
dangers were in greatest part overcome to the great ease and security of such
as have been since that time transported thither We do therefore hereby ordain
that all such persons as sithence the coming away of the said Sr Thomas Dale
have at their own charges been transported thither to inhabit and so continued
as aforesaid there be allotted and set out upon a first division fifty acres of
land to them and their heirs for ever for their personal Adventure paying a
free rent of one Shilling yearly in manner aforesaid And that all persons which
since the going away of the said Sr Thomas Dale have been transported thither
at the Companies charges or which hereafter shall be so transported be placed
as tenants on the Companies lands for term of seven years occupy the same to
the half part of the profits as is abovesaid We therefore will and ordain that
other three thousand Acres of Land be set out in the fields and territory of
Charles City and other three thousand Acres of Land in the fields and territories of Henrico And other three thousand Acres of land in the fields and
territory of Kiccowtan all which to be and be called the Companies lands and
to be occupied by the Companies Tenants for half profits as afore said And
that the profits belonging to the Company be disposed by their several moieties
in the same manner as before set down touching the Companies lands in the
territory of James town with like allowance to the Bailies and reservation of
ground for the common Store of Cattle in those several places as is there set
down And our will is that such of the Companies tenants as already inhabite
in those several Cities or Burroughs be not removed to any other City or
Burrough but placed on the Companies Lands belonging to those Cities or Burroughs where they now inhabite *Provided* alwaies that if any private person
without fraud or injurious intent to the public at his own charges have freed
any of the said Lands formerly appointed to the Governor he may continue and
inhabite there till a valuable recompence be made him for his said Charges . . .

A MORE POWERFUL GENERAL ASSEMBLY

In 1619 the Company created a General Assembly in Virginia. It had very little power beyond advising the Governor, but it created an illusion of self-government and acted as a sounding board for colonial grievances. Two years later, in 1621, the Company created two councils, an upper and a lower house, as it were. The upper house or Council was appointed by the Company to assist the Governor, while the lower house or General Assembly, made up of two representatives from each of the towns or plantation "hundreds," was to pass laws which were subject only to the veto of the Company's home Council so long as they were not repugnant to the laws of England. Likewise, laws proposed by the Governor and Council had to be ratified by the General Assembly before they became operational. This document provides evidence of the increased local power which developed in the two short years since the meeting of the first assembly in 1619.

THE ORDINANCE OF 1621

To all people to whom these presents shall come bee seen or heard, the Treasuror, Council and Company of Adventurers and Planters of the Citty of London for the First Collony in Virginia send greeting: knowe yee that wee, the said Treasuror, Counsell and Company, takeing into our carefull consideracion the present state of the said Colony in Virginia, and intending by the Devine assistance to settle such a forme of government ther as may bee to the greatest benefitt and comfort of the people and wherby all injustice, grevance and oppression may bee prevented and kept of as much as is possible from the said Colony, have thought fitt to make our entrance by ordaining & establishing such supreme Counsells as may not only bee assisting to the Governor for the time being in administracion of justice and the executing of other duties to his office belonging, but also by ther vigilent care & prudence may provide as well for remedy of all inconveniencies groweing from time to time as also for the advancing of encrease, strength, stabillitie and prosperitie of the said Colony:

Wee therefore, the said Treasuror, Counsell and Company, by authoritie directed to us from His Majestie under his Great Seale, upon mature delibera-

S. M. Kingsbury, ed., *The Records of the Virginia Company*, III, pp. 482–484.

cion doe hereby order & declare that from hence forward ther bee towe su-
preame Counsells in Virginia for the better government of the said Colony as
aforesaid: the one of which Counsells to bee called the Counsell of State and
whose office shall cheiflie bee assisting, wth ther care, advise & circomspec-
tion, to the said Governor; shall be chosen, nominated, placed and displaced
from time to time by us, the said Treasurer, Counsell & Company and our
successors; which Counsell of State shall consiste for the present onlie of
those persons whose names are here inserted, vizt.: Sir Francis Wyatt, Governor of Virginia; Captaine Francis West; Sir George Yeardley, Knight; Sir
William Newce, Knight, Marshall of Virginia; Mr. George Sandys, Tresuror;
Mr. George Thorpe, Deputy of the Colledge; Captaine Thomas Newce, Deputy
for the Company; Mr. Christopher Davison, Secretarie; Doctor Potts, Phesition
to the Company; Mr. Paulet; Mr. Leech; Captaine Nathaniell Powell; Mr.
Roger Smith; Mr. John Berkley; Mr. John Rolfe; Mr. Ralfe Hamer; Mr. John
Pountus; Mr. Michael Lapworth; Mr. Harwood; [and] Mr. Samuel Macocke.
Which said Counsellors and Counsell wee earnestlie pray & desier, and in
His Majesties name strictlie charge and command, that all factious parcialties
and sinister respects laid aside, they bend ther care and endeavors to assist
the said Governor first and principallie in advancement of the honor and
service of Almightie God and the enlargement of His kingdome amongste
those heathen people; and next in the erecting of the said Colonie in one
obedience to His Majestie and all lawful authoritie from His Majestis dirived;
and lastlie in maitaining the said people in justice and Christian conversation
among themselves and in strength and habillitie to wth stand ther ennimies.
And this Counsell is to bee alwaies, or for the most part, residing about or
neere the said Governor. The other Counsell, more generall, to bee called by
the Governor, and yeerly, of course, & no oftner but for very extreordinarie &
important occasions, shall consist for present of the said Counsell of State and
of tow burgesses out of every towne, hunder [hundred] and other particuler
plantacion to bee respetially chosen by the inhabitants. Which Counsell
shalbee called the Generall Assemblie, wherein as also in the said Counsell of
State, all matters shall be decided, determined & ordered by the greater part
of the voices then present, reserveing alwaies to the Governor a negative
voice. And this Generall Assembly shall have free power to treat, consult &
conclude as well of all emergent occasions concerning the publiqe weale of
the said Colony and evrie parte therof as also to make, ordeine & enact such
generall lawes & orders for the behoof of the said Colony and the good gov-
ermt therof as shall time to time appeare necessarie or requisite. Wherin
as in all other things wee requier the said Gennerall Assembly, as also the said
Counsell of State, to imitate and followe the policy of the forme of goverment,
lawes, custome, manners of loyall and other administracion of justice used

in the realme of England, as neere as may bee even as ourselves by His Majesties lettres patents are required; provided that noe lawes or ordinance made in the said Generall Assembly shalbe and continew in force and validitie, unlese the same shalbe sollemlie ratified and confirmed in a generall greater court of the said court here in England and so ratified and returned to them under our seale. It being our intent to affoord the like measure also unto the said Colony that after the goverment of the [said Colony, shall once have been well framed & settled accordingly, which is to be done by us as by authoritie derived from] his Majestie and the sa[me shall] have bene soe by us declared, no orders of our court afterwarde shall binde [the said] Colony unles they bee ratified in like manner in ther Generall Assembly.

In wittnes wherof wee have hereunto sett our common seale the 24th day of [July] 1621, and in the yeare of the raigne of our governoure, Lord James by the . . . of God of England, Scotland, France & Ireland, King, Defendor of the . . . vizt., of England, France and Scotland the nineteenth and of Scotland the fower and fiftieth.

THE MASSACRE OF 1622

How wisely the General Assembly ruled is revealed by the results of its paternalistic Indian policy, which sought to make the savage redmen docile slaves. The following is a report of the massacre of 1622 in which 347 men, women, and children were killed. Such an uprising had been brewing since 1607, shortly after the first landing. Thanks to the shrewd policy of Captain John Smith, however, and the forbearance of Chief Powhatan, no general uprising had occurred. Only with the death of Powhatan did the Indian leaders succeed in arousing the tribesmen to the warpath. What is the official attitude of the colonists toward the Indians in this report? What are the reasons for this attitude?

An Indian dance, drawn by John White.

FAILURE OF THE ASSEMBLY'S INDIAN POLICY

And such was the conceit of firme peace and amitie, as that there was seldome or neuer a sword worne, and a Peece seldomer, except for a Deere or Fowle. By which assurance of securitie, the Plantations of particular Aduenturers and Planters were placed scatteringly and straglingly as a choyce veyne of rich ground inuited them, and the further from neighbors held the better. The houses generally set open to the Sauages, who were alwaies friendly entertained at the tables of the English, and commonly lodged in their bed-chambers. The old planters (as they thought now come to reape the benefit of their long trauels) placed with wonderfull content vpon their priuate diuidents, and the planting of particular Hundreds and Colonies pursued with an hopefull alacrity, all our proiects (saith he) in a faire way, and their familarity with the Natiues, seeming to open a faire gate for their conuersion to Christianitie.

The Country being in this estate, an occasion was ministred of sending to *Opachankano* the King of these Sauages, about the middle of *March* last, what time the Messenger returned backe with these words from him, That he held the peace concluded so firme, as the Skie should sooner fall then it dissolue: yea, such was the treacherous dissimulation of that people who then had contriued our destruction, that even two dayes before the Massacre, some of our men were guided thorow the woods by them in safety: and one *Browne*, who then to learne the language liued among the *Warrascoyacks* (a Prouince of that King) was in friendly manner sent backe by them to Captaine *Hamor* his Master, and many the like passages, rather increasing our former confidence, then any wise in the world ministring the least suspition of the breach of the peace, or of what instantly ensued; yea, they borrowed our owne Boates to conuey themselues crosse the Riuer (on the bankes of both sides whereof all our Plantations were) to consult of the diuellish murder that ensued, and of our vtter extirpation, which God of his mercy (by the meanes of some of themselues conuerted to Christianitie) preuented; and as well on the Friday morning (the fatal day) the 22 of *March*, as also in the euening, as in other dayes before, they came vnarmed into our houses, without Bowes or arrowes, or other weapons, with Deere, Turkies, Fish, Furres, and other prouisions, to sell, and trucke with vs for glasse, beades, and other trifles: yea in some places, sate downe at Breakfast with our people at their tables, whom immediately with their owne tooles and weapons, eyther laid downe, or standing in their houses, they basely and barbarously murthered, not sparing eyther age or sexe, man, woman or childe; so sodaine in their cruell execution, that

S. M. Kingsbury, ed., *The Records of the Virginia Company*, III, pp. 550–551, 554–555.

few or none discerned the weapon or blow that brought them to destruction. In which manner they also slew many of our people then at their seuerall workes and husbandries in the fields, and without their houses, some in planting Corne and Tobacco, some in gardening, some in making Bricke, building, sawing, and other kindes of husbandry, they well knowing in what places and quarters each of our men were, in regard of their daily familiarity, and resort to vs for trading and other negotiations, which the more willingly was by vs continued and cherished for the desire we had of effecting that great masterpeece of workes, their conuersion. And by this meanes that fatall Friday morning, there fell vnder the bloudy and barbarous hands of that perfidious and inhumane people, contrary to all lawes of God and men, of Nature & Nations, three hundred forty seuen men, women, and children, most by their owne weapons; and not being content with taking away life alone, they fell after againe vpon the dead, making as well as they could, a fresh murder, defacing, dragging, and mangling the dead carkasses into many pieces, and carrying some parts away in derision, with base and bruitish triumph.

Neither yet did these beasts spare those amongst the rest well knowne vntthem, from whom they had daily receiued many benefitts and fauours, but spitefully also massacred them, without remorse or pitty, being in this more fell then Lyons and Dragons, which (as Histories record) haue beene so farre from hurting, as they haue both acknowledged, and gratefully requited their Benefactors; such is the force of good deeds, though done to cruell beasts, as to make them put off the very nature of beasts, and to put on humanity vpon them. But these miscreants, contrariwise in this kinde, put not off onely all humanity, but put on a worse and more then vnnaturall bruitishnesse. . . .

The Letters of Mr. *George Sandis* a worthy Gentleman and Treasurer there, likewise haue aduertised (as many others from many particular persons of note and worth) besides the Relations of many returned in the Sea-flower (the ship that brought vs this vnwelcome newes) haue beene heard at large in the publike Courts, that whilst all their affayres were full of successe, and such intercourse of familiaritie, as if the *Indians* and themselues had beene of one Nation, those treacherous Natiues, after fiue yeares peace, by a generall combination in one day plotted to subuert their whole Colony, and at one instant of time, though our seuerall Plantations were an hundred and forty miles vp one Riuer on both sides. . . .

They certifie further, that besides Master *George Thorpe*, before mentioned, Master *Iohn Berkeley*, Captaine *Nathanael Powel*, and his wife, (daughter of Master *William Tracy*, and great with childe) and Captaine *Maycock*, all Gentlemen of birth, vertue, and industry, and of the Councell there, suffered vnder this their cruelty and treason.

That the slaughter had beene vniuersall, if God had not put it into the heart of an Indian belonging to one *Perry*, to disclose it, who liuing in the house of one *Pace*, was vrged by another Indian his Brother (who came the night before and lay with him) to kill *Pace*, (so commanded by their King as he declared) as hee would kill *Perry*: telling further that by such an houre in the morning a number would come from diuers places to finish the Execution, who failed not at the time: *Perries* Indian rose out of his bed and reueales it to *Pace*, that vsed him as a Sonne: And thus the rest of the Colony that had warning giuen them, by this meanes was saued. Such was (God bee thanked for it) the good fruit of an Infidell conuerted to Christianity; for though three hundred and more of ours died by many of these Pagan Infidels, yet thousands of ours were saued by the means of one of them alone which was made a Christian. . . .

GOVERNMENT BY ROYAL INSTRUCTIONS

After the dissolution of the Company and the creation of Virginia as a royal colony in 1624, government was conducted by means of royal instructions to governors appointed by the King. These instructions were often extremely detailed, frequently unrealistic, and invariably out of date with developments in the colony. Through the Governor and his appointed council, the Crown tried to exercise more and more control over the colony, as the following document—instructions to Governor George Yeardley in 1626—indicates. Note especially the attempts to control the marketing of tobacco, which by this time was beginning to be the main staple of the colony. Crown policy appears to have been to encourage self-sufficiency in the production of food-stuffs, and to control tobacco export by making Jamestown the only shipping point. This policy failed.

INSTRUCTIONS TO GOVERNOR GEORGE YEARDLEY IN 1626

Instructions from the Lords of His Maties Most Honble Privy Councill, To Sir George Yardly, Knt., Governor of Virginia, and to the Honble Councill of State there:

Ye 19th day of April, 1626.

1. That you, ye s^d Sir George Yardly, do use your best endeavours to be ready with such ships and vessels, Men and Provisions as ye have furnished for ye purpose upon ye first fair wind and weather, to put to sea, and to sail directly for Virginia, unless ye shall find it requisite for ye good of ye Plantacon and peoples to touch at ye Summer Islands by ye way. When after ye have refreshed ye shall proceed to Virginia, and upon yor arrival there according to your commission granted by His Most Xtian Maj^ty under ye great Seal, take upon you ye present government of the Colony.

2. That in the first place you be carefull that Almighty God may be duly and daily served, both by yourself and all the people under yor charge, wch may draw down a blessing upon all your Endeavours.

3. That you faile not by the first Ship to send us a list of all the severall plantacons, ye places where they are planted, the distance between the Plantations, the number of people in every Plantation distinguished by their sexes, ages, Professions and Condition, and also by ye place of every ones birth, and the manner of their Patents here in England. What arms, Ammunition, Boats or Ships, Dwelling Houses and other Buildings?

What unpaled ground? Provision of Food or store of Tame Cattle in every of ye s^d Plantations.

4. That you diligently and particularly enquire by oath and all other lawfull means what Lands, Woods, Serv^ts, Tenem^ts, Houses, Boats, Ships were in November, 1623, belonging unto ye late Company. How and to whom they have been disposed? By what order and authority they have been so disposed and what ye shall find remaining to reserve to the public use. All which you are to certify under ye Hands and Seale of the Colony.

5. That all new comers be well entertained and lodged in houses by the old Planters untill they can lodge themselves, that they be not suffered to sit down stragling, but enjoyned to live by those already planted or in sufficient number by themselves. And if be unprovided of Land fit to manure, then to be permitted to sit down upon the Company's Land upon the conditions expressed in the Treas^y and Councills Letter sent immediately after the Massacre in August, 1623.

The Virginia Magazine of History and Biography, **2,** April 1895, pp. 393–396.

6. That all new comers be exempted ye 1st year from going in p^son or contributing to the war save only in defence of the place where they shall inhabit, and that only when the enemy shall assail it. But all others in the colony shall be rated to ye maintenance of ye warrs proportionally to their abilities. Neither shall any man be priviledged from going to the wars that is above seventeen years old and under 60. Respect being had to the quality of the persons, that officers be not forced to go as private soldiers, or in places inferior to their degrees, unless in cases of extream necessity.

7. That the merchants be not constrained to take Tobacco at 3. p. Pound in exchange for his wares, but that it be lawfull for him to make his own bargain for his goods be so changable notwithstanding any Proclamation published there to the contrary.

8. That ye call for ye charter parties that the Masters of ships bring along with them and straightly examine whether they have truly performed ye condicon of their contracts, especially to enquire whether they have not pestred their ships with passengers, and whether they have given sufficient and wholesom food and drink during ye voyage, and as ye find to certify ye Lords of his Maj^tys privy councill or ye comm^rs of Virginia.

9. That ye be carefull that the good ship the Annie wherein ye are to embarque yourself and the James that goeth in concert wth you be not pestred with passengers and y^t ye Masters of ye same ships do give the Passengers sufficient and wholesom food and drink during the voyage.

10. That in regard ye may daily expect ye coming of a fforaign Enemy, Wee require you after your first landing that you publish by Proclamation through the Colony that no person whatsoever upon ye arrivall of any Ship or Ships shall dare to go aboard without express warrant from you ye Gove^nr and Councill, least by that means they be surprised to the great prejudice if not overthrow of the Plantacon.

11. To avoid that intollerable abuse of Ingrossing comodities and forestalling ye Market, That you require all Masters of ships not to break Bulk till their arrivall at James City, or other wise without special order from you ye Governor and Councill.

12. That you endeavour by severe punishment to suppress drunkeness and that you be carefull that great Quantities of Wine and strong Drink be not sold into the hands of those who are likeliest to abuse it, but that as near as you can, it may be equally disposed of for the comfort and reliefe of ye whole Plantacon. And if any Merc^ht or any other for private lucre shall bring in any rotten and unwholesome wines or strong drink, such as may endanger ye health of ye people, That ye suffer it not to be sold there, but do cause them to ship it back again.

13. That whereas the Tobacco falleth every day more and more to a baser price, We require you to use your best Endeavours to cause ye people there to

apply themselves more to ye raising of more staple comodities as likewise to ye impaling of Gardens and Orchards and enclosing of Grounds for all manner of Cattle, whereby the Hire of the Country may be advanced in abundance.

14. That you cause ye people to plant such store of corn as there may be a whole year's provision before hand in ye Colony, least relying upon ye Single Harvest by Drought, blasting or other waies they fall into such wants & fammines as formerly they have endured.

15. That you may the better avoid the Treachery of ye Savages and prevent such Dangers as heretofore have fallen upon the Country, you strictly forbid all persons whatsoever to receive into their Houses any of ye Indians, or to parly, converse or trade with them without especiall License and warrant given to that purpose, according to y^{or} Commission, inflicting severe Punishment upon ye Offenders.

16. That whereas by y^{or} last Letters from Virginia, wee are given to understand that of those who are now nominated for Councellors there, some are Dead and others are coming home. Wee do authorize you ye Gov^{er} to make choice of such as you in y^{or} Judgment shall think most fitt to supply their places, and to administer to them an oath as you are directed by y^{r} Commission that so in these dangerous times there may not be wanting a sufficient number to assist in ye Government of the affairs of that Colony.

As also to administer the Oaths of Allegiance and Supremacy to all such as come hither w^{h} an intention to plant & reside there, which if they shall refuse he is to be returned or shipped from thence home. The same oath to be administered to all other p^{sons} when ye shall see it fitt, as Mariners, Merch^{ts}, &c., to prevent danger by Spyes.

17. And to conclude, That in all things according to your best endeavour, you endeavour the extirpating of vice and the encouragement of virtue and goodness.

> Thos. Coventry, C.,
> Marlbrugh,
> Worster,
> Pembroke &
> Montgomery,
> E. Comby,
> J. Edmonds,
> J. Suckling,
> D. Charleton,
> John Cook,
> Humphrey May,
> C. R.

BEHIND THE SCENES OF ROYAL GOVERNMENT

The following letter from Captain Young (otherwise unidentified) to a political confidant back in England reveals something of the factional strife and spirit of untrammeled opportunism that existed behind the facade of royal government. Samuel Mathews (1600–1660) of Blunt Point, Virginia, though somewhat anomalous in that he was a Puritan, was nonetheless a characteristic figure in Virginia politics. A wealthy planter and merchant who had secured much of his status by marriage to the daughter of Sir Thomas Hinton, M. P., a rich and influential British politician, Mathews was a power in colonial Virginia for over thirty years. Variously a member of the Royal Commission to investigate the Virginia Company, a Governor's Councillor, and the last Commonwealth Governor of Virginia, Mathews was continually embroiled in politics, but derived his main strength from his connections back home. These connections enabled him to survive temporary imprisonment and the confiscation of his estates by the hostile Governor John Harvey. They also enabled him to maintain his power during both the Cromwell and the Stuart regimes.

In the selection included here, Mathews is seen as intriguing against Lord Baltimore and the Catholic colonists of Maryland. The activities described took place in the period 1652–1657, and were eventually terminated when, in November 1657, Mathews signed an agreement with Lord Baltimore relinquishing Virginia's claims to Maryland.

SAMUEL MATHEWS INTRIGUES AGAINST
THE AUTHORITIES IN VIRGINIA AND MARYLAND

This, so farre as I can learne, is the true state wherein my Lord of Baltimores plantation stands with those of Virginia, wch perhaps may prove dangerous enough for them if there be not some present order taken in England for the suppressing the insolence of Cleyborne and force his complines and for disjoynting this faction, wch is soe fast linked and united as I am perswaded will not by the Governor be easily dissevered or over ruled with[out] some strong

C. C. Hall, ed., "Narratives of Early Maryland, 1633–1684," in J. Franklin Jameson, ed., *Original Narratives of Early American History* (New York, Charles Scribner's Sons, 1910), pp. 58–61. The footnotes are those of C. C. Hall.

and powerful addition to his present authority by some new power from England, and it will be to little purpose for my Lord to proceed in his colony against which they have so exasperated and incensed all the English Colony of Virginia as heere it is accounted a crime almost as heynous as treason to favor, nay allmost to speak well of that Colony of my Lords. And I have observed myself a palpable kind of strangenesse and distance between those of the best sort in the country who have formerly bene very familiar and loving one to another, only because the one hath bene suspected but to have bene a well wisher to the Plantation in Maryland.

The Governor only of Virginia (a gentleman in good faith in my judgment of a noble mynde and worthy heart) out of his care to observe his Maties commands signified to him by his Royall l^{res} [letters] and also out of his own good inclinations hath carried himself very worthily and respectively towards them and is ready on all occasions to give them all the assistance and furtherance that possibly he can, though thereby he hath acquired to himself extreame hatred and malice from all the rest of the country, to whom I can find only two of his councell indifferent, the one of them called Captaine Purfree a souldier and a man of an open heart, honest and free, hating for ought I can [see?] all kinds of dissimulation and basenesse, the other an honest playne man but of small capacity and lesse power.*

The person on whom the strength and sinewes of this faction depends is one Captayne Mathews an ancient planter heere, a man of a bold spiritt, turbulent and strong in the faction of the more refractory sort of the countrey, and as I have bene informed by persons of good creditt a great opposer and interpreter of all letters and commands that come from the King and state of England, apt also to possesse and preoccupate the judgments of the rest of his fellow councellors, that letters from the King and from the Lords are surreptitiously gotten and that the obedience to them may and ought to be suspended till they be warranted by second commands from England, which may issue from them after the Lords have bene informed by them, for that many times the Lords are not sufficiently instructed in the necessities and conveniencies of this Government heere, pretending and making them beleeve that evry kind of disobedience doe oftentimes become gratefull to the State. This gentleman as I heare is lately married to the daughter of one Sir Thomas Hinton, who is lately retired hither into these parts,† and he grows, as is conceaved, much bolder by this alliance, as hoping by his power to find great strength in England, though for my part I conceave he hath but small grounds for those hopes, yet heere we have it very confidently and very frequently

---

* Sir John Harvey continued to be the staunch friend of Lord Baltimore and the Maryland Colony and to entertain suspicions as to the loyalty of Claiborne.
† Sir Thomas Hinton, M. P., 1620–1626.

reported that a sonne of S[r] Thomas Hintons, who is a gentleman of the Privie Chamber, is to come over hither Governor.

S[r] John Harvye invited me very earnestly that during the time that my ship was making ready and my shallopp building I would accompany him to James Towne, whither he was then going, wch I accepted as a favor, partly led thereunto with desire to see the country, partly also to see the event of my Lords buisnesse, and likewise a little to recreate myself after my long voyage, wherein I thank God I have yet had my health very well. We lay two nights by the way, at a gentlemans house a planter of the country one night, and the other most parte of it aboard S[r] Johns barge. This countrey aboundeth with very great plentie insomuch as in ordinary planters houses of the better sort we found tables fournished with porke, kidd, chickens, turkeyes, young geese, Caponetts and such other foules as the season of the yeare affords, besides plentie of milk, cheese, butter and corne, wch latter almost every planter in the country hath.

The country is very good and fertill, the climate pleasant and wholesome, the land fertile enough and with good husbandry will soone grow into great abundance, and a great Trade may quickly be driven heere, if good providence and care be taken, wch will much advance his Ma[ties] customes.

While I stay heere at James Towne, where Now I am, I meet dayly with severall of the best and most understanding sort of the Inhabitants of this place, by whome I enforme myself as much as I can of the State of this countrey and I find really that the present Governor hath carried himselfe heere with very good prudence, hath bene extraordinary diligent in advancing and furthering the Colony, a great reformer of the abuses in the Governement, especially in point of justice, wch at his first entrance was full of corruption and partiality, the richest and most powerfull oppressing and swallowing up the poorer, though now much amended by his care and zeale to justice, though even in that also he is sometimes overborne by the strength and power of some factious and turbulent spiritts of his councell, for heere in this place all things are carried by the most voyces of the Councell, and they are for the most part united in a kind of faction against the Governor, insomuch as they make their publike consultations give strength and authority to their faction, and it is hard for the Governors to determine or order any thing heere contrary to their dreaming, for they come all hither preoccupated and resolved to follow and concurr with the votes of their leaders. Of this faction Captain Mathews, of whom before I spake, is the head and cheefe supporte. This gentleman, as I am told, tooke the boldenesse publikely when the kings letter was delivered and read in favor of my Lord of Baltimore was there read, to question whether they were not surreptitiously procured, and it is vehemently suspected, and they say not without reason, that he hath bene the incendiary of all this wicked plott of Cleybourne's and yet continues to bee the supporter and upholder of him, and except my Lord finde some meanes speedily and in a very exemplar manner to curb and suppresse this mans insolencies, he will dayly find more and more practizes and treacherous conspiracies contrived against him, and veryly I beleeve if my Lord could finde meanes over heere to ecclipse his power and greatnesse, or to remove him from hence, the backe of this faction would soone be broken and this strong knot would untie of itselfe. Nor is that other instrument of his of whome I spake before, namely Cleybourne, lesse carefully to be lookt unto, since his practizes, though they be not so publike as the others insolencies, yet are they not lesse dangerous to that Colony, yea and to the security of the peace of this very land and governement of Virginia, where I have bene informed that some of the Councellors have bene bold enough in a presumptuous manner to say, to such as told them that perhaps their disobedience might cause them to be sent for into England, That if the King would have them he must come himself and fetch them.

MERCANTILISM AND EMPIRE

We have seen that, in the instructions to the royal governors, the Crown attempted to control the commerce of the American colonies, but with only indifferent success. As early as 1645 the first of a series of general Navigation Acts, which were meant to control trade throughout all British colonial lands, was passed. It was a clear recognition of the fact of empire and an attempt to make the empire pay.

The most important of these early Navigation Acts was that of 1660, which was more generally applicable than any of the others. Essentially it controlled trade between the colonies and foreign nations. No longer, for example, could a Virginian consign his tobacco to Holland. Sugar or molasses could not be acquired from French or Spanish islands to be made into rum for sale in territories outside the British Empire, such as the French fishing provinces of Canada. More important, no produce of English colonies could be carried in anything but English or colonial ships manned by predominantly English or colonial crews. The Navigation Act was, in effect, a shrewd recognition that the major profits of the empire were to be made in shipping.

This Act, which imitated traditional Spanish exclusion policies, was not an innovation. It was designed, as Spanish commercial laws had been, to benefit the mother country at the expense of the colonies. However, unlike the Spanish laws, it was directed specifically at excluding foreign rivals like the Dutch, thus enabling Britain to secure maximum advantage from the produce of the empire. The Navigation Acts were the antithesis of the later free-trade policies advocated by Adam Smith, whereby buyers and sellers exchanged goods all over the world for whatever the market would bring. They were mercantilistic; that is, they enabled the mother country to protect "home" markets from foreign goods, artificially control prices, and thus work toward a favorable balance of trade. This was a worldwide extension of the traditional practice of monopoly by a chartered company, as exemplified by the Levant Company and the East India Company. Until British productivity rose to the point where English goods could undersell foreign goods in world markets, and until the colonies made Britain relatively self-sufficient, a mercantilist policy was vital to Britain's economic health, though perhaps not to that of her colonies.

For the most part, Virginia merchants honored the Navigation Act of 1660, though smuggling and illicit trading increased throughout the period. As a result of this Act and the flooding of English markets with Virginia tobacco, the first genuine depression in the North American colonies took place.

THE NAVIGATION ACT OF 1660

An Act for the Encouraging and Increasing of Shipping and Navigation

For the increase of shipping and encouragement of the navigation of this nation, wherein, under the good providence and protection of God, the wealth, safety and strength of this kingdom is so much concerned; (2) be it enacted by the King's most excellent majesty, and by the lords and commons in this present parliament assembled, and by the authority thereof, That from and after the first day of December one thousand six hundred and sixty, and from thenceforward, no goods or commodities whatsoever shall be imported into or exported out of any lands, islands, plantations or territories to his Majesty belonging or in his possession, or which may hereafter belong unto

Danby Pickering, The Statutes at Large, From The Thirty-Ninth Year of Queen Elizabeth to the Twelfth Year of King Charles II, inclusive (Cambridge, 1763), VII, pp. 452–459.

or be in the possession of his Majesty, his heirs and successors, in *Asia, Africa* or *America*, in any other ship or ships, vessel or vessels whatsoever, but in such ships or vessels as do truly and without fraud belong only to the people of *England* or *Ireland*, dominion of *Wales* or town of *Berwick* upon *Tweed*, or are of the built of and belonging to any the said lands, islands, plantations or territories, as the proprietors and right owners thereof, and whereof the master and three fourths of the mariners at least are *English*; (3) under the penalty of the forfeiture and loss of all the goods and commodities which shall be imported into or exported out of any the aforesaid places in any other ship or vessel, as also of the ship or vessel. . . .

II. And be it enacted, That no alien or person not born within the allegiance of our sovereign lord the King, his heirs and successors, or naturalized, or made a free denizen, shall from and after the first day of *February*, which will be in the year of our Lord one thousand six hundred sixty-one, exercise the trade or occupation of a merchant or factor in any the said places; (2) upon pain of the forfeiture and loss of all his goods and chattels. . . .

III. And it is further enacted by the authority aforesaid, That no goods or commodities whatsoever, of the growth, production or manufacture of *Africa, Asia* or *America*, or of any part thereof, or which are described or laid down in the usual maps or cards of those places, be imported into *England, Ireland* or *Wales*, islands of *Guernsey* and *Jersey*, or town of *Berwick* upon *Tweed*, in any other ship or ships, vessel or vessels whatsoever, but in such as do truly and without fraud belong only to the people of *England* or *Ireland*, dominion of *Wales*, or town of *Berwick* upon *Tweed*, or of the lands, islands, plantations or territories in *Asia, Africa* or *America*, to his Majesty belonging, as the proprietors and right owners thereof, and whereof the master, and three fourths at least of the mariners are *English*; (2) under the penalty of the forfeiture of all such goods and commodities, and of the ship or vessel in which they were imported. . . .

IV. And it is further enacted . . . That no goods or commodities that are of foreign growth, production or manufacture, and which are to be brought into *England, Ireland, Wales*, the islands of *Guernsey* and *Jersey*, or town of *Berwick* upon *Tweed*, in *English*-built shipping, or other shipping belonging to some of the aforesaid places, and navigated by *English* mariners, as aforesaid, shall be shipped or brought from any other place or places, country or countries, but only from those of the said growth, production or manufacture, or from those ports where the said goods and commodities can only, or are, or usually have been, first shipped for transportation, and from none other places or countries; (2) under the penalty of the forfeiture of all such of the aforesaid goods as shall be imported from any other place or country contrary to the true intent and meaning hereof, as also of the ship in which they were imported. . . .

V. And it is further enacted . . . That any sort of ling, stock-fish, pilchard, or any other kind of dried or salted fish, usually fished for and caught by the people of *England, Ireland, Wales,* or town of *Berwick* upon *Tweed;* or any sort of cod-fish or herring, or any oil or blubber made or that shall be made of any kind of fish whatsoever, or any whale-fins or whale-bones, which shall be imported into *England, Ireland, Wales,* or town of *Berwick* upon *Tweed,* not having been caught in vessels truly and properly belonging thereunto as proprietors and right owners thereof, and the said fish cured saved and dried, and the oil and blubber aforesaid (which shall be accounted and pay as oil) not made by the people thereof, and shall be imported into *England, Ireland* or *Wales,* or town of *Berwick* upon *Tweed,* shall pay double aliens custom.

VI. And be it further enacted . . . That from henceforth it shall not be lawful to any person or persons whatsoever, to load or cause to be loaden and carried in any bottom or bottoms, ship or ships, vessel or vessels whatsoever, whereof any stranger or strangers-born (unless such as shall be denizens or naturalized) be owners, part-owners or master, and whereof three fourths of the mariners at least shall not be *English,* any fish, victual, wares, goods, commodities or things, of what kind or nature soever the same shall be, from one port or creek of *England, Ireland, Wales,* islands of *Guernsey* or *Jersey,* or town of *Berwick* upon *Tweed,* to another port or creek of the same, or of any of them; under penalty for every one that shall offend contrary to the true meaning of this branch of this present act, to forfeit all such goods as shall be loaden and carried in any such ship or vessel, together with the ship or vessel. . . .

VII. And it is further enacted . . . That where any ease, abatement or privilege is given in the book of rates to goods or commodities imported or exported in *English*-built shipping, that is to say, shipping built in *England, Ireland, Wales,* islands of *Guernsey* or *Jersey,* or town of *Berwick* upon *Tweed,* or in any the lands, islands, dominions and territories to his Majesty in *Africa, Asia,* or *America,* belonging, or in his possession, that it is always to be understood and provided, that the master and three fourths of the mariners of the said ships at least be also *English;* (2) and that where it is required that the master and three fourths of the mariners be *English,* that the true intent and meaning thereof is, that they should be such during the whole voyage, unless in case of sickness, death, or being taken prisoners in the voyage, to be proved by the oath of the master or other chief officer of such ships.

VIII. And it is further enacted . . . That no goods or commodities of the growth, production or manufacture of *Muscovy,* or to any the countries, dominions or territories to the great duke or emperor of *Muscovy* or *Russia* belonging, as also that no sort of masts, timber or boards, no foreign salt, pitch, tar, rosin, hemp or flax, raisins, figs, prunes, olive-oils, no sorts of corn or grain, sugar, pot-ashes, wines, vinegar, or spirits called *aqua-vitae,* or brandy-wine, shall from and after the first day of *April*, which shall be in the year of our Lord one thousand six hundred sixty-one, be imported into *England*, *Ireland*, *Wales*, or town of *Berwick* upon *Tweed*, in any ship or ships, vessel or vessels whatsoever, but in such as do truly and without fraud belong to the people thereof, or some of them, as the true owners and proprietors thereof, and whereof the master and three fourths of the mariners at least are *English*; and that no currans nor commodities of the growth, production or manufacture of any the countries, islands, dominions or territories to the *Othoman* or *Turkish* empire belonging, shall from and after the first day of *September*, which shall be in the year of our Lord one thousand six hundred sixty-one, be imported into any the afore-mentioned places in any ship or vessel, but which is of *English*-built, and navigated. . . .

IX. Provided always, and be it hereby enacted by the authority aforesaid, That for the prevention of the great frauds daily used in colouring and concealing of aliens goods, all wines of the growth of *France* or *Germany*, which from and after the twentieth day of *October* one thousand six hundred and sixty shall be imported into any the ports or places aforesaid, in any other ship or vessel than which doth truly and without fraud belong to *England*, *Ireland*, *Wales*, or town of *Berwick* upon *Tweed*, and navigated with the mariners thereof, as aforesaid, shall be deemed aliens goods, and pay all strangers customs and duties to his Majesty, his heirs and successors, as also to the town or port into which they shall be imported; (2) and that all sorts of masts, timber or boards, as also all foreign salt, pitch, tar, rosin, hemp, flax, raisins, figs, prunes, olive-oils, all sorts of corn or grain, sugar, pot-ashes, spirits commonly called brandy-wine, or *aqua-vitae*, wines of the growth of *Spain*, the islands of the *Canaries* or *Portugal*, *Madera*, or western islands; (3) and all the goods of the growth, production or manufacture of *Muscovy* or *Russia*, which from and after the first day of *April*, which shall be in the year of our Lord one thousand six hundred sixty-one, shall be imported into any the aforesaid places in any other than such shipping, and so navigated; (4) and all currans and *Turkey* commodities which from and after the first day of *September* one thousand six hundred sixty-one, shall be imported into any the places aforesaid, in any other than *English*-built shipping, and navigated as aforesaid, (5) shall be deemed aliens goods, and pay accordingly to his Majesty, his heirs and successors, and to the town or port into which they shall be imported.

X. And for prevention of all frauds which may be used in colouring or buying of foreign ships, be it enacted by the authority aforesaid, and it is hereby enacted, That from and after the first day of *April*, which shall be in the year of our Lord one thousand six hundred sixty-one, no foreign-built ship or vessel whatsoever shall be deemed or pass as a ship to *England*, *Ireland*, *Wales*, or town of *Berwick*, or any of them belonging, or enjoy the benefit or privilege of such a ship or vessel, until such time that he or they claiming the said ship or vessel to be theirs, shall make appear to the chief officer or officers of the customs in the port next to the place of his or their abode, that he or they are not aliens, and shall have taken an oath before such chief officer or officers, who are hereby authorized to administer the same, that such ship or vessel was *bona fide* and without fraud by him or them bought for a valuable consideration. . . .

XIII. Provided also, That this act or any thing therein contained, extend not, or be meant, to restrain the importing of any *East-India* commodities loaden in *English* built shipping, and whereof the master and three fourths of the mariners at least are *English*, from the usual place or places for lading of them in any part of those seas, to the southward and eastward of *Cabo bona Esperanza*, although the said ports be not the very places of their growth. . . .

XV. Provided, That this act, or any thing therein contained, extend not to bullion, nor yet to any goods taken, or that shall be *bona fide* taken, by way of reprisal by any ship or ships belonging to *England*, *Ireland* or *Wales*, islands of *Guernsey* or *Jersey*, or town of *Berwick* upon *Tweed*, and whereof the master and three fourths of the mariners at least are *English*, having commission from his Majesty, his heirs or successors. . . .

XVIII. And it is further enacted . . . That from and after the first day of *April*, which shall be in the year of our Lord one thousand six hundred sixty-one, no sugars, tobacco, cotton-wool, indicoes, ginger, fustick, or other dying wood, of the growth, production or manufacture of any *English* plantations in *America*, *Asia* or *Africa*, shall be shipped, carried, conveyed or transported from any of the said *English* plantations to any land, island, territory, dominion, port or place whatsoever, other than to such other *English* plantations as do belong to his Majesty, his heirs and successors, or to the kingdom of *England* or *Ireland*, or principality of *Wales*, or town of *Berwick* upon *Tweed*, there to be laid on shore, (2) under the penalty of the forfeiture of the said goods, or the full value thereof, as also of the ship, with all her guns, tackle, apparel, ammunition and furniture; the one moiety to the King's majesty, his heirs and successors, and the other moiety to him or them that shall seize, inform or sue for the same in any court of record, by bill, plaint, or information, wherein no essoin, protection or wager of law shall be allowed.

XIX. And be it further enacted by the authority aforesaid, That for every ship or vessel, which from and after the five and twentieth day of *December* in the year of our Lord one thousand six hundred and sixty shall set sail out of or from *England*, *Ireland*, *Wales*, or town of *Berwick* upon *Tweed*, for any *English* plantation in *America*, *Asia* or *Africa*, sufficient bond shall be given with one surety to the chief officers of the custom-house of such port or place from whence the said ship shall set sail, to the value of one thousand pounds. . . .

AMERICAN TOBACCO IMPORTED BY ENGLAND, 1616–1693

(In thousands of pounds. For years ending September 28 except 1637–1640, unknown; 1672–1682, December 24; 1690–1693, November. Leaders denote no satisfactory data available. Outports are English ports other than London)

Year	Total	London	Outports	Year	Total	London	Outports	Year	Total	London	Outports
1693	.....	19,866.0	.....	1679	.....	12,983.0	.....	1629	178.7	89.0	89.7
1692	.....	13,423.5	.....	1678	.....	14,455.0	.....	1628	552.9	420.1	132.8
1691	.....	14,830.5	.....	1677	.....	11,735.0	.....	1627	376.9	335.3	41.6
1690	.....	12,638.0	.....	1676	.....	11,127.0	.....	1626	333.1	213.3	119.8
1689	.....	14,392.6	.....	1672	17,559.0	10,539.0	7,020.0	1625	131.8	111.1	20.7
1688	28,385.5	14,890.5	13,495.0	1669	.....	9,037.3	.....	1624	203.0	187.3	15.6
1687	27,567.0	14,072.0	13,495.0	1663	.....	7,371.1	.....	1623	134.6	119.4	15.2
1686	28,036.5	14,541.5	13,495.0	1640	.....	1,257.0	.....	1622	61.6	59.4	2.2
1684	.....	.....	13,495.0	1639	.....	1,345.0	.....	1621	73.8	73.8	.....
1683	.....	.....	13,495.0	1638	.....	3,134.0	.....	1620	119.0	118.0	1.0
1682	21,399.0	12,592.0	8,807.0	1637	.....	1,537.0	.....	1619	45.8	45.8	.....
1681	.....	14,472.0	.....	1631	272.3	209.7	62.5	1618	49.7	49.5	0.2
1680	.....	11,943.0	.....	1630	458.2	360.6	97.5	1617	18.8	18.8	.....
								1616	2.5	2.3	0.2

United States Bureau of the Census, *Historical Statistics of the United States, Colonial Times to 1957* (Washington, D.C., Government Printing Office, 1960), p. 766.

AMERICAN TOBACCO IMPORTED
BY ENGLAND, 1616–1693

The table on the facing page gives some indication of the trade in tobacco between the colonies and the mother country. It enables the historian to chart the steady overall increase in production of the commodity while at the same time observing the short-run fluctuations. There is a noticeable "jump" in imports after the passage of the Navigation Acts of mid-century, but, without any figures as to prices, it is difficult to draw conclusions as to whether depressed or inflated prices prevailed in the market. Modern agricultural studies do indicate, however, that in times of falling prices farmers tend to market more of their produce so as to maintain as much as possible their accustomed income, especially if they are unorganized and hence unable to control prices among themselves, as was the case in colonial Virginia. In 1662, protesting the Navigation Acts, Governor William Berkeley of Virginia had written to the King, "we cannot but resent, that forty thousand people should be impoverish'd to enrich little more than forty Merchants, who being the only buyers of our Tobacco, give us what they please for it, and after it is here, sell it how they please; and indeed have forty thousand servants in us at cheaper rates, then any other men have slaves. . . ."*

THE VIRGINIAN AS COSMOPOLITAN MERCHANT

The development of Virginia from an isolated company plantation to a complex cosmopolitan trading society in the seventeenth century is epitomized in the career of William Fitzhugh (1651–1701), some of whose letters are reproduced below. Fitzhugh was a comparatively wealthy tobacco planter

---

* Quoted in Wilcomb E. Washburn, *The Governor and the Rebel: a History of Bacon's Rebellion in Virginia* (Chapel Hill, N. C., University of North Carolina Press, 1957), p. 105.

who was also a merchant, a storekeeper, a lawyer, a militia officer, a justice of the peace, and a member of the House of Burgesses (as the Assembly came to be called). In addition, he was a slave trader and an intellectual of sorts who imported and read books from England. His letters indicate above all how direct the relationship of the Virginia planter was to the British world empire. Neither local government nor geographical isolation appears to have presented any obstacles. And all attempts to organize towns, thereby placing middlemen between the planter and the shipmasters, failed.

These letters give some additional insight into such things as tobacco prices, the planter-factor-shipper relationship, the standard of living, the local trading network, the local prices of slaves, their position in society even at this early time, and the interrelationship between New England slave importers and Southern planters.

THE LETTERS OF WILLIAM FITZHUGH

To Captain Francis Partis

Sir   The above is Copy of my former June 11th. 1680 I have no new matter to add, only I would have you be very carefull of my flax, hemp & hayseed, two bushels of each of which I have sent for, because we now have resolved a cessation from making Tobo. next year. We are also going to make Towns, if you can meet with any tradesmen, that will come in & live at the Towns, they may have large priviledges & immunitys. I would have you to bring me in a good Housewife, I do not intend or mean to be brought in as the ordinary servants are, but to pay for her passage, & agree to give her fifty shillings or three pound a year, during the space of five years, upon which terms I suppose good servants may be had, because they have their passage clear, & as much wages as they can have there, I would have a good one or none: I look upon the generality of wenches you usually bring in not worth the keeping. I expect to hear from you by all conveniencys, for I assure you I let slip none to tell you I am &c. I would have you bring me two large Paper books, one to contain about fourteen or fifteen Quire of Paper, the other about ten Quire, & one other small one

July 1st. 1680   W. ff.
Capt. Fowler

William Fitzhugh, *William Fitzhugh and His Chesapeake World, 1676–1701; The Fitzhugh Letters and other Documents,* Edited and with an Introduction by Richard Beale Davis, Virginia Historical Society, Doc. 3 (Chapel Hill, N. C., University of North Carolina Press, 1963), pp. 82–84, 90–92, 119, 127–128. Reprinted by permission of the University of North Carolina Press.

To Captain Francis Partis

Sir   Decr. 4th. 1680

Both your's I have receiv'd by Capt. Paine am glad of your health, sorry you came to no better a market. I hope this year Tobo.* will rise by reason there's but small Crops made throughout this Country and Maryland too. I have got ready the Tobo. I owe you, which when your brother comes or any one by your order may receive, we now look out every day for his Arrival, by whom I intend to ship thirty or fourty hhds. Crops are so small & debts comes in so badly that I cannot send so much as I thought by twenty hhds. But what I do send is pretty good. What friend, I can advise shall assuredly secure you. Mr. Scarlet has promised me to consign you twenty hhds. and I believe shall get you some more this year. Sr. I kindly observe two passages in your letter, one is that if I have occasion for fourty or fifty pound sterling you will pay it, though you have none of my effects in your hands, the other that you paid my last bills of £7 . . 13 . . 4 at sight. The one gives me credit the other honour for both which I thank you. I understand by the said letter that you have sent me all I sent for which you inform me comes to something more than you have in your hands. Yet being encouraged by your letter & assured of money, that I shall remit home if my Tobo. should either miscarry or come to a bad market, for I shall certainly remit home a hundred pound sterling certain, if not more from good hands & sure paymasters. I have ventured on a bargain of 29£ sterling for two Negroes of Mr. Vincent Goddard for which I have drawn bills of Exchange upon you which please give due acceptance I know not yet what to inlarge, by the first opportunity after your brother's Arrival, shall give you a larger account, & therefore at present shall only tell you that I shall always continue

Sr.
Your   W. ff.

To Captain John Lucum

Mr. John Lucum   May 31st. 1681

If nobody should come from me or by my order, to take the bills of Exchange for the Pipe Staves, & the bills of loading for the eleven hhds. of Tobo. consigned to Mr. John Cooper of London Merchant, I am so far satisfy'd of your Integrity & fidelity, that I request you to do it your self, that is to pass bills of Exchange for your full debt, according to the number of Pipe Staves you receive, & bills of Loading for the eleven hhds. Tobo. according to the agreement, & yr. receipt for the other one hhd., consigned to your self, which I

---

* Tobacco.

would have you thus order. Inclose one of the bills of Loading & one of the bills of Exchange, in this letter to Mr. Jno. Cooper which you have open, & write a letter your self to me, & inclose the other two bills of Loading & the two bills of Exchange, & your Receipt for the hhd. Tobo. well sealed up, & leave them either with Mr. William Hardidge or Mr. Secretary & deliver them to themselves with request to keep them, till I send for them for fear of miscarriages, if they should chance to convey them up to me by an uncertain hand.

Also I farther request you to acquaint Mr. Cooper, the reason that I could not indorse the bills of Exchange to him, which upon your information will give him the opportunity of demanding & receiving it without Indorsement. I hope you'll keep this letter by you, for your Instructions & follow it, if I have not the opportunity of sending one to do it for me which will oblige

Sir Yr.   W. ff.

To John Cooper

Mr. John Cooper   June 2nd 1681

This is Copy of my former by Capt. Jno. Lucum bearing date 31st. May last, I have sent another by the said Lucum, of the same date & of the same purport but open, for a bill of loading & a bill of Exchange to be inclosed therein, for the above Tobo. Sr. In my particulars mentioned & here inclosed, you'll find I send for a feather bed & furniture, curtains & vallens. The furniture Curtains & Vallens I would have new, but the bed at second hand, because I am informed new ones are very full of dust. The Curtains & Vallens I would have plain & not very costly. I desire you to take notice in the purchase of these things in the Note of Particulars here inclosed, & if it should so happen by accident, or some other mischance, I should not have the opportunity of giving you farther advice please to take care to send those particulars, by the first ships, by Capt. Norrington if he comes forth early

[no signature]

To John Cooper

Sir   June 7th. 1681

By Mr. Lucum & Mr. Lymes bearing date 31st. May & 2nd. June I have given you an account of eleven hhds. Tobo. consigned to you, together with several bills of Exchange to the value of £31 sterling, besides Mr. Lucum's bills of Exchange for what value I know not yet, which according to my order receive of him. I desire your Care in sending me in those things I sent for, & do now send for, which are for my own particular use, therefore I desire you to take care in the goodness of them, & what my money comes to more than I have given you advice of, please to send me it in Linnen, of which let gentish holland be finest except, one piece of Kenting, & let there be two pieces of white Dimmity, & one piece of colour'd. I refer the sorting the linnen to your self, being mindfull of blue Linnen in the Parcel. If you could possibly procure me a Bricklayer or Carpenter or both, it would do me a great kindness, & save me a great deal of money in my present building, & I should be willing to advance something extraordinary for the procuration of them or either of them. If you send in any tradesmen be sure send in their tools with them. Sr. My small acquaintance begs my excuse for not giving you an account of news stirring. Although I have sent none yet I hope to receive some from you, together with the present transactions of affairs in England, if the market gives any encouragement, you may be sure to hear more from me for the future I am

Your   W. ff.

Instructions for John Withers

Instructions for Mr. Jno. Withers his proceedings in his York journey June 5th. 1682

First to Majr. Beverley there's two letters, & two bills drawn for him to sign for £20 . . . 5. as ℈ the bills you'll see, which remember to take, except he will give you bills of Exchange to Mr. Jno. Buckner for the said Sum 2ndly. To take of Madam Hull, Roger Hull's widow two bills of Exchange for £3. each payable to Mr. Brent & myself. Thirdly to take Mr. Fantleroy's bills for £8 . . 10, if he will pass for so much, but be sure for £6. or else tell him I shall sue him for his Protest Fourthly To deliver Mr. Brody's letter, & take bills of him for £5 sterling, or ready money if he pleases Fifthly To deliver Herriot's letter & take bills for £3. in your own name, or else to receive the same in ready money, & deliver his papers after paymt. Sixthly To Deliver Mr. Christopher Robinson his letter, & take bills for £7 . . 10. for Mr. Brent, & as much for me in my own name, & to acquaint him that you are to pay them away as you come up Seventhly To pass Leftidge's bill away, though it be for fourty shillings. Eighthly To purchase what likely Negroes you can, either 1, 2, 3, 4, 5, or 6. what boys & men you possibly can, as few women as may be, but be sure not above two, to purchase neither men nor women above thirty years old, not to exceed £20 for the price of a man, unless he be extraordinary likely, to buy Mr. Walkers boy alone for £20 if you can, or to give £54 for the three at most, what under you can, if you cannot purchase him alone. To proceed to £34 for Majr. Peyton's two boys, if you can't get them under or can't hear of a better purchase to do for me as for your self in choosing & purchasing. Ninthly To pass Haverton's bills away in the purchase of Negroes if you can. Tenthly To pass George Boyce his two bills in the Purchase of Negros, or any other Swap to advantage, nay though with loss. Eleventhly To pass Corbets bills of £6 for any thing to my best advantage, though at halves, or for any truck Twelfthly To Deliver Gullock's letter, & to take bills of Exchange for Mr. Brent for £5 & the same for me in your own name, if you see occasion,

Your   W. ff.

To [John] Jackson

Mr. Jackson   February 11th. 1682/3

 As to your Proposal about the bringing in Negros next fall, I have this to offer, & you may communicate the same to your owners & Employers, that I will deal with them for so many as shall amount to 50000lb Tobo. & cash which will be about 120 hhds., under the Condition & at these ages & prices following, to say to give 3000lb. Tobo. for every Negro boy or girl, that shall be between the age of seven & eleven years old, to give 4000lb. Tobo. for every youth or girle that shall be between the age of 11 & 15 & to give 5000lb. Tobo. for every young man or woman that shall be above 15 years of age, & not exceed 24. the said Negroes to be delivered at my Landing, some time in Septr. next & I to have notice whether they will so agree some time in August next, And I do assure you & so you may acquaint them that upon your delivery & my receipt of the Negroes, according to the ages abovementioned, & that they be sound & healthfull at their Delivery I will give such sufficient Caution for the payment of the Tobo., accordingly, by the 20th. Decr. then next following, as shall be approved of. The ages of the Negros to be judged & determined by two or three such honest & reasonable men here, as your self shall nominate & appoint. The whole Sum of the Tobo. to be paid in the Compass of twenty miles perhaps not so remote I am

Your   W. ff.

A NEW CIVILIZATION AND ITS DISCONTENTS

In the spring of 1676, as Virginian frontiersmen moved into the interior from the Tidewater country in search of new lands, they found themselves confronted by the warlike Susquehannocks whose hunting grounds they were invading. A series of bloody frontier skirmishes occurred which brought to the fore one of Virginia's most famous heroes, the Indian-fighter Nathaniel Bacon (1647–1676). Dubbed "The Torchbearer of the Revolution" by one American historian,* Bacon advocated vigorous repression of all Indians, hostile and friendly alike. In the summer of 1676 he destroyed the village of the friendly Occaneechees on the Roanoke River; then, using his Indian-fighters as a nucleus, he assembled an army which captured Jamestown, overthrew Governor William Berkeley, and for a brief time ruled Virginia. The Governor, however, who was then seventy years old, refused to acknowledge Bacon's power and, gaining control of the waterways, brought the fight to the rebels, who in turn burned Jamestown to the ground. At the height of the rebellion Bacon died, infested by lice and infected with "bloody flux." With his death, the rebellion collapsed and the Governor regained control of the colony.

Until the publication of Wilcomb Washburn's The Governor and the Rebel: a History of Bacon's Rebellion in Virginia in 1957, the story of Bacon's Rebellion had been a simple one, with Bacon, the champion of frontier democracy, pitted against Governor William Berkeley, the Tidewater tyrant. Washburn's convincing study, however, largely reversed the roles of the two men, thus destroying one of America's most cherished historical myths. In addition, his careful analysis of the causes of the Rebellion revealed a great deal about late seventeenth-century Virginia and its discontents. Washburn's analysis takes its cue from Robert Beverley's The History and Present State of Virginia published in 1705. Beverley (1673–1722) was the son of Robert Beverley (1641–1687), who served as one of Berkeley's chief lieutenants in the fight against Bacon; hence, his account, while shrewd, may not have been altogether unbiased. The selection that follows from Beverley's work is presented,

---

* Thomas Jefferson Wertenbaker, Torchbearer of the Revolution: the Story of Bacon's Rebellion and Its Leader (Princeton, N.J., Princeton University Press, 1940).

however, for the insight it affords into the difficulties confronting late seven-teenth-century Virginians, rather than as a basis for judging the merits of the Rebellion. The student should relate this document to those immediately preceding it.

BACON'S REBELLION, 1676

The occasion of this rebellion is not easy to be discovered: but 'tis certain there were many things that concurred towards it. For it cannot be imagined, that upon the instigation of two or three traders only, who aimed at a monopoly of the Indian trade, as some pretend to say, the whole country would have fallen into so much distraction; in which people did not only hazard their necks by rebellion, but endeavored to ruin a governor, whom they all entirely loved, and had unanimously chosen; a gentleman who had devoted his whole life and estates to the service of the country, and against whom in thirty-five years experience there had never been one single complaint. Neither can it be supposed, that upon so slight grounds, they would make choice of a leader they hardly knew, to oppose a gentleman that had been so long and so deserv-edly the darling of the people. So that in all probability there was something else in the wind, without which the body of the country had never been en-gaged in that insurrection.

Four things may be reckoned to have been the main ingredients towards this intestine commotion, viz., First, The extreme low price of tobacco, and the ill usage of the planters in the exchange of goods for it, which the country, with all their earnest endeavors, could not remedy. Secondly, The splitting the colony into proprieties, contrary to the original charters; and the extrav-agant taxes they were forced to undergo, to relieve themselves from those grants. Thirdly, The heavy restraints and burdens laid upon their trade by act of Parliament in England. Fourthly, The disturbance given by the Indians. Of all which in their order.

First, Of the low price of tobacco, and the disappointment of all sort of remedy, I have spoken sufficiently before. Secondly, Of splitting the country into proprieties.

King Charles the Second, to gratify some nobles about him, made two great grants out of that country. These grants were not of the uncultivated wood land only, but also of plantations, which for many years had been seated and

Robert Beverley, *The History of Virginia, in Four Parts* (Reprinted, Richmond, Va., J. W. Randolph, 1855), pp. 60–64, 66–67, 69. Beverley's work was originally titled *The History and Present State of Virginia.*

improved, under the encouragement of several charters granted by his royal ancestors to that colony. Those grants were distinguished by the names of the Northern and Southern grants of Virginia, and the same men were concerned in both. They were kept dormant some years after they were made, and in the year 1674 begun to be put in execution. As soon as ever the country came to know this, they remonstrated against them; and the assembly drew up an humble address to his majesty, complaining of the said grants, as derogatory to the previous charters and privileges granted to that colony, by his majesty and his royal progenitors. They sent to England Mr. Secretary Ludwell and Colonel Park, as their agents to address the king, to vacate those grants. And the better to defray that charge, they laid a tax of fifty pounds of tobacco per poll, for two years together, over and above all other taxes, which was an excessive burden. They likewise laid amercements of seventy, fifty, or thirty pounds of tobacco, as the cause was on every law case tried throughout the country. Besides all this, they applied the balance, remaining due upon account of the two shilling per hogshead, and fort duties, to this use. Which taxes and amercements fell heaviest on the poor people, the effect of whose labor would not clothe their wives and children. This made them desperately uneasy, especially when, after a whole year's patience under all these pressures, they had no encouragement from their agents in England, to hope for remedy; nor any certainty when they should be eased of those heavy impositions.

Thirdly, Upon the back of all these misfortunes came out the act of 25 Car. II. for better securing the plantation trade. By this act several duties were laid on the trade from one plantation to another. This was a new hardship, and the rather, because the revenue arising by this act was not applied to the use of the plantations wherein it was raised: but given clear away; nay, in that country it seemed to be of no other use, but to burden the trade, or create a good income to the officers; for the collector had half, the comptroller a quarter, and the remaining quarter was subdivided into salaries, till it was lost.

By the same act also very great duties were laid on the fisheries of the plantations, if manufactured by the English inhabitants there; while the people of England were absolutely free from all customs. Nay, though the oil, blubber and whale bone, which were made by the inhabitants of the plantations, were carried to England by Englishmen, and in English built ships, yet it was held to a considerable duty, more than the inhabitants of England paid.

These were the afflictions that country labored under when the fourth accident happened, viz., the disturbance offered by the Indians to the frontiers.

This was occasioned, first, by the Indians on the head of the bay. Secondly, by the Indians on their own frontiers.

First. The Indians at the head of the bay drove a constant trade with the Dutch in Monadas, now called New York; and to carry on this, they used to come every year by the frontiers of Virginia, to hunt and purchase skins and furs of the Indians to the southward. This trade was carried on peaceably while the Dutch held Monadas; and the Indians used to call on the English in Virginia on their return, to whom they would sell part of their furs, and with the rest go on to Monadas. But after the English came to possess that place, and understood the advantages the Virginians made by the trade of their Indians, they inspired them with such a hatred to the inhabitants of Virginia that, instead of coming peaceably to trade with them, as they had done for several years before, they afterwards never came, but only to commit robberies and murders upon the people.

Secondly. The Indians upon their own frontiers were likewise inspired with ill thoughts of them. For their Indian merchants had lost a considerable branch of their trade they knew not how; and apprehended the consequences of Sir William Berkeley's intended discoveries, (espoused by the assembly,) might take away the remaining part of their profit. This made them very troublesome to the neighbor Indians; who on their part, observing an unusual uneasiness in the English, and being terrified by their rough usage, immediately suspected some wicked design against their lives, and so fled to their remoter habitations. This confirmed the English in the belief, that they had been the murderers, till at last they provoked them to be so in earnest.

This addition of mischief to minds already full of discontent, made people ready to vent all their resentment against the poor Indians. There was nothing to be got by tobacco; neither could they turn any other manufacture to advantage; so that most of the poorer sort were willing to quit their unprofitable employments, and go volunteers against the Indians.

At first they flocked together tumultuously, running in troops from one plantation to another without a head, till at last the seditious humor of Colonel Nath. Bacon led him to be of the party. This gentleman had been brought up at one of the Inns of court in England, and had a moderate fortune. He was young, bold, active, of an inviting aspect, and powerful elocution. In a word, he was every way qualified to head a giddy and unthinking multitude. Before he had been three years in the country, he was, for his extraordinary qualifications, made one of the council, and in great honor and esteem among the people. For this reason he no sooner gave countenance to this riotous mob, but they all presently fixed their eyes upon him for their general, and accordingly made their addresses to him. As soon as he found this, he harangued them publicly. He aggravated the Indian mischiefs, complaining that they were occasioned for want of a due regulation of their trade. He recounted particularly the other grievances and pressures they lay under, and pretended that he accepted of their command with no other intention but to do them and the country service, in which he was willing to encounter the greatest difficulties and dangers. He farther assured them he would never lay down his arms till he had revenged their sufferings upon the Indians, and redressed all their other grievances.

By these insinuations he wrought his men into so perfect an unanimity, that they were one and all at his devotion. He took care to exasperate them to the utmost, by representing all their misfortunes. After he had begun to muster them, he dispatched a messenger to the governor, by whom he aggravated the mischiefs done by the Indians, and desired a commission of general to go out against them. This gentleman was in so great esteem at that time with the council, that the governor did not think fit to give him a flat refusal; but sent him word he would consult the council, and return him a farther answer. . . .

The governor . . . obstinately refused to grant him anything, offering his naked breast against the presented arms of his followers. But the assembly, fearing the fatal consequences of provoking a discontented multitude ready armed, who had the governor, council and assembly entirely in their power, addressed the governor to grant Bacon his request. They prepared themselves the commission, constituting him general of the forces of Virginia, and brought it to the governor to be signed.

With much reluctancy the governor signed it, and thereby put the power of war and peace into Bacon's hands. Upon this he marched away immediately, having gained his end, which was in effect a power to secure a monopoly of the Indian trade to himself and his friends.

As soon as General Bacon had marched to such a convenient distance from Jamestown that the assembly thought they might deliberate with safety, the governor, by their advice, issued a proclamation of rebellion against him, commanding his followers to surrender him, and forthwith disperse themselves, giving orders at the same time for raising the militia of the country against him.

The people being much exasperated, and General Bacon by his address and eloquence having gained an absolute dominion over their hearts, they unanimously resolved that not a hair of his head should be touched, much less that they should surrender him as a rebel. Therefore they kept to their arms, and instead of proceeding against the Indians they marched back to Jamestown, directing their fury against such of their friends and countrymen as should dare to oppose them.

The governor seeing this, fled over the bay to Accomac, whither he hoped the infection of Bacon's conspiracy had not reached. But there, instead of that people's receiving him with open arms, in remembrance of the former services he had done them, they began to make terms with him for redress of their grievances, and for the ease and liberty of trade against the acts of parliament. Thus Sir William, who had been almost the idol of the people, was, by reason of their calamity and jealousy, abandoned by all, except some few, who went over to him from the western shore in sloops and boats, among which one Major Robert Beverley was the most active and successful commander; so that it was sometime before he could make head against Bacon, but left him to range through the country at discretion.

General Bacon at first held a convention, of such of the chief gentlemen of the country as would come to him, especially of those about Middle Plantation, who were near at hand. At this convention they made a declaration to justify his unlawful proceedings, and obliged people to take an oath of obedience to him as their general. Then, by their advice, on pretence of the governor's abdication, he called an assembly, by writs signed by himself and four others of the council. . . .

By this time the governor had got together a small party to side with him. These he furnished with sloops, arms and ammunition, under command of Major Robert Beverley, in order to cross the bay and oppose the malcontents. By this means there happened some skirmishes, in which several were killed, and others taken prisoners. Thus they were going on by a civil war to destroy one another, and lay waste their infant country, when it pleased God, after some months' confusion, to put an end to their misfortunes, as well as to Bacon's designs, by his natural death. He died at Dr. Green's in Gloucester county. But where he was buried was never yet discovered, though afterward there was great inquiry made, with design to expose his bones to public infamy.

In the meanwhile those disorders occasioned a general neglect of husbandry, and a great destruction of the stocks of cattle, so that people had a dreadful prospect of want and famine. But the malcontents being thus disunited by the loss of their general, in whom they all confided, they began to squabble among themselves, and every man's business was, how to make the best terms he could for himself.

Lieutenant General Ingram, (whose true name was Johnson) and Major General Walklate, surrendered, on condition of pardon for themselves and their followers, though they were both forced to submit to an incapacity of bearing office in that country for the future.

Peace being thus restored, Sir William Berkeley returned to his former seat of government, and every man to his several habitation.

VIRGINIA SOCIETY AT THE END
OF THE SEVENTEENTH CENTURY

The following document, published in 1697, entitled "An Account of the Present State and Government of Virginia," was written by three Virginians: Henry Hartwell, a merchant and planter; James Blair, a clergyman; and Edward Chilton, a lawyer. It was designed to present a case to the Crown. At the same time, however, it provides a useful survey of Virginia society at the end of the seventeenth century. What does the lack of towns in Virginia suggest about the nature of its society? From what economic and political points of view is the document written?

AN OVERVIEW OF THE STATE AND GOVERNMENT OF VIRGINIA

Of the Natural Advantages of the Country

It is astonishing to hear what contrary characters are given of the country of Virginia, even by those who have often seen it, and know it very well; some of them representing it as the best, others as the worst country in the world. Perhaps they are both in the right. For the most general true character of Virginia is this, that as to the natural advantages of a country, it is one of the best; but as to the improved ones, one of the worst of all the English plantations in America. When one considers the wholesomeness of its air, the fertility of its soil, the commodiousness of its navigable rivers, and creeks, the openness of its coast all the year long, the conveniency of its fresh-water runs, and springs, the plenty of its fish, fowl, and wild beasts, the variety of its simples, and dying woods, the abundance of its timbers, minerals, wild vines and fruits, the temperature of its climate, being situated betwixt the extremities of both heat and cold; in short, if it be looked upon in all respects, as it came out of the hand of God, it is certainly one of the best countries in the world. But on the other hand, if we inquire for well-built towns, for convenient ports and markets, for plenty of ships and seamen, for well improved trades

Massachusetts Historical Collections, 1st series (Boston, 1798), V, pp. 124–131. Note that this selection amounts to about one-third of the entire document, which includes, in addition, a description of land policy, the Governor, the Council, the Assembly, the judiciary, the Secretary's Office, money and tobacco, the militia, the Church and religion, and William and Mary College.

and manufactures, for well-educated children, for an industrious and thriving people, or for an happy government in church and state; and in short, for all the other advantages of human improvements, it is certainly, for all these things, one of the poorest, miserablest, and worst countries in all America that is inhabited by christians.

It is a common saying among themselves, that if any other nation had had Virginia, but the English, they would have made it an happy country. But it is easier to see their misery, than to find out the causes of it. No doubt it is chiefly to be imputed to the first wrong measures that were taken *in not seating themselves in towns,* and to the narrow, selfish ends of most of their governors, who go easily into any projects, whereby they may make a present gain, but very difficultly into the expensive and generous undertakings of doing good amongst them, which seldom turn to a present, or to a quick account. But after all, perhaps as much is to be imputed to the obstinacy of the people, as to any other mismanagements, as will be seen in the sequel of this narrative, which will discover a sad truth, viz. that the bringing the people of that country to the improvements of cohabitation, must be against their will, by virtue of the king's prerogative, and not by expecting the concurrence of their general assemblies, the major part of the members whereof having never seen a town, nor a well improved country, in their lives, cannot therefore imagine the benefit of it, and are afraid of every innovation, that will put them to a present charge, whatever may be the future benefit.

It is impossible to reckon up all the improvements which might be made in such a country, where many useful inventions would present themselves to the industrious. The following ones are such as naturally offer to any judicious spectator.

The manufacture of iron and other minerals, with which that country, to all appearance, is well stored, together with all the advantages of wood to burn them, and water to make the carriage easy. They have likewise, in several places, a great deal of a curious transparent stone, finer than marble, which, together with the iron and minerals, might be carried for England as ballast for ships, and so of little or no freight.

It is a good country for the manufacture of silks; for mulberry trees, the proper food for silk worms, thrive as well there, as any tree whatsoever; and a great deal of this work, being the feeding of the worms, and winding off of the silk, might be performed by negro children, that are now so many useless hands. A plant, likewise, called silkgrass, out of which several fine things might be made, is there in great plenty.

It is likewise very fit for potash for soap, by reason of the infinite number of trees; which make that country more to resemble a forest than one of the countries of Europe.

It abounds also in pitch, tar, rosin, masts, and all timbers for shipping, which the Bristol men being sensible of, make use of the opportunity to build ships there at very easy rates.

Wheat, rye, indian corn, oats, barley, pease, and many other sorts of pulse grow there in great plenty, and are very useful for the supply of Barbadoes, and the other Leeward islands, as also of New-England, which produces very little wheat, or indian corn, the frost of late years often taking it, before it is ripe.

That country has also great advantages for the making of cider, wine, oil, distilled spirits, figs, raisins, and conserved fruits. The country producing huge quantities of the best apples, pears, peaches, quinces, cherries, straw-berries, mulberries, raspberries, putchamins, and melons, and abounding every where with several sorts of wild grapes, the woods also bringing good store of chestnuts, walnuts, hickery nuts, chincopins, and other shell fruit of a very oily substance.

Flax, hemp, and cotton grow there very fine. Here might be a great trade for sturgeon, drums, sheepsheads, and several other fish, as also for whales.

There might be a vast Indian trade for skins and furs carried on there, they lying near a great many Indians to the west and southwest.

It is an excellent country for dying stuff, and curious simples, as also for several other curious woods used in wainscoting and cabinet-making, such as cedar, cypress, sassafras, black walnut, &c.

In many places of that country, there is great store of the myrtleberries, which being boiled up to a wax, make as good candles as the best wax candles whatsoever, the snuff whereof, instead of stinking, does really perfume like incense.

We need not mention tobacco, which would likewise be an excellent staple commodity of that country, if they would make it good, without trash; but so it is at present, that tobacco swallows up all other things, every thing else is neglected, and all markets are often so glutted with bad tobacco, that it be-comes a mere drug, and will not clear the freight and custom.

Of the Several Sorts of Inhabitants and Cultivation of Virginia

So much for the natural (we cannot say commodities, but) disposition and advantageous circumstances of the country.

But now, if it be inquired, what sort of a country it is? after all this, we must represent it after a quite different manner from what might be expected from the first and eldest of all the English plantations in America. As to the outward appearance, it looks all like a wild desert, the high lands overgrown with trees, and the low lands sunk with water, marsh, and swamp: The few plantations and cleared grounds bearing no proportion to the rough and uncultivated.

The inhabitants are of three sorts, planters, tradesmen, and merchants.

Though the planters are the most numerous, perhaps not the hundredth part of the country is yet cleared from the woods, and not one foot of the marsh and swamp drained. As fast as the ground is worn out with tobacco and corn, it runs up again in underwoods; and in many places of the country, that which has been cleared is thicker in woods than it was before the clearing. It is but in very few places that the plough is made use of; for in their first clearing they never grub up the stumps, but cut the trees down about two or three feet from the ground, so that all the roots and stumps being left, that ground must be tended with hoes; and by that time the stumps are rotten, the ground is worn out. And having fresh land enough, of which they must clear some for fire wood, they take but little care to recruit the old fields with dung. Of grain and pulse, they commonly provide only as much as they expect they themselves shall have occasion for, for the use of their families, there being no towns or markets, where they can have a ready vent for them, and scarce any money to serve for a common exchange in buying and selling. The only thing whereof they make as much as they can is tobacco; there being always a vent for that, at one time of the year or other; besides that their want of cloaths and household furniture, and all their other necessaries, instigate them to make as much tobacco as they can, this being the money of that country which answers all things. But the great labour about tobacco being only in summer time, they acquire great habits of idleness all the rest of the year.

For want of towns, markets, and money, there is but little encouragement for tradesmen and artificers, and therefore little choice of them, and their labour very dear in the country. A tradesman having no opportunity of a market, where he can buy meat, milk, corn, and all other things, must either make corn, keep cows, and raise stocks himself; or must ride about the country to buy meat and corn where he can find it; and then is puzzled to find carriers, drovers, butchers; salting (for he cannot buy one joint or two) and a great many other things, which there would be no occasion for if there were towns and markets. Then a great deal of the tradesmen's time being necessarily spent in going and coming to and from his work, in dispersed country plantations, and his pay being generally in straggling parcels of tobacco, the collection whereof costs about 10 per cent. and the best of this pay coming but once a year, so that he cannot turn his hand frequently with a small stock, as tradesmen do in England and elsewhere; all this occasions the dearth of all tradesmen's labours, and likewise the discouragement, scarcity and insufficiency of tradesmen.

The merchants live the best of any in that country; but yet are subject to great inconveniencies in the way of their trade, which might be avoided if they had towns, markets, and money: For, first, they are obliged to sell upon trust all the year long, except just a little while when tobacco is ready. 2. They likewise drive a pitiful retail trade to serve every man's little occasions, being all, in effect, but country chapmen, for want of towns to be a center of trade and business. 3. Besides the charge of it they are necessitated to trust all their concerns to their receivers, who go about among the planters that owe them tobacco, and receive and mark it for them, which receivers, if they want either skill or honesty, it proves very fatal to the merchant. 4. They are at the charge of carting this tobacco, so marked and received, to convenient landings; or if it lies not far from these landings, they must trust to the seamen for their careful rolling it on board of their sloops and shallops: and if the seamen roll it in bad weather, or dirty ways, it is exposed to a great deal of damage. 5. It is a great while before the ships can be loaded, their freight lying at such a distance, and being to be brought together in this scrambling manner. By reason of this, it is an usual thing with ships to lie three or four months in the country, which might be dispatched in a fortnight's time, if the tobacco were ready at certain ports; and this inflames the freight to almost double the price of what it needed to be, if the ships had a quick dispatch.

In New-England, they were obliged at their first settlement to settle in towns, and would not permit a single man to take up land, till a certain number of men agreed together, as many as might make a township; then they laid them out a town, with home lots for gardens and orchards, out lots for cornfields, and meadows and country lots for plantations, with overseers and gangs of hands, which would have proved an excellent way in such a country as Virginia is. But this opportunity being lost, they seated themselves, without any rule or order, in country plantations; and being often sensible of the inconveniencies of that dispersed way of living, their General Assemblies have made several attempts to bring the people into towns, which have proved all ineffectual.

One error has generally run through all these undertakings, viz. that they always appointed too many towns, which will be still the fault of them, if they are contrived by a General Assembly: For every man desiring the town to be as near as is possible to his own door, and the burgesses setting up every one of them for his own county, they have commonly contrived a town for every county, which might be reasonable enough hereafter, when the country comes to be well peopled; but at present is utterly impracticable, for want of people to inhabit them, and money to build them. And therefore we cannot but think the Governor and Assembly of Maryland have taken a much wiser course, who, in their law for towns, have ordered only two towns, in that whole province, viz. one on the eastern and another on the western shore. So perhaps two or three towns in Virginia would be enough at first. The country might add more afterwards, as they increase in wealth and people.

Another error they ran into, in their last law for towns, was, that they made it utterly unlawful to buy or sell any goods exported or imported but at these towns, under no less a penalty than the forfeiture of ship and goods; which was a great force upon trade, and would have made all people very uneasy at present; though on the other hand there is this to be said for it, that their merchants being already seated with their stores in country plantations, and having their customers all round about them, without some considerable force, could not be induced to leave all these, and to come and live in towns.

Some are of opinion, that the King's constituting ports for exportation and importation would do the business, i.e. would bring the trade to these ports; and perhaps it would at the long run; for all that set up for merchants, after such a constitution of ports, would probably set up at these places; but it would be a long time before the old merchants, who are in the present possession of the trade, would be persuaded to leave their country houses, and stores, to come and live at towns. Perhaps if there were great care taken to encourage these port towns with privileges and immunities, and likewise to discourage the country stores, the thing would quickly be more effectual. However, it is *hoc opus hic labor est,* if towns and ports can be brought to bear, the chief obstruction to the improvement of that country will be removed. It is certain that little help towards it is to be expected from the General Assembly; except they should come to have a Governor, in whom they have a most mighty confidence, that he acts for the public good, which was the case in Governor Nicholson's time, when we see they were not only willing to have towns, but to force them with many visible inconveniencies. But for their own temper, they showed it as soon as he was gone, i.e. they are daily more and more averse to cohabitation; the major part of the house of burgesses consisting of Virginians that never saw a town, nor have no notion of the conveniency of any other but a country life. As a proof whereof, perhaps it may not be unfit to give an account of an argument which was brought against towns, by an ingenious Virginian, who had never been out of the country. His argument was this: "That they might observe already, wherever they were thick seated, they could hardly raise any stocks, or live by one another; much more, concluded he, would it be impossible for us to live when a matter of an hundred families are cooped up within the compass of half a mile of ground." . . .

3 / MASSACHUSETTS BAY: THE SHIFTING STANCES OF PURITANISM

INTRODUCTION

Having savored the delights and frustrations of the intellectual historian and the institutional historian, the student should now be in a position to appreciate the problems faced by the historian of early New England. In this case institutional history is further complicated by the existence of a highly technical and subtle theology which in large measure defined still another important institution—religion—which stood at the center of life in seventeenth-century New England. Without some understanding of the complex intellectual phenomenon of Puritanism, it is virtually impossible to understand politics, economics, or society in Massachusetts Bay.

The historian Perry Miller, author of the focal article for this section, devoted most of his life to sifting through long-neglected Puritan sermons and theological tracts, court records, diaries, letters, Harvard College archives, antique literature, and early scientific papers in an effort to understand the Puritan mind. He succeeded brilliantly in revealing the subtleties and complexities of Puritanism which had been obscured by the stereotyped view of the Puritan as a rather dull person in a high-crowned hat, carrying a blunderbuss and a dead turkey. What Miller found was a drama of intense human interest: the efforts of highly intellectual and sincere men to bend society and the environment to their holy purposes. In some ways it was a tragic story, because it was the story of failure on an almost heroic scale. Like the Elizabethans before them, and their contemporaries the Virginians, the Puritans, too, were forced to yield to conditions in the New World and changing relationships in the Old World. They did not, however, yield easily; and the story that may be derived from a study of the documents that follow—each written for a particular purpose and from a special point of view—is a story of constant skirmishes, grudging adjustments, and furious rearguard action.

INTERPRETATION

The late Perry Miller, author of "The Puritan State and Puritan Society," was Powell M. Cabot Professor of American Literature at Harvard University. His major works include Orthodoxy in Massachusetts, The New England Mind (2 vols.), Roger Williams, Jonathan Edwards, and Errand Into the Wilderness.

PERRY MILLER, The Puritan State and Puritan Society

It has often been said that the end of the seventeenth and the beginning of the eighteenth century mark the first real break with the Middle Ages in the history of European thought. Even though the Renaissance and Reformation transformed many aspects of the Western intellect, still it was not until the time of Newton that the modern scientific era began; only then could men commence to regard life in this world as something more than preparation for life beyond the grave. Certainly if the eighteenth century inaugurated the modern epoch in natural sciences, so also did it in the political and social sciences. For the first time since the fall of the Roman Empire religion could be separated from politics, doctrinal orthodoxy divorced from loyalty to the state, and the citizens of a nation be permitted to worship in diverse churches and to believe different creeds without endangering the public peace. Various factors contributed to effecting this revolution; the triumph of scientific method and of rationalism made impossible the older belief that government was of divine origin; the rise of capitalism, of the middle class, and eventually of democracy, necessitated new conceptions of the role of the state. Social leadership in England and America was assumed by a group of gentlemen who were, by and large, deists or skeptics, and to them all religious issues had become supremely boring. At the same time the churches themselves, particularly the newer evangelical denominations, were swinging round to a theology that made religious belief the subjective experience of individual men, entirely unrelated to any particular political philosophy or social theory. In order to understand Puritanism we must go behind these eighteenth-century developments to an age when the unity of religion and politics was

Perry Miller, Errand Into the Wilderness (Cambridge, Mass., The Belknap Press of Harvard University Press, 1956), pp. 141–152. Reprinted by permission of the publishers. Copyright 1956 by the President and Fellows of Harvard College.

so axiomatic that very few men would even have grasped the idea that church and state could be distinct. For the Puritan mind it was not possible to segregate a man's spiritual life from his communal life. Massachusetts was settled for religious reasons, but as John Winthrop announced, religious reasons included "a due forme of Government both ciuill and ecclesiasticall," and the civil was quite as important in his eyes as the ecclesiastical. Only in recent years has it become possible for us to view the political aspects of Puritanism with something like comprehension and justice. For two centuries our social thinking has been dominated by ideas that were generated in the course of a sweeping revolt against everything for which the Puritans stood; the political beliefs of the Puritans were forgotten, or, if remembered at all, either deplored or condemned as unfortunate remnants of medievalism. Puritanism has been viewed mainly as a religious and ethical movement. But of late years the standards of the eighteenth century have for the first time come under serious criticism and in many quarters are showing the strain. In these circumstances the social philosophy of Puritanism takes on a new interest, and quite possibly becomes for us the most instructive and valuable portion of the Puritan heritage.

The Puritan theory of the state began with the hypothesis of original sin. Had Adam transmitted undiminished to his descendants the image of God in which he had been created, no government would ever have been necessary among men; they would all then have done justice to each other without the supervision of a judge, they would have respected each other's rights without the intervention of a policeman. But the Bible said—and experience proved—that since the Fall, without the policeman, the judge, the jail, the law, and the magistrate, men will rob, murder, and fight among themselves; without a coercive state to restrain evil impulses and administer punishments, no life will be safe, no property secure, no honor observed. Therefore, upon Adam's apostasy, God Himself instituted governments among men. He left the particular form to be determined by circumstance—this was one important human art on which the Puritans said the Bible was not an absolute and imperious lawgiver—but He enacted that all men should be under some sort of corporate rule, that they should all submit to the sway of their superiors, that no man should live apart from his fellows, that the government should have full power to enforce obedience and to inflict every punishment that the crimes of men deserved.

There was, it is true, a strong element of individualism in the Puritan creed; every man had to work out his own salvation, each soul had to face his maker alone. But at the same time, the Puritan philosophy demanded that in society all men, at least all regenerate men, be marshaled into one united array. The lone horseman, the single trapper, the solitary hunter was not a figure of the Puritan frontier; Puritans moved in groups and towns, settled in whole communities, and maintained firm government over all units. Neither were the individualistic business man, the shopkeeper who seized every opportunity to enlarge his profits, the speculator who contrived to gain wealth at the expense of his fellows, neither were these typical figures of the original Puritan society. Puritan opinion was at the opposite pole from Jefferson's feeling that the best government governs as little as possible. The theorists of New England thought of society as a unit, bound together by inviolable ties; they thought of it not as an aggregation of individuals but as an organism, functioning for a definite purpose, with all parts subordinate to the whole, all members contributing a definite share, every person occupying a particular status. "Society in all sorts of humane affaires is better then Solitariness," said John Cotton. The society of early New England was decidedly "regimented." Puritans did not think that the state was merely an umpire, standing on the side lines of a contest, limited to checking egregious fouls but otherwise allowing men free play according to their abilities and the breaks of the game. They would have expected *laissez faire* to result in a reign of rapine and horror. The state to them was an active instrument of leadership, discipline, and, wherever necessary, of coercion; it legislated over any or all aspects of human behavior, it not merely regulated misconduct but undertook to inspire and direct all conduct. The commanders were not to trim their policies by the desires of the people, but to drive ahead upon the predetermined course; the people were all to turn out as they were ordered, and together they were to crowd sail to the full capacity of the vessel. The officers were above the common men, as the quarter-deck is above the forecastle. There was no idea of the equality of all men. There was no questioning that men who would not serve the purposes of the society should be whipped into line. The objectives were clear and unmistakable; any one's disinclination to dedicate himself to them was obviously so much recalcitrancy and depravity. The government of Massachusetts, and of Connecticut as well, was a dictatorship, and never pretended to be anything else; it was a dictatorship, not of a single tyrant, or of an economic class, or of a political faction, but of the holy and regenerate. Those who did not hold with the ideals entertained by the righteous, or who believed God had preached other principles, or who desired that in religious belief, morality, and ecclesiastical preferences all men should be left at liberty to do as they wished—such persons had every liberty, as Nathaniel Ward said, to stay away from New England. If they did come, they were expected to keep their opinions to themselves; if they discussed them in public or attempted to act upon them, they were exiled; if they persisted in returning, they were cast out again; if they still came back, as did four Quakers, they were hanged on Boston Common. And from the Puritan point of view, it was good riddance.

These views of the nature and function of the state were not peculiar to the Puritans of New England; they were the heritage of the past, the ideals, if not always the actuality, of the previous centuries. That government was established by God in order to save depraved men from their own depravity had been orthodox Christian teaching for centuries; that men should be arranged in serried ranks, inferiors obeying superiors, was the essence of feudalism; that men should live a social life, that profit-making should be restrained within the limits of the "just price," that the welfare of the whole took precedence over any individual advantage, was the doctrine of the medieval church, and of the Church of England in the early seventeenth century. Furthermore, in addition to these general principles, there were two or three more doctrines in the New England philosophy which also were common to the age and the background: all the world at that moment believed with them that the church was to be maintained and protected by the civil authority, and a certain part of the world was contending that government must be limited by fundamental law and that it takes its origin from the consent of the people.

Every respectable state in the Western world assumed that it could allow only one church to exist within its borders, that every citizen should be compelled to attend it and conform to its requirements, and that all inhabitants should pay taxes for its support. When the Puritans came to New England the idea had not yet dawned that a government could safely permit several creeds to exist side by side within the confines of a single nation. They had not been fighting in England for any milk-and-water toleration, and had they been offered such religious freedom as dissenters now enjoy in Great Britain they would have scorned to accept the terms. Only a hypocrite, a person who did not really believe what he professed, would be content to practice his religion under those conditions. The Puritans were assured that they alone knew the exact truth, as it was contained in the written word of God, and they were fighting to enthrone it in England and to extirpate utterly and mercilessly all other pretended versions of Christianity. When they could not succeed at home, they came to America, where they could establish a society in which the one and only truth should reign forever. There is nothing so idle as to praise the Puritans for being in any sense conscious or deliberate pioneers of religious liberty—unless, indeed, it is still more idle to berate them because in America they persecuted dissenters for their beliefs after themselves had undergone persecution for differing with the bishops. To allow no dissent from the truth was exactly the reason they had come to America. They maintained here precisely what they had maintained in England, and if they exiled, fined, jailed, whipped, or hanged those who disagreed with them in New England, they would have done the same thing in England could they have secured the power. It is almost pathetic to trace the puzzlement of New England leaders at the end of the seventeenth century, when the idea of toleration was becoming more and more respectable in European thought. They could hardly understand what was happening in the world, and they could not for a long time be persuaded that they had any reason to be ashamed of their record of so many Quakers whipped, blasphemers punished by the amputation of ears, Antinomians exiled, Anabaptists fined, or witches executed. By all the lights which had prevailed in Europe at the time the Puritans had left, these were achievements to which any government could point with pride. In 1681 a congregation of Anabaptists, who led a stormy and precarious existence for several years in Charlestown, published an attack upon the government of Massachusetts Bay; they justified themselves by appealing to the example of the first settlers, claiming that like themselves the founders had been nonconformists and had fled to New England to establish a refuge for persecuted consciences. When Samuel Willard, minister of the Third Church in Boston, read this, he could hardly believe his eyes; he hastened to assure the authors that they did not know what they were talking about:

> I perceive they are mistaken in the design of our first Planters, whose business was not Toleration; but were professed Enemies of it, and could leave the World professing they *died no Libertines*. Their business was to settle, and (as much as in them lay) secure Religion to Posterity, according to that way which they believed was of God.

For the pamphlet in which Willard penned these lines Increase Mather wrote an approving preface. Forty years later, he and his son Cotton participated in the ordination of a Baptist minister in Boston, and he then preached on the need for harmony between differing sects. But by that time much water had gone under the bridge, the old charter had been revoked, there was danger that the Church of England might be made the established church of the colonies, theology had come to be of less importance in men's minds than morality, the tone of the eighteenth century was beginning to influence opinion— even in Boston. Increase was old and weary. Puritanism, in the true sense of the word, was dead.

Of course, the whole Puritan philosophy of church and state rested upon the assumption that the Word of God was clear and explicit, that the divines had interpreted it correctly, and that no one who was not either a knave or a fool could deny their demonstrations. *Ergo*, it seemed plain, those who did deny them should be punished for being obstinate. John Cotton said that offenders should not be disciplined for their wrong opinions, but for persisting in them; he said that Roger Williams was turned out of Massachusetts not for his conscience but for sinning against his own conscience. Roger Williams and John Cotton debated the question of "persecution" through several hundred pages; after they had finished, I think it is very doubtful whether Cotton had even begun to see his adversary's point. And still today it is hard to make

clear the exact grounds upon which Roger Williams became the great apostle
of religious liberty. Williams was not, like Thomas Jefferson, a man to whom
theology and divine grace had become stuff and nonsense; on the contrary
he was pious with a fervor and passion that went beyond most of his contemporaries. So exalted was his conception of the spiritual life that he could
not bear to have it polluted with earthly considerations. He did not believe
that any man could determine the precise intention of Scripture with such
dreadful certainty as the New England clergy claimed to possess. Furthermore, it seemed to him that even if their version were true, submission to
truth itself was worth nothing at all when forced upon men by the sword.
Williams evolved from an orthodox Puritan into the champion of religious
liberty because he came to see spiritual truth as so rare, so elevated, so supernal
a loveliness that it could not be chained to a worldly establishment and a
vested interest. He was a libertarian because he contemned the world, and he
wanted to separate church and state so that the church would not be contaminated by the state; Thomas Jefferson loved the world and was dubious about
the spirit, and he sought to separate church and state so that the state would
not be contaminated by the church. But John Cotton believed that the state
and church were partners in furthering the cause of truth; he knew that the
truth was clear, definite, reasonable, and undeniable; he expected all good
men to live by it voluntarily, and he was sure that all men who did not do so
were obviously bad men. Bad men were criminals, whether their offense was
theft or a belief in the "inner light," and they should be punished. Moses and
Aaron, the priest and the statesman, were equally the vice-regents of God,
and the notion that one could contaminate the other was utter insanity.

The two other ideas derived from the background of the age, rule by fundamental law and the social compact, were also special tenets of English Puritanism. For three decades before the settlement of Massachusetts the Puritan
party in England had been working hand in glove with the Parliament against
the King. The absolutist Stuarts were allied with the bishops, and the Puritan
agitator and the Parliamentary leader made common cause against them both.
As a result of this combination, the Puritan theorists had taken over the essen-
tials of the Parliamentary conception of society, the contention that the power
of the ruler should be exercised in accordance with established fundamental
law, and that the government should owe its existence to a compact of the
governed. Because these ideas were strategically invaluable in England, they
became ingrained in the Puritan consciousness; they were carried to the New
England wilderness and were preached from every pulpit in the land.

The Puritans did not see any conflict between them and their religious
intentions. In New England the fundamental law was the Bible. The magistrates were to have full power to rule men for the specific purposes to which
the society was dedicated; but they as well as their subordinates were tied to

the specific purposes, and could not go beyond the prescribed limits. The Bible was clear and definite on the form of the church, on the code of punishments for crimes, on the general purposes of social existence; its specifications were binding on all, magistrates, ministers, and citizens. Consequently, the Puritans did not find it difficult to conclude that in those matters upon which the Bible left men free to follow their own discretion, the society itself should establish basic rules. The New England leaders and the people frequently disagreed about what these rules were, or how detailed they should be made, but neither side ever doubted that the community must abide by whatever laws had been enacted, either by God or by the state. The government of New England was, as I have said, a dictatorship, but the dictators were not absolute and irresponsible. John Cotton was the clerical spokesman for the Massachusetts rulers, but he stoutly demanded "that all power that is on earth be limited."

The belief that government originated in the consent of the governed was equally congenial to the Puritan creed. The theology is often enough described as deterministic, because it held that men were predestined to Heaven or Hell; but we are always in danger of forgetting that the life of the Puritan was completely voluntaristic. The natural man was indeed bound in slavery to sin and unable to make exertions toward his own salvation; but the man into whose soul grace had been infused was liberated from that bondage and made free to undertake the responsibilities and obligations of virtue and decency. The holy society was erected upon the belief that the right sort of men could of their own free will and choice carry through the creation and administration of the right sort of community. The churches of New England were made up of "saints," who came into the church because they wanted membership, not because they were born in it, or were forced into it, or joined because of policy and convention. Though every resident was obliged to attend and to pay taxes for the support of the churches, no one became an actual member who did not signify his strong desire to be one. The saints were expected to act positively because they had in them a spirit of God that made them capable of every exertion. No doubt the Puritans maintained that government originated in the consent of the people because that theory was an implement for chastening the absolutism of the Stuarts; but they maintained it also because they did not believe that any society, civil or ecclesiastical, into which men did not enter of themselves was worthy of the name.

Consequently, the social theory of Puritanism, based upon the law of God, was posited also upon the voluntary submission of the citizens. As men exist in nature, said Thomas Hooker, no one person has any power over another; "there must of necessity be a mutuall ingagement, each of the other, by their free consent, before by any rule of God they have any right or power, or can exercise either, each towards the other." This truth appears, he argues, from all relations among men, that of husband and wife, master and servant; there must be a compact drawn up and sealed between them.

> From *mutuall acts* of consenting and ingaging each of other, there is an impression of *ingagement* results, as a *relative bond*, betwixt the contractours and confederatours, wherein the *formalis ratio*, or *specificall nature* of the covenant lieth, in all the former instances especially *that of* corporations. So that however it is true, the rule bindes such to the duties of their places and relations, yet it is certain, it requires that they should *first freely ingage* themselves in such covenants, and *then* be carefull to fulfill such duties. A man is allowed freely to make choice of his wife, and she of her husband, before they need or should perform the duties of husband and wife one towards another.

The rules and regulations of society, the objectives and the duties, are erected by God; but in a healthy state the citizens must first agree to abide by those regulations, must first create the society by willing consent and active participation.

These ideas, of a uniform church supported by the civil authority, of rule by explicit law, of the derivation of the state from the consent of the people, were transported to the wilderness because they were the stock ideas of the time and place. What the New England Puritans added of their own was the unique fashion in which they combined them into one coherent and rounded theory. The classic expression of this theory is the speech on liberty delivered by John Winthrop to the General Court in 1645. In that year Winthrop was serving as lieutenant governor, and as such was a justice of the peace; a squabble broke out in the town of Hingham over the election of a militia officer; Winthrop intervened, committing one faction for contempt of court when they would not give bond to appear peaceably before the legislature and let the affair be adjudicated. Some of the citizens were enraged, and the lower house of the General Court impeached Winthrop for exceeding his commission and going beyond the basic law of the land. He was tried and acquitted; thereupon he pronounced his magnificent oration, setting before the people the unified theory of the Puritan commonwealth.

As he expounds it, the political doctrine becomes part and parcel of the theological, and the cord that binds all ideas together is the covenant. Winthrop argues that individuals, in a natural state, before grace has been given them, are at absolute liberty to do anything they can, to lie, steal, murder; obviously he is certain that natural men, being what they are, will do exactly these things unless prevented. But when men become regenerate they are then at "liberty" to do only what God commands. And God commands certain things for the group as a whole as well as for each individual. Regenerate men, therefore, by the very fact of being regenerate, come together, form churches and a state upon explicit agreements, in which they all promise to live with one another according to the laws and for the purposes of God. Thus the government is brought into being by the act of the people; but the people do not create just any sort of government, but the one kind of government which God has outlined. The governors are elected by the people, but elected into an office which has been established by God. God engenders the society by acting through the people, as in nature He secures His effects by guiding secondary causes; the collective will of regenerate men, bound together by the social compact, projects and continues the will of God into the state. As John Davenport expressed it, "In regular actings of the creature, God is the first Agent; there are not two several and distinct actings, one of God, another of the People: but in one and the same action, God, by the Peoples suffrages, makes such an one Governour, or Magistrate, and not another." So, when men have made a covenant with God they have thereby promised Him, in the very terms of that agreement, to compact among themselves in order to form a holy state in which His discipline will be practiced. As one of the ministers phrased it:

> Where the Lord sets himselfe over a people, he frames them unto a willing and voluntary subjection unto him, that they desire nothing more then to be under his government . . . . When the Lord is in Covenant with a people, they follow him not forcedly, but as farre as they are sanctified by grace, they submit willingly to his regiment.

When men have entered these covenants, first with God, then with each other in the church and again in the state, they have thrice committed themselves to the rule of law and the control of authority. Winthrop can thus insist that though the government of Massachusetts is bound by fundamental law, and though it takes its rise from the people, and though the people elect the officials, still the people's liberty in Massachusetts consists in a "liberty to that only which is good, just and honest." By entering the covenant with God, and the covenant with each other, the citizens renounce all natural liberty, surrender the right to seek for anything that they themselves might lust after, and retain only the freedom that "is maintained and exercised in a way of subjection to authority."

The theory furnishes an excellent illustration of the intellectual ideal toward which all Puritan thought aspired; in the realm of government as of nature, the Puritan thinker strove to harmonize the determination of God with the exertion of men, the edicts of revelation with the counsels of reason and experience. On one side, this account exhibits the creation of society as flowing from the promptings and coaction of God; on the other side it attributes the origination to the teachings of nature and necessity. The social compact may be engineered by God, but it is also an eminently reasonable method of bringing a state into being. Delimitation of the ruler's power by basic law may be a divine ordinance to restrain the innate sinfulness of men, but it is also a very natural device to avoid oppression and despotism; the constitution may be promulgated to men from on high, but it is in fact very much the sort which, had they been left to their own devices, they might have contrived in the interests of efficiency and practicality. Men might conceivably have come upon the erection of governments through explicit compacts, in which they incorporated certain inviolable regulations and a guarantee of rights, quite as much by their own intelligence as by divine instruction. As always in Puritan thought, there was no intention to discredit either source, but rather to integrate the divine and the natural, revelation and reason, into a single inspiration. "Power of Civil Rule, by men orderly chosen, is Gods Ordinance," said John Davenport, even if "It is from the Light and Law of Nature," because "the Law of Nature is God's Law." The Puritan state was thus from one point of view purely and simply a "theocracy"; God was the sovereign; His fiats were law and His wishes took precedence over all other considerations; the magistrates and ministers were His viceroys. But from another point of view, the Puritan state was built upon reason and the law of nature; it was set up by the covenant of the people, the scope of its power was determined by the compact, and the magistrates and ministers were the commissioned servants of the people.

As this theory stands on paper it is, like so many edifices of the Puritan mind, almost perfect. When it was realized in practice, however, there were at least two difficulties that soon became apparent. For one, not all the people, even in New England, were regenerate; in fact, the provable elect were a minority, probably no more than one-fifth of the total population. But this did not dismay the original theorists, for they had never thought that mere numerical majorities proved anything. Consequently, though the social compact furnished the theoretical basis of society in New England, nevertheless it was confined to the special few; the election of officers and the passing of laws was given to those only who could demonstrate their justification and sanctification. The congregational system, with its membership limited to those who had proved before the church that they possessed the signs of grace, offered a ready machinery for winnowing the wheat from the chaff. Therefore, under the first charter the suffrage in Massachusetts was limited to the church members. In Connecticut the franchise was not officially restrained in this fashion, but other means served as well to keep the electorate pure and orthodox. The "citizens," as they were called, elected delegates to the General Court, chose judges, and passed laws. The others, the "inhabitants," had equality before the law, property rights, police protection; they were taxed no more than the citizens or submitted to no indignities, but they were allowed no voice in the government or in the choice of ministers, and only by the mere force of numbers gained any influence in town meetings.

The restriction of the franchise to church membership seemed to solve the first difficulty confronted by the Puritan theorists. But in time it only brought them face to face with the second and more serious problem: the whole structure of theory which Winthrop outlined in his speech, and which the sermons of the 1660's and 1670's reiterated fell apart the moment the "citizens" were no longer really and ardently holy. Just as soon as the early zeal began to die down, and the distinction between the citizens and the inhabitants became difficult to discern, then the purely naturalistic, rational, practical aspect of the political theory became detached from the theological, began to stand alone and by itself. As the religious inspiration waned, there remained no reason why all the people should not be held partners to the social compact; the idea that God worked His ends through the covenant of the people grew vague and obscure, while the notion that all the people made the covenant for their own reasons and created the state for their own purposes took on more and more definite outlines. As toleration was forced upon the colonies by royal command, or became more estimable as religious passions abated, the necessity for the social bond being considered a commitment of the nation to the will of God disappeared. Instead, men perceived the charms and usefulness of claiming that the compact had been an agreement of the people, not to God's terms, but to their own terms. The divine ordinance and the spirit of God, which were supposed to have presided over the political process, vanished, leaving a government founded on the self-evident truths of the law of nature, brought into being by social compact, instituted not for the glory of God, but to secure men's "inalienable rights" of life, liberty, and the pursuit of happiness. Except that, until Jefferson rewrote the phrase, the sacred trinity of interests which government could not tamper with were more candidly summarized as life, liberty—and property.

After the new charter of 1691—which Increase Mather negotiated and which for him was a diplomatic triumph, but which nevertheless was an imposition upon Massachusetts from the outside—leaders of the colony made various efforts to accommodate the original conception of social purpose to the constitutional requirements of the document. I have elsewhere described their flounderings (*The New England Mind: From Colony to Province*, 1953), and the literature of the eighteenth century clearly yields up the evolution of a political philosophy which, by the time of the revolution, was entirely perfected (see Alice M. Baldwin, *The New England Clergy and the American Revolution*, Durham, North Carolina, 1928). Historians now agree that the first clear break with the seventeenth-century complex was John Wise's *Vindication of the Government of the New England Churches* in 1717. Though actually this book had little or no effect on colonial thinking, and does not appear to have been cited even in the revolutionary debates, still it was far ahead of its own time in proclaiming that a contractual system of government, with inalienable rights preserved in society from the original state of nature, was the dictate of aboriginal reason, that it could be said to have only subsequently obtained "the Royal Approbation" of the Creator. The transformation of the doctrine of the founders into a weapon for burgeoning nationalism was virtually completed in 1750 when Jonathan Mayhew, preaching on the anniversary of the day on which the Puritans had decapitated Charles I, delivered "A Discourse Concerning Unlimited Subjection." To this enlightened Puritan it now appeared that the purposes of society are not at all those of the deity but of the subjects. The advantage to be derived from corporate existence is no longer the salvation but the well-being of the citizen. The power even of the Puritan God—and therefore, naturally, that of an English king—is bound by the terms of compact. New England's errand into the wilderness—having set out from the federal theology—had now developed into an assurance that God Himself would respect the laws we have agreed upon. As for King George, if he imposes a tax to which we do not ourselves consent, and if we thereupon resist him, "even to the dethroning him," we are not criminals: we have only taken "a reasonable way" of vindicating our natural rights.

In 1750 Mayhew's boldness still dismayed most of his contemporaries, as did also his theological liberalism, but it was only a matter of time before the community caught up with at least his political argument. Hence he is the most obvious link between Puritan and revolutionary ideas. However, in the excitement of embracing Mayhew's radicalism, few at the time of the war had the leisure or inclination to look back to Winthrop or to inquire how they had managed to travel the tortuous road from his doctrine of federal liberty to their constitutionalism. There ceased to survive even the faintest memory of an era when the social contract had incorporated absolute subjection to the ontological realities of the good, just, and honest—those anterior verities which existed from eternity, long before any peoples anywhere were gathered into societies and which no mere convention of the citizens could alter or redefine.

THE HISTORIAN'S HEROIC VIEW

Edward Johnson, the author of Wonder-Working Providence of Sions Saviour in New England, *from which this selection is taken, was one of the Puritans who landed at Massachusetts Bay in 1630. He wrote his history between 1650 and 1654, at which date it was published in London. Johnson was variously a proprietor, clerk, selectman, militia captain, and speaker of the Massachusetts House of Deputies, and hence an important person who played many roles. Not the least of his roles was that of historian.*

Johnson's approach to history, as represented by this document, is a curious one. Wonder-Working Providence *can be read as a straightforward narrative by an eyewitness of the Puritan landing and the founding, after great hardship, of the first inland settlement at Concord. It may also be considered, however, as functional literature in that it seeks to dramatize the working of God's divine providence in aiding the Puritans in their holy mission to the New World. It is, in Voltaire's phrase, "philosophy teaching by example," or a "usable past."*

EDWARD JOHNSON'S WONDER-WORKING PROVIDENCE

Chap. XII. Of the voluntary banishment, chosen by this People of Christ, and their last farewell taken of their Country and Friends

And now behold the severall Regiments of these Souldiers of Christ, as they are shipped for his service in the Westerne World, Part thereof being come to the Towne and Port of Southamptan in England, where they were to be shipped, that they might prosecute this designe to the full, one Ship called the *Eagle*,* they wholy purchase, and many more they hire, filling them with the seede of man and beast to sow this yet untilled Wildernesse withall, making sale of such Land as they possesse, to the great admiration of their Friends and Acquaintance, who thus expostulate with them, "What, will not the large

---

Edward Johnson, Wonder-Working Providence of Sions Saviour in New England, 1628–1651, in J. Franklin Jameson, ed., Original Narratives of Early American History (New York, Charles Scribner's Sons, 1910), pp. 50–54, 63–66, 111–115.
* Winthrop's "admiral" or flagship, a ship of 350 tons. Johnson probably was a passenger in this ship.

income of your yearly revenue content you, which in all reason cannot chuse but be more advantagious both to you and yours, then all that Rocky Wildernesse, whither you are going, to run the hazard of your life? Have you not here your Tables filled with great variety of Foode, your Coffers filled with Coyne, your Houses beautifully built and filled with all rich Furniture? (or otherwise) have you not such a gainfull Trade as none the like in the Towne where you live? Are you not inriched daily? Are not your Children very well provided for as they come to years? (nay) may you not here as pithily practise the two chiefe Duties of a Christian (if Christ give strength), namely Mortification and Sanctification, as in any place of the World? What helps can you have there that you must not carry from hence?" With bold resolvednesse these stout Souldiers of Christ reply; as Death, the King of terror, with all his dreadfull attendance, inhumane and barbarous tortures, doubled and trebled by all the infernal furies, have appeared but light and momentary to the Souldiers of Christ Jesus, so also the Pleasure, Profits and Honours of this World set forth in their most glorious splendor and magnitude by the alluring Lady of Delight, proffering pleasant embraces, cannot intice with her Syren Songs, such Souldiers of Christ, whose aymes are elevated by him, many Millions above that brave Warrier Ulysses.

Now seeing all can be said will but barely set forth the immoveable Resolutions that Christ continued in these men; Passe on and attend with teares, if thou hast any, the following discourse, while these Men, Women and Children are taking their last farwell of their Native Country, Kindred, Friends and Acquaintance, while the Ships attend them; Many make choise of some solitary place to eccho out their bowell-breaking affections in bidding their Friends farwell. "Deare friends" (sayes one) "as neare as my owne soule doth thy love lodge in my brest, with thought of the heart-burning Ravishments, that thy Heavenly speeches have wrought: my melting soule is poured out at present with these words." Both of them had their farther speach strangled from the depth of their inward dolor, with breast-breaking sobs, till leaning their heads each on others shoulders, they let fall the salt-dropping dews of vehement affection, striving to exceede one another, much like the departure of David and Jonathan: having a little eased their hearts with the still streames of Teares, they recovered speech againe. "Ah! my much honoured friend, hath Christ given thee so great a charge as to be Leader of his People into that far remote, and vast Wildernesse, I [ay], oh, and alas, thou must die there and never shall I see thy Face in the flesh againe. Wert thou called to so great a taske as to passe the pretious Ocean, and hazard thy person in Battell against thousands of Malignant Enemies there, there were hopes of thy return with triumph; but now after two, three, or foure moneths spent with daily expectation of swallowing Waves and cruell Pirates, you are to be Landed among barbarous Indians, famous for nothing but cruelty, where you are like to spend your days in a famishing condition for a long space." Scarce had he uttered this, but presently hee lockes his friend fast in his armes; holding each other thus for some space of time, they weepe againe. But as Paul to his beloved flock, the other replies, "What doe you weeping and breaking my heart? [Acts 21:13] I am now prest for the service of our Lord Christ, to re-build the most glorious Edifice of Mount Sion in a Wildernesse, and as John Baptist, I must cry, Prepare yee the way of the Lord, make his paths strait, for behold hee is comming againe, hee is comming to destroy Antichrist, and give the whore double to drinke the very dregs of his wrath. Then my deare friend unfold thy hands, for thou and I have much worke to doe, I [ay] and all Christian Souldiers the World throughout."

Then hand in hand they leade each other to the Sandy-banks of the brinish Ocean, when clenching their hands fast, they unloose not til inforced to wipe their watery-eyes, whose constant streames forced a watery-path upon their Cheekes, which to hide from the eyes of others they shun society for a time, but being called by occasion, whose bauld back-part none can lay hold one [on]; They thrust in among the throng now ready to take Ship, where they beheld the like affections with their own among divers Relations. Husbands and Wives with mutuall consent are now purposed to part for a time 900 Leagues asunder, since some providence at present will not suffer them to goe together; they resolve their tender affections shall not hinder this worke of Christ. The new Married and betrothed man, exempt by the Law of God from war, now will not claime their priviledge, but being constrained by the Love of Christ, lock up their naturall affections for a time, till the Lord shall be pleased to give them a meeting in this Westerne World, sweetly mixing it with spirituall love in the meane time. Many Fathers now take their yong Samuells, and give them to this service of Christ all their Lives. Brethren, Sisters, Unkles, Nephewes, Neeces, together with all Kindred of bloud that binds the bowells of affection in a true Lovers knot, can now take their last farewell, each of other, although naturall affection will still claime her right, and manifest her selfe to bee in the body by looking out at the Windowes in a mournefull manner. Among this company, thus disposed, doth many Reverend and godly Pastors of Christ present themselves, some in a Seamans Habit, and their scattered sheepe comming as a poore Convoy loftily take their leave of them as followeth, "What dolefull dayes are these, when the best choice our Orthodox Ministers can make is to take up a perpetuall banishment from their native soile, together with their Wives and Children; wee their poore sheepe they may not feede, but by stoledred [stealth] should they abide here. Lord Christ, here they are at thy command, they go; this is the doore thou hast opened upon our earnest request, and we hope it shall never be shut: for Englands sake they are going from England to pray without ceasing for England. O England! thou shalt finde New England prayers prevailing with their God for thee, but now woe alas, what great hardship must these our indeared Pastors indure for a long season." With these words they lift up their voyces and wept, adding many drops of salt liquor to the ebbing Ocean; Then shaking hands they bid adue with much cordiall affection to all their Brethren, and Sisters in Christ, yet now the Scorne and Derision of those times, and for this their great enterprise counted as so many crackt-braines; but Christ will make all the earth know the wisdome he hath indued them with, shall over-top all the humane policy in the World, as the sequell wee hope will shew; Thus much shall suffice in generall to speak of their peoples farewell they tooke from time to time of their Country and Friends. . . .

Chap. XVII. Of the first leading of these People of Christ, when the Civill Government was Established

But to goe on with the Story, the 12 of July or thereabout, 1630, these Souldiers of Christ first set foote one this Westerne end of the World; where arriveing in safety, both Men, Women and Children, on the North side of Charles River, they landed neare a small Island, called Noddells Island, where one Mr. Samuel Mavereck then living, a man of a very loving and curteous behaviour, very ready to entertaine strangers, yet an enemy to the Reformation in hand, being strong for the Lordly Prelaticall power, one [on] this Island he had built a small Fort with the helpe of one Mr. David Tompson, placing therein foure Murtherers to protect him from the Indians. About one mile distant upon the River ran a small creeke, taking its Name from Major Gen. Edward Gibbons, who dwelt there for some yeares after; One [on] the South side of the River one [on] a point of Land called Blaxtons point, planted Mr. William Blaxton, of whom we have former spoken: to the South-East of him, neare an Island called Tompsons Island lived some few Planters more. These persons were the first Planters of those parts, having some small Trading with the Indians for Beaver-Skins, which moved them to make their aboade in those parts, whom these first Troopes of Christs Army, found as fit helpes to further their worke. At their arrivall those small number of Christians gathered at Salem, greatly rejoycing, and the more, because they saw so many that came chiefly for promoting the great Work of Christ in hand. The Lady Arrabella and some other godly Women aboad at Salem, but their Husbands continued at Charles Town, both for the settling the civill Government, and gathering another Church of Christ. The first Court was holden aboard the *Arrabella* the 23. of August. When the much honoured John Wintrope Esq. was chosen Governour for the remainder of that yeare, 1630. Also the worthy Thomus Dudly Esq. was chosen Deputy Governour, and Mr. Simon Brodestreet Secretary, the people after their long Voyage were many of them troubled with the Scurvy,

and some of them died. The first station they tooke up was at Charles Towne, where they pitched some Tents of Cloath, other built them small Huts, in which they lodged their Wifes and Children. The first beginning of this worke seemed very dolorous; First for the death of that worthy personage Izaac Johnson Esq. whom the Lord had indued with many pretious gifts, insomuch that he was had in high esteeme among all the people of God, and as a chiefe Pillar to support this new erected building. He very much rejoyced at his death, that the Lord had been pleased to keepe his eyes open so long, as to see one Church of Christ gathered before his death, at whose departure there was not onely many weeping eyes, but some fainting hearts, fearing the fall of the present worke. For future Remembrance of him mind this Meeter.

Izaac Johnson Esquire, beloved of Christ and his people, and one of
the Magistrates of New England

What mov'd thee on the Seas upon such toyle with Lady-taking;
    Christs drawing love all strength's above, when way for his hee's making.
Christ will have thee example be, honoured with's graces, yeilding
    His Churches aid, foundation laid, now new one Christ a building.
Thy Faith, Hope, Love, Joy, Meeknesse prove improved for thy Lord,
    As he to thee, to people be, in Government accord.
Oh! people why doth Christ deny this worthies life to lengthen?
    Christ onely trust, Johnsons turnd dust, and yet hee's crownd and strengthend.

The griefe of this people was further increased by the sore sicknesse which befell among them, so that almost in every Family Lamentation, Mourning, and woe was heard, and no fresh food to be had to cherish them. It would assuredly have moved the most lockt up affections to Teares no doubt, had they past from one Hut to another, and beheld the piteous case these people were in, and that which added to their present distresse was the want of fresh water, for although the place did afford plenty, yet for present they could finde but one Spring, and that not to be come at but when the tide was downe, which caused many to passe over to the Southside of the River, where they afterward erected some other Townes, yet most admirable it was to see with what Christian courage many of these Souldiers of Christ carried it amidst all these calamities, and in October, the Governour Deputy and Assistants held their second Court on the South-side of the River; Where they then began to build, holding correspondency with Charles Towne, as one and the same.

At this Court many of the first Planters came, and were made free, yet afterward none were admitted to this fellowship, or freedome, but such as were

---

Facing page: map of New England, from Travels and Works of Captain John Smith, *Vol. II, A. G. Bradley, ed. (Edinburgh, 1910).*

first joyned in fellowship with some one of the Churches of Christ, their chiefest aime being bent to promote his worke altogether. The number of Freemen this yeare was 110. or thereabout.

Chap. XXXVI. Of the laborious worke Christ's people have in planting this wildernesse, set forth in the building the Towne of Concord, being the first in-land Towne

Now because it is one of the admirable acts of Christ['s] Providence in leading his people forth into these Westerne Fields, in his providing of Huts for them, to defend them from the bitter stormes this place is subject unto, therefore here is a short Epitome of the manner how they placed downe their dwellings in this Desart Wildernesse, the Lord being pleased to hide from the Eyes of his people the difficulties they are to encounter withall in a new Plantation, that they might not thereby be hindered from taking the worke in hand; upon some inquiry of the Indians, who lived to the North-west of the Bay, one Captaine Simon Willard being acquainted with them, by reason of his Trade, became a chiefe instrument in erecting this Town, the land they purchase of the Indians, and with much difficulties traveling through unknowne woods, and through watery scrampes [swampes], they discover the fitnesse of the place, sometimes passing through the Thickets, where their hands are forced to make way for their bodies passage, and their feete clambering over the crossed Trees, which when they missed they sunke into an uncertaine bottome in water, and wade up to the knees, tumbling sometimes higher and sometimes lower, wearied with this toile, they at end of this meete with a scorching plaine, yet not so plaine, but that the ragged Bushes scratch their legs fouly, even to wearing their stockings to their bare skin in two or three houres; if they be not otherwise well defended with Bootes, or Buskings, their flesh will be torne: (that some being forced to passe on without further provision) have had the bloud trickle downe at every step, and in the time of Summer the Sun casts such a reflecting heate from the sweet Ferne, whose scent is very strong so that some herewith have beene very nere fainting, although very able bodies to undergoe much travell, and this not to be indured for one day, but for many, and verily did not the Lord incourage their naturall parts (with hopes of a new and strange discovery, expecting every houre to see some rare sight never seene before) they were never able to hold out, and breake through: but above all, the thirsting desires these servants of Christ have had to Plant his Churches, among whom the forenamed Mr. Jones* shall not be forgotten.

---

* John Jones, pastor of the Concord church.

In Desart's depth where Wolves and Beares abide,
    There Jones sets down a wary watch to keepe,
O're Christs deare flock, who now are wandered wide;
    But not from him, whose eyes ne're close with sleepe.
Surely it sutes thy melancholly minde,
    Thus solitary for to spend thy dayes,
Much more thy soule in Christ content doth finde,
    To worke for him, who thee to joy will raise.
Leading thy son to Land, yet more remote,
    To feede his flock upon this Westerne wast:
Exhort him then Christs Kingdome to promote;
    That he with thee of lasting joyes may tast.

Yet farther to tell of the hard labours this people found in Planting this Wildernesse, after some dayes spent in search, toyling in the day time as formerly is said; like true Jacobites they rest them one [on] the Rocks where the night takes them, their short repast is some small pittance of Bread, if it hold out, but as for Drinke they have plenty, the Countrey being well watered in all places that yet are found out. Their farther hardship is to travell, sometimes they know not whether, bewildred indeed without sight of Sun, their compasse miscarrying in crouding through the Bushes, they sadly search up and down for a known way, the Indians paths being not above one foot broad, so that a man may travell many dayes and never find one. But to be sure the directing Providence of Christ hath beene better unto them than many paths, as might here be inserted, did not hast call my Pen away to more waighty matters; yet by the way a touch thus, it befell with a servant maide, who was travelling about three or foure miles from one Towne to another, loosing her selfe in the Woods, had very diligent search made after her for the space of three dayes, and could not possible be found, then being given over as quite lost, after three dayes and nights, the Lord was pleased to bring her feeble body to her own home in safety, to the great admiration of all that heard of it. This intricate worke no whit daunted these resolved servants of Christ to goe on with the worke in hand, but lying in the open aire, while the watery Clouds poure down all the night season, and sometimes the driving Snow dissolving on their backs, they keep their wet cloathes warme with a continued fire, till the renewed morning give fresh opportunity of further travell; after they have thus found out a place of aboad, they burrow themselves in the Earth for their first shelter under some Hill-side, casting the Earth aloft upon Timber; they make a smoaky fire against the Earth at the highest side, and thus these poore servants of Christ provide shelter for themselves, their Wives and little ones, keeping off the short showers from their Lodgings, but the long raines penetrate through, to their great disturbance in the night season: yet in these poore

Wigwames they sing Psalmes, pray and praise their God, till they can provide them houses, which ordinarily was not wont to be with many till the Earth, by the Lords blessing, brought forth Bread to feed them, their Wives and little ones, which with sore labours they attaine every one that can lift a hawe [hoe] to strike it into the Earth, standing stoutly to their labours, and teare up the Rootes and Bushes, which the first yeare beares them a very thin crop, till the soard [sward] of the Earth be rotten, and therefore they have been forced to cut their bread very thin for a long season. But the Lord is pleased to provide for them great store of Fish in the spring time, and especially Alewives about the bignesse of a Herring; many thousands of these, they used to put under their Indian Corne, which they plant in Hills five foote asunder, and assuredly when the Lord created this Corne, hee had a speciall eye to supply these his peoples wants with it, for ordinarily five or six graines doth produce six hundred.

As for flesh they looked not for any in those times (although now they have plenty) unlesse they could barter with the Indians for Venison or Rockoons, whose flesh is not much inferiour unto Lambe, the toile of a new Plantation being like the labours of Hercules never at an end, yet are none so barbarously bent (under the Mattacusets especially) but with a new Plantation they ordinarily gather into Church-fellowship, so that Pastors and people suffer the inconveniences together, which is a great meanes to season the sore labours they undergoe, and verily the edge of their appetite was greater to spirituall duties at their first comming in time of wants, than afterward: many in new Plantations have been forced to go barefoot, and bareleg, till these latter dayes, and some in time of Frost and Snow: Yet were they then very healthy more then now they are: in this Wildernesse-worke men of Estates speed no better than others, and some much worse for want of being inured to such hard labour, having laid out their estate upon cattell at five and twenty pound a Cow, when they came to winter them with in-land Hay, and feed upon such wild Fother as was never cut before, they could not hold out the Winter, but ordinarily the first or second yeare after their comming up to a new Plantation, many of their Cattell died, especially if they wanted Salt-marshes: and also those, who supposed they should feed upon Swines flesh were cut short, the Wolves commonly feasting themselves before them, who never leave neither flesh nor bones, if they be not scared away before they have made an end of their meale. As for those who laid out their Estate upon Sheepe, they speed worst of any at the beginning (although some have sped the best of any now) for untill the Land be often fed with other Cattell Sheepe cannot live; And therefore they never thrived till these latter dayes: Horse had then no better successe, which made many an honest Gentleman travell a foot for a long time, and some have even perished with extreame heate in their travells: as also the want of English graine, Wheate, Barly and Rie proved a sore affliction to some stomacks, who could not live upon Indian Bread and water, yet were they compelled to it till Cattell increased, and the Plowes could but goe: instead of Apples and Peares, they had Pomkins and Squashes of divers kinds. Their lonesome condition was very grievous to some, which was much aggravated by continuall feare of the Indians approach, whose cruelties were much spoken of, and more especially during the time of the Peqot wars.

Thus this poore people populate this howling Desart, marching manfully on (the Lord assisting) through the greatest difficulties, and forest labours that ever any with such weak means have done.

A MODEL OF THE PURITAN STATE

The selections that follow are from the works of John Winthrop, at various times Governor or Deputy Governor of the Massachusetts Bay Colony from the time of his landing in 1630 until his death in 1649. It fell to Winthrop, as a leader of the Massachusetts Bay Puritans, to define the nature and objectives of the community, and then to bend his every effort toward holding it together in piety and efficient service to God. The documents below reveal his efforts in that direction. The first is one draft of his analysis of the reasons for sailing to the New World in the first place. The second is a copy of the Cambridge Agreement of August 1629, which outlines the structure of the Company and incidentally indicates that it was no accident that the Puritans brought their charter to Massachusetts with them. These two documents should be compared with the other models and plans for New World colonies in Part I of the present work.

The third document is Winthrop's famous sermon aboard the ship Arabella, delivered even before the landing in Massachusetts. It outlines the communal nature of the Puritan enterprise and, with religious sanction, stresses the need for mutual charity and avoidance of class-oriented strife. It describes the idea of the "covenant" or bargain struck between the Puritan community and their God.

The last document in this sequence is Winthrop's speech to the General Court (or Assembly) of July 3, 1645. It is, as Perry Miller remarks, "the classical expression of Puritan political theory."

JOHN WINTHROP ON THE AIMS OF THE BAY COLONY

1. Generall considerations for the plantation in New England, with an answer to several objections

First, it will be a service to the church of great consequence, to carry the gospell into those parts of the world, and to raise a bulwarke against the kingdom of Antichrist which the Jesuits labour to rear up in all places of the world.

Secondly, all other churches of Europe are brought to desolation, and it may be justly feared that the like judgment is coming upon us; and who knows but that God hath provided this place to be a refuge for many whom he meanes to save out of the general destruction.

Thirdly, the land growes weary of her inhabitants, so that man, which is the most precious of all creatures, is here more vile and base than the earth they tread upon; so as children, neighbors and friends, especially of the poore, are counted the greatest burdens which, if things were right, would be the highest earthly blessings.

Fourthly. Wee are growen to that excess and intemperance in all excess of riot as no meane estate almost will suffice to keep saile with his equals, and he that fayles in it must live in sorrow and contempt. Hence it comes to passe that all arts and trades are carried in that deceitful manner and unrighteous course as it is almost impossible for a good upright man to maintayne his chardge and live comfortably in any of them.

Fifthly. The schools of learning and religion are so corrupted, as (besides the unsupportable chardge of this education) most children, (even the best wittiest and of fayerest hopes) are perverted, corrupted and utterly over powered by the multitude of evill examples and licentious governors of those seminaries.

Sixthly. The whole earth is the Lord's garden and hee hath given it to the sons of Adam to bee tilled and improved by them, why then should we stand starving here for places of habitation (many men spending as much labour and cost to recover or keepe sometymes an acre or two of lands, as would procure him many hundreds of acres, as good or better in another place) and in the meane tyme suffer whole countryes as profitable for the use of man, to lye waste without any improvement?

The first three selections are from *Winthrop Papers* (Boston, Massachusetts Historical Society, 1931), II, pp. 117–118, 151–152, 282–284, 292–295, and are reprinted by permission of the Massachusetts Historical Society. The last selection is from John Winthrop, *Winthrop's Journal: "History of New England," 1630–1649,* in James Kendall Hosmer, ed., *Original Narratives of Early American History* (New York, Charles Scribner's Sons, 1908), II, pp. 237–239.

Seventhly. What can bee a better worke and more noble and worthy a christian, than to helpe to raise and support a particular church while it is in its infancy, and to join our forces with such a company of faithfull people, as by a tymely assistance may grow stronger and prosper, and for want of it may be put to great hazzard if not wholly ruined?

Eightly. If any such as are known to bee godly and live in wealth and prosperity here, shall forsake all this to joyn themselves with this church, and runne in hazard with them of hard and meane condition, it will be an example of great use both for the removing of scandall and sinister and worldly respects, to give more lyfe to the faith of God's people in their prayers for the plantation and also to encourage others to joyne the more willingly in it.

2. The Agreement at Cambridge, August 26, 1629

Vpon due consideracion of the state of the plantacion now in hand for new England, wherein wee (whose names are hervnto subscribed) haue ingaged ourselves: and having weighed the greatnes of the worke in regard of the consequence, Gods glory and the churches good: As also in regard of the difficultyes and discouragements which in all probabilityes must be forcast vpon the prosecution of this businesse: Considering withall that this whole adventure growes vpon the joynt confidence we haue in each others fidelity and resolucion herein, so as no man of vs would haue adventured it without assurance of the rest: Now for the better encourragement of ourselves and others that shall joyne with vs in this action, and to the end that euery man may without scruple dispose of his estate and afayres as may best fitt his preparacion for this voyage, It is fully and faithfully agreed amongst vs, and euery of vs doth hereby freely and sincerely promise and bynd himselfe in the word of a Christian and in the presence of God who is the searcher of all hearts, that we will so really endevour the prosecucion of this worke, as by Gods assistaunce we will be ready in our persons, and with such of our seuerall familyes as are to go with vs and such provisions as we are able conveniently to furnish ourselves withall, to embarke for the said plantacion by the first of march next, at such port or ports of this land as shall be agreed vpon by the Company, to the end to passe the Seas (vnder Gods protection) to inhabite and continue in new England. Provided always that before the last of September next the whole gouernement together with the Patent for the said plantacion bee first by an order of Court legally transferred and established to remayne with vs and others which shall inhabite vpon the said plantacion. And provided also that if any shall be hindered by such just and inevitable Lett or other cause to be allowed by 3 parts of foure of these whose names are herevnto subscribed, then such persons for such tymes and during such letts to be dischardged of this bond. And we do further promise euery one for himselfe that shall fayle to be ready through his owne default by the day appointed, to pay for euery dayes default the summe of 3 *li.* to the vse of the rest of the Company who shall be ready by the same day and tyme.

This was done by order of Court the 29th of August. 1629.

Rich: Saltonstall	John Winthrop	Isaack Johnson
Tho: Dudley	Will: Pinchon	John Humfrey
William Vassall	Kellam Browne	Tho: Sharp
Nicho: West	William Colbron	Increase Nowell

3. A Modell of Christian Charity. Written On Boarde the Arrabella, On the Attlantick Ocean. By the Honorable John Winthrop Esquire.

In His passage, (with the great Company of Religious people, of which Christian Tribes he was the Brave Leader and famous Governor;) from the Island of Great Brittaine, to New-England in the North America. Anno 1630.

Christian Charitie

A MODELL HEREOF

God Almightie in his most holy and wise providence hath soe disposed of the Condicion of mankinde, as in all times some must be rich some poore, some highe and eminent in power and dignitie; others meane and in subieccion.

THE REASON HEREOF

1. REAS: *First,* to hold conformity with the rest of his workes, being delighted to shewe forthe the glory of his wisdome in the variety and differance of the Creatures and the glory of his power, in ordering all these differences for the preservacion and good of the whole, and the glory of his greatnes that as it is the glory of princes to haue many officers, soe this great King will haue many Stewards counting himselfe more honoured in dispenceing his guifts to man by man, then if hee did it by his owne immediate hand.

2. REAS: *Secondly,* That he might haue the more occasion to manifest the worke of his Spirit: first, vpon the wicked in moderateing and restraineing them: soe that the riche and mighty should not eate vpp the poore, nor the poore, and dispised rise vpp against theire superiours, and shake off theire yoake; 2ly in the regenerate in exerciseing his graces in them, as in the greate ones, theire loue mercy, gentlenes, temperance etc., in the poore and inferiour sorte, theire faithe patience, obedience etc:

3. REAS: Thirdly, That every man might haue need of other, and from hence they might be all knitt more nearly together in the Bond of brotherly affec-

cion: from hence it appeares plainely that noe man is made more honourable then another or more wealthy etc., out of any perticuler and singuler respect to himselfe but for the glory of his Creator and the Common good of the Creature, Man; Therefore God still reserues the propperty of these guifts to himselfe as Ezek: 16. 17. he there calls wealthe his gold and his silver etc. Prov: 3. 9. he claimes theire seruice as his due honour the Lord with thy riches etc. All men being thus (by divine providence) rancked into two sortes, riche and poore; vnder the first, are comprehended all such as are able to liue comfortably by theire owne meanes duely improued; and all others are poore according to the former distribution. There are two rules whereby wee are to walke one towards another: Justice and Mercy. These are allwayes distinguished in theire Act and in theire obiect, yet may they both concurre in the same Subiect in eache respect; as sometimes there may be an occasion of shewing mercy to a rich man, in some sudden danger of distresse, and allsoe doeing of meere Justice to a poor man in regard of some perticuler contract etc. There is likewise a double Lawe by which wee are regulated in our conversacion one towardes another: in both the former respects, the lawe of nature and the lawe of grace, or the morrall lawe or the lawe of the gospell, to omitt the rule of Justice as not propperly belonging to this purpose otherwise then it may fall into consideracion in some perticuler Cases: By the first of these lawes man as he was enabled soe withall [is] commaunded to loue his neighbour as himselfe vpon this ground stands all the precepts of the morrall lawe, which concernes our dealings with men. To apply this to the works of mercy this lawe requires two things first that every man afford his help to another in every want or distresse Secondly, That hee performe this out of the same affeccion, which makes him carefull of his owne good according to that of our Saviour Math: [7.12] Whatsoever ye would that men should doe to you. This was practised by Abraham and Lott in entertaineing the Angells and the old man of Gibea.

The Lawe of Grace or the Gospell hath some differance from the former as in these respectes first the lawe of nature was giuen to man in the estate of innocency; this of the gospell in the estate of regeneracy: 2ly, the former propounds one man to another, as the same fleshe and Image of god, this as a brother in Christ allsoe, and in the Communion of the same spirit and soe teacheth vs to put a difference betweene Christians and others. Doe good to all especially to the household of faith; vpon this ground the Israelites were to putt a difference betweene the brethren of such as were strangers though not of the Canaanites. 3ly. The Lawe of nature could giue noe rules for dealeing with enemies for all are to be considered as freinds in the estate of innocency, but the Gospell commaunds loue to an enemy. proofe. If thine Enemie hunger feede him; Loue your Enemies doe good to them that hate you Math: 5.44.

This Lawe of the Gospell propoundes likewise a difference of seasons and occasions there is a time when a christian must sell all and giue to the poore as they did in the Apostles times. There is a tyme allsoe when a christian (though they giue not all yet) must giue beyond theire abillity, as they of Macedonia. Cor: 2. 6. likewise community of perills calls for extraordinary liberallity and soe doth Community in some speciall seruice for the Churche. Lastly, when there is noe other meanes whereby our Christian brother may be releiued in this distresse, wee must help him beyond our ability, rather then tempt God, in putting him vpon help by miraculous or extraordinary meanes. . . .

From the former Consideracions ariseth these Conclusions.

1 First, This loue among Christians is a reall thing not Imaginarie.

2ly. This loue is as absolutely necessary to the being of the body of Christ, as the sinewes and other ligaments of a naturall body are to the being of that body.

3ly. This loue is a divine spirituall nature free, actiue strong Couragious permanent vnder valueing all things beneathe its propper obiect, and of all the graces this makes vs nearer to resemble the virtues of our heavenly father.

4ly, It restes in the loue and wellfare of its beloued, for the full and certaine knowledge of these truthes concerning the nature vse, [and] excellency of this grace, that which the holy ghost hath left recorded 1. Cor. 13. may giue full satisfaccion which is needfull for every true member of this louely body of the Lord Jesus, to worke vpon theire heartes, by prayer meditacion continuall exercise at least of the speciall [power] of this grace till Christ be formed in them and they in him all in eache other knitt together by this bond of loue.

It rests now to make some applicacion of this discourse by the present designe which gaue the occasion of writeing of it. Herein are 4 things to be propounded: first the persons, 2ly, the worke, 3ly, the end, 4ly the meanes.

1. For the persons, wee are a Company professing our selues fellow members of Christ, In which respect onely though wee were absent from eache other many miles, and had our imploymentes as farre distant, yet wee ought to account our selues knitt together by this bond of loue, and liue in the excercise of it, if wee would haue comforte of our being in Christ, this was notorious in the practise of the Christians in former times, as is testified of the Waldenses from the mouth of one of the adversaries Aeneas Syluius, mutuo [solent amare] pene antequam norint, they vse to loue any of theire owne religion even before they were acquainted with them.

2ly. for the worke wee haue in hand, it is by a mutuall consent through a speciall overruleing providence, and a more then an ordinary approbation of the Churches of Christ to seeke out a place of Cohabitation and Consorteshipp vnder a due forme of Goverment both ciuill and ecclesiasticall. In such cases as this the care of the publique must oversway all private respects, by which not onely conscience,* but meare Ciuill pollicy doth binde vs; for it is a true rule that perticuler estates cannott subsist in the ruine of the publique.

3ly. The end is to improue our liues to doe more seruice to the Lord the comforte and encrease of the body of christe whereof wee are members that our selues and posterity may be the better preserued from the Common corrupcions of this euill world to serue the Lord and worke out our Salvacion vnder the power and purity of his holy Ordinances.

4ly for the meanes whereby this must bee effected, they are 2fold, a Conformity with the worke and end wee aime at, these wee see are extraordinary, therefore wee must not content our selues with vsuall ordinary meanes whatsoever wee did or ought to haue done when wee liued in England, the same must wee doe and more allsoe where wee goe: That which the most in theire Churches maineteine as a truthe in profession onely, wee must bring into familiar and constant practise, as in this duty of loue wee must loue brotherly without dissimulation, wee must loue one another with a pure hearte feruently wee must beare one anothers burthens, wee must not looke onely on our owne things, but allsoe on the things of our brethren, neither must wee think that the lord will beare with such faileings at our hands as hee dothe from those among whome wee haue liued, and that for 3 Reasons.

1. In regard of the more neare bond of mariage, betweene him and vs, wherein he hath taken vs to be his after a most strickt and peculiar manner which will make him the more Jealous of our loue and obedience soe he tells the people of Israell, you onely haue I knowne of all the families of the Earthe therefore will I punishe you for your Transgressions.

2ly, because the lord will be sanctified in them that come neare him. Wee know that there were many that corrupted the seruice of the Lord some setting vpp Alters before his owne, others offering both strange fire and strange Sacrifices allsoe; yet there came noe fire from heaven, or other sudden Judgement vpon them as did vpon Nadab and Abihu whoe yet wee may thinke did not sinne presumptuously.

3ly When God giues a speciall Commission he lookes to haue it stricktly obserued in every Article, when hee gaue Saule a Commission to destroy Amaleck hee indented with him vpon certaine Articles and because hee failed in one of the least, and that vpon a faire pretence, it lost him the kingdome, which should haue beene his reward, if hee had obserued his Commission: Thus stands the cause betweene God and vs, wee are entered into Covenant with him for this worke, wee haue taken out a Commission, the Lord hath giuen vs leaue to drawe our owne Articles wee haue professed to enterprise these Accions vpon these and these ends, wee haue herevpon besought him of favour and blessing: Now if the Lord shall please to heare vs, and

---

* The copyist wrote "consequence," above which a later hand has interlined "conscience."

bring vs in peace to the place wee desire, then hath hee ratified this Covenant and sealed our Commission, [and] will expect a strickt performance of the Articles contained in it, but if wee shall neglect the observacion of these Articles which are the ends wee haue propounded, and dissembling with our God, shall fall to embrace this present world and prosecute our carnall intencions, seekeing greate things for our selues and our posterity, the Lord will surely breake out in wrathe against vs be revenged of such a periured people and make vs knowe the price of the breache of such a Covenant.

Now the onely way to avoyde this shipwracke and to provide for our posterity is to followe the Counsell of Micah, to doe Justly, to loue mercy, to walke humbly with our God, for this end, wee must be knitt together in this worke as one man, wee must entertaine each other in brotherly Affeccion, wee must be willing to abridge our selues of our superfluities, for the supply of others necessities, wee must vphold a familiar Commerce together in all meekenes, gentlenes, patience and liberallity, wee must delight in eache other, make others Condicions our owne reioyce together, mourne together, labour, and suffer together, allwayes haueing before our eyes our Commission and Community in the worke, our Community as members of the same body, soe shall wee keepe the vnitie of the spirit in the bond of peace, the Lord will be our God and delight to dwell among vs, as his owne people and will commaund a blessing vpon vs in all our wayes, soe that wee shall see much more of his wisdome power goodnes and truthe then formerly wee haue beene acquainted with, wee shall finde that the God of Israell is among vs, when tenn of vs shall be able to resist a thousand of our enemies, when hee shall make vs a prayse and glory, that men shall say of succeeding plantacions: the lord make it like that of New England: for wee must Consider that wee shall be as a Citty vpon a Hill, the eies of all people are vppon vs; soe that if wee shall deale falsely with our god in this worke wee haue vndertaken and soe cause him to withdrawe his present help from vs, wee shall be made a story and a by-word through the world, wee shall open the mouthes of enemies to speake euill of the wayes of god and all professours for Gods sake; wee shall shame the faces of many of gods worthy seruants, and cause theire prayers to be turned into Cursses vpon vs till wee be consumed out of the good land whether wee are goeing: And to shutt vpp this discourse with that exhortacion of Moses that faithfull seruant of the Lord in his last farewell to Israell Deut. 30. Beloued there is now sett before vs life, and good, deathe and euill in that wee are Commaunded this day to loue the Lord our God, and to loue one another to walke in his wayes and to keepe his Commaundements and his Ordinance, and his lawes, and the Articles of our Covenant with him that wee may liue and be multiplyed, and that the Lord our God may blesse vs in the land whether wee goe to possesse it: But if our heartes shall turne away soe that wee will not obey, but shall be seduced and worshipp other Gods our pleasures, and proffitts, and serue them; it is propounded vnto vs this day, wee shall surely perishe out of the good Land whether wee passe over this vast Sea to possesse it;

> Therefore lett vs choose life,
> that wee, and our Seede,
> may liue; by obeyeing his
> voyce, and cleaueing to him,
> for hee is our life, and
> our prosperity.

4. Deputy Governor John Winthrop's Speech to the General Court, July 3, 1645

I suppose something may be expected from me, upon this charge that is befallen me, which moves me to speak now to you; yet I intend not to intermeddle in the proceedings of the court, or with any of the persons concerned therein. Only I bless God, that I see an issue of this troublesome business. I also acknowledge the justice of the court, and, for mine own part, I am well satisfied, I was publicly charged, and I am publicly and legally acquitted, which is all I did expect or desire. And though this be sufficient for my justification before men, yet not so before the God, who hath seen so much amiss in my dispensations (and even in this affair) as calls me to be humble. For to be publicly and criminally charged in this court, is matter of humiliation, (and I desire to make a right use of it,) notwithstanding I be thus acquitted. If her father had spit in her face, (saith the Lord concerning Miriam,) should she not have been ashamed seven days? Shame had lien upon her, whatever the occasion had been. I am unwilling to stay you from your urgent affairs, yet give me leave (upon this special occasion) to speak a little more to this assembly. It may be of some good use, to inform and rectify the judgments of some of the people, and may prevent such distempers as have arisen amongst us. The great questions that have troubled the country, are about the authority of the magistrates and the liberty of the people. It is yourselves who have called us to this office, and being called by you, we have our authority from God, in way of an ordinance, such as hath the image of God eminently stamped upon it, the contempt and violation whereof hath been vindicated with examples of divine vengeance. I entreat you to consider, that when you choose magistrates, you take them from among yourselves, men subject to like passions as you are. Therefore when you see infirmities in us, you should reflect upon your own, and that would make you bear the more with us, and not be severe censurers of the failings of your magistrates, when you have continual experience of the like infirmities in yourselves and others. We account him a good servant, who breaks not his covenant. The covenant between you and us is the oath you have taken of us, which is to this purpose, that we shall govern you and judge your causes by the rules of God's laws and our own, according to our best skill. When you agree with a workman to build you a ship or house, etc., he undertakes as well for his skill as for his faithfulness, for it is his profession, and you pay him for both. But when you call one to be a magistrate, he doth not profess nor undertake to have sufficient skill for that office, nor can you furnish him with gifts, etc., therefore you must run the hazard of his skill and ability. But if he fail in faithfulness, which by his oath he is bound unto, that he must answer for. If it fall out that the case be clear to common apprehension, and the rule clear also, if he transgress here, the error is not in the skill, but in the evil of the will: it must be required of him. But if the case be doubtful, or the rule doubtful, to men of such understanding and parts as your magistrates are, if your magistrates should err here, yourselves must bear it.

For the other point concerning liberty, I observe a great mistake in the country about that. There is a twofold liberty, natural (I mean as our nature is now corrupt) and civil or federal. The first is common to man with beasts and other creatures. By this, man, as he stands in relation to man simply, hath liberty to do what he lists; it is a liberty to evil as well as to good. This liberty is incompatible and inconsistent with authority, and cannot endure the least restraint of the most just authority. The exercise and maintaining of this liberty makes men grow more evil, and in time to be worse than brute beasts: omnes sumus licentia deteriores. This is that great enemy of truth and peace, that wild beast, which all the ordinances of God are bent against, to restrain and subdue it. The other kind of liberty I call civil or federal, it may also be termed moral, in reference to the covenant between God and man, in the moral law, and the politic covenants and constitutions, amongst men themselves. This liberty is the proper end and object of authority, and cannot subsist without it; and it is a liberty to that only which is good, just, and honest. This liberty you are to stand for, with the hazard (not only of your goods, but) of your lives, if need be. Whatsoever crosseth this, is not authority, but a distemper thereof. This liberty is maintained and exercised in a way of subjection to authority; it is of the same kind of liberty wherewith Christ hath made us free. The woman's own choice makes such a man her husband; yet being so chosen, he is her lord, and she is to be subject to him, yet in a way of liberty, not of bondage; and a true wife accounts her subjection her honor and freedom, and would not think her condition safe and free, but in her subjection to her husband's authority. Such is the liberty of the church under the authority of Christ, her king and husband; his yoke is so easy and sweet to her as a bride's ornaments; and if through frowardness or wantonness, etc., she shake it off, at any time, she is at no rest in her spirit, until she take it up again; and whether her lord smiles upon her, and embraceth her in his arms, or whether he frowns, or rebukes, or smites her, she apprehends the sweetness of his love in all, and is refreshed, supported, and instructed by every such dispensation of his authority over her. On the other side, ye know who they are that complain of this yoke and say, let us break their bands, etc., we will not have this man to rule over us. Even so, brethren, it will be between you and your magistrates. If you stand for your natural corrupt liberties, and will do what is good in your own eyes, you will not endure the least weight of authority, but will murmur, and oppose, and be always striving to shake off that yoke; but if you will be satisfied to enjoy such civil and lawful liberties, such as Christ allows you, then will you quietly and cheerfully submit unto that authority which is set over you, in all the administrations of it, for your good. Wherein, if we fail at any time, we hope we shall be willing (by God's assistance) to hearken to good advice from any of you, or in any other way of God; so shall your liberties be preserved, in upholding the honor and power of authority amongst you.

THE IDEA OF THE COVENANT

Peter Bulkeley, one of the founders and the leading minister of the back-country settlement of Concord from 1630 until his death in 1659, was one of the most thoughtful and most important New England theologians. The document printed below is from his book The Gospel-Covenant (London, 1646). Entitled "New England and Her Covenant," it outlines the entire covenant relationship and reinforces the remarks of Winthrop in the previous selection.

PETER BULKELEY ON THE COVENANT

New England and Her Covenant

And thou, New England, which art exalted in privileges of the Gospel above many other people, know thou the time of thy visitation, and consider the great things the Lord hath done for thee. The Gospel hath free passage in all

---

Edmund Clarence Stedman and Ellen Mackay Hutchinson, eds., *A Library of American Literature from the Earliest Settlement to the Present Time* (New York, Charles L. Webster and Co., 1891), I, pp. 244–245.

places where thou dwellest; oh that it might be glorified also by thee! Thou enjoyest many faithful witnesses, which have testified unto thee the Gospel of the grace of God. Thou hast many bright stars shining in thy firmament to give thee the knowledge of salvation from on high, to guide thy feet in the way of peace. Be not high-minded, because of thy privileges, but fear because of thy danger. The more thou hast committed unto thee, the more thou must account for. No people's account will be heavier than thine if thou do not walk worthy of the means of thy salvation. The Lord looks for more from thee than from other people; more zeal for God, more love to his truth, more justice and equity in thy ways. Thou shouldst be a special people, an only people, none like thee in all the earth; oh, be so in loving the Gospel and Ministers of it, having them in singular love for their work's sake. Glorify thou that word of the Lord, which hath glorified thee. Take heed lest for neglect of either God remove thy candlestick out of the midst of thee; lest being now as a city upon an hill which many seek unto, thou be left like a beacon upon the top of a mountain desolate and forsaken. If we walk unworthy of the Gospel brought unto us, the greater our mercy hath been in the enjoying of it, the greater will our judgment be for the contempt. Be instructed and take heed.

The things of the covenant are great things. Princes and monarchs when they enter into covenant with other nations, they do not make covenants about children's toys and light matters, but such as concern the welfare of the kingdom; so when the great Monarch of heaven and earth enters into covenant with us, it is about the great things of our salvation, the great things of heaven, yea, of God himself. The covenant is full of blessings, it is a rich store-house, replenished with all manner of blessings. It is not dry nor barren, but like the fat olive or fruitful vine the fruit whereof cheers the heart of God and man. God himself is delighted in the communication of his grace to his people; and they are delighted with the participation of his grace from him. The covenant is a tree of life to those that feed upon it; they shall live forever. It is a well of salvation. It's a fountain of good things to satisfy every thirsty soul. It is a treasure full of goods.

Here is unsearchable riches in this covenant, which can never be emptied nor come to an end. Our finite narrow understandings can never apprehend the infinite grace this covenant contains no more than an egg-shell is able to contain the water of the whole sea. Yet it is not in vain to consider them as we are able to express them, though they be above that which we are able to speak or think. As Moses, though he could not see God's face, nor discern his glory to the full, yet he was permitted to see his back parts; so we may take a little view of the blessings promised, though the full cannot be seen. As in a map, we have the bounds of a Lordship set forth, the rivers, woods, meadows, pastures, etc. These are seen darkly in the map, but they are nothing to that when they are seen in their own beauty and greenness: to see the silver streams in the rivers, the beautiful woods, the large meadows, fat pastures, and goodly orchards, which are far more excellent in themselves, than when they are seen in the map. So we can show you but a little map of those glorious things which the covenant contains; but by that little you do see, you may be raised up to the consideration of the things that are not seen, but are to be revealed in due time.

THE ANTINOMIAN CRISIS

In 1637 Anne Hutchinson was brought before the General Court in a trial presided over by Governor John Winthrop. She had been accused of holding to the doctrine of "enthusiasm" or the idea of personal, private divine inspiration. A small group of followers had gathered around her, including the influential minister John Cotton. Anne Hutchinson's doctrines were, of course, a threat to established ministerial authority, since if each person were free to follow his own "inner light," then there would be no need of ministerial guidance and no need of a theocratic state. Without proper communal piety, the state would fall apart, the holy mission would fail, and God's wrath would descend upon New England for failure to keep the covenant. This, at least, was Winthrop's reasoning, and there is no doubt but what he was a sincere man. Anne Hutchinson was, of course, equally sincere, as her acceptance of suffering and banishment indicates. During the trial John Cotton, on whom Anne Hutchinson had depended for support, disavowed his connection with her and denied any sympathy for her doctrines. Though the doctrines on which the controversy centered seem somewhat obscure today, the Antinomian Crisis aroused the emotions of the entire colony because it threatened the very basis of its existence.

The version of Anne Hutchinson's trial printed below is an unusual one taken from the Tory Governor Thomas Hutchinson's "Appendix" to The History of the Colony of Massachusetts Bay. *It is based, in Governor Hutchinson's words, on "An ancient manuscript of the trial at large, having been preserved. . . ." Could this have been a trial transcript preserved by a member of Anne Hutchinson's own family? The student should compare this version with that contained in John Winthrop's* The History of New England . . . *(James Savage, ed.).*

GOVERNOR THOMAS HUTCHINSON'S VERSION
OF THE TRIAL OF ANNE HUTCHINSON

The Examination of Mrs. Anne Hutchinson at the Court of Newtown

Mr. Winthrop, governor. Mrs. Hutchinson, you are called here as one of those that have troubled the peace of the commonwealth and the churches here; you are known to be a woman that hath had a great share in the promoting and divulging of those opinions that are causes of this trouble, and to be nearly joined not only in affinity and affection with some of those the court had taken notice of and passed censure upon, but you have spoken divers things as we have been informed very prejudicial to the honour of the churches and ministers thereof, and you have maintained a meeting and an assembly in your house that hath been condemned by the general assembly as a thing not tolerable nor comely in the sight of God nor fitting for your sex, and notwithstanding that was cried down you have continued the same, therefore we have thought good to send for you to understand how things are, that if you be in an erroneous way we may reduce you that so you may become a profitable member here among us, otherwise if you be obstinate in your course that then the court may take such course that you may trouble us no further, therefore I would intreat you to express whether you do not assent and hold in practice to those opinions and factions that have been handled in court already, that is to say, whether you do not justify Mr. Wheelwright's sermon and the petition.

Mrs. Hutchinson. I am called here to answer before you but I hear no things laid to my charge.

Gov. I have told you some already and more I can tell you. (Mrs. H.) Name one Sir.

Gov. Have I not named some already?

Mrs. H. What have I said or done?

Gov. Why for your doings, this you did harbour and countenance those that are parties in this faction that you have heard of. (Mrs. H.) That's matter of conscience, Sir.

Gov. Your conscience you must keep or it must be kept for you.

Mrs. H. I pray Sir prove it that I said they preached nothing but a covenant of works.

Dep. Gov. Nothing but a covenant of works, why a Jesuit may preach truth sometimes.

Mrs. H. Did I ever say they preached a covenant of works then?

The Publications of the Prince Society (Boston, 1894), XXI, pp. 235–236, 244, 246–247.

Dep. Gov. If they do not preach a covenant of grace clearly, then they preach a covenant of works.

Mrs. H. No Sir, one may preach a covenant of grace more clearly than another, so I said.

D. Gov. We are not upon that now but upon position.

Mrs. H. Prove this then Sir that you say I said.

D. Gov. When they do preach a covenant of works do they preach truth?

Mrs. H. Yes Sir, but when they preach a covenant of works for salvation, that is not truth.

D. Gov. I do but ask you this, when the ministers do preach a covenant of works do they preach a way of salvation?

Mrs. H. I did not come hither to answer to questions of that sort.

D. Gov. Because you will deny the thing.

Mrs. H. Ey, but that is to be proved first.

D. Gov. I will make it plain that you did say that the ministers did preach a covenant of works.

Mrs. H. I deny that.

D. Gov. And that you said they were not able ministers of the new testament, but Mr. Cotton only.

Mrs. H. If ever I spake that I proved it by God's word.

Court. Very well, very well. . . .

Mr. Peters. We shall give you a fair account of what was said and desire that we may not be thought to come as informers against the gentlewoman, but as it may be serviceable for the country and our posterity to give you a brief account. This gentlewoman went under suspicion not only from her landing, that she was a woman not only difficult in her opinions, but also of an intemperate spirit. What was done at her landing I do not well remember, but assoon as Mr. Vane and ourselves came this controversy began yet it did reflect upon Mrs. Hutchinson and some of our brethren had dealt with her and it so fell out that some of our ministry doth suffer as if it were not according to the gospel and as if we taught a covenant of works instead of a covenant of grace. Upon these and the like we did address ourselves to the teacher of that church, and the court then assembled being sensible of these things, and this gentlewoman being as we understood a chief agent, our desire to the teacher was to tell us wherein the difference lay between him and us, for the spring did then arise as we did conceive from this gentlewoman, and so we told him. He said that he thought it not according to God to commend this to the magistrates but to take some other course, and so going on in the discourse we thought it good to send for this gentlewoman, and she willingly came, and at the very first we gave her notice that such reports there were that she did conceive our ministry to be different from the ministry of the gospel, and that we taught a covenant of works, &c. and this was her table talk, and therefore we desired her to clear herself and deal plainly. She was very tender at the first. Some of our brethren did desire to put this upon proof, and then her words upon that were The fear of man is a snare why should I be afraid. These were her words. I did then take upon me to ask her this question. What difference do you conceive to be between your teacher and us? She did not request us that we should preserve her from danger or that we should be silent. Briefly, she told me there was a wide and a broad difference between our brother Mr. Cotton and our selves. I desired to know the difference. She answered that he preaches the covenant of grace and you the covenant of works and that you are not able ministers of the new testament and know no more than the apostles did before the resurrection of Christ. I did then put it to her, What do you conceive of such a brother? She answered he had not the seal of the spirit. And other things we asked her but generally the frame of her course was this, that she did conceive that we were not able ministers of the gospel. And that day being past our brother Cotton was sorry that she should lay us under a covenant of works, and could have wished she had not done so. The elders being there present we did charge them with her, and the teacher of the place said they would speak further with her, and after some time she answered that we were gone as far as the apostles were before Christ's ascension. And since that we have gone with tears some of us to her.

Mrs. H. If our pastor would shew his writings you should see what I said, and that many things are not so as is reported.

THE CAMBRIDGE PLATFORM

In 1646, because of rumblings of dissatisfaction among freemen and church members in the Colony, the Puritans were forced to revise the structural relationships of church and state. The Cambridge Platform, finally ratified in 1651, represents a redefinition and a clarification of the relative positions of church and state in Massachusetts Bay. Eleven years later the whole structure of church membership had to be revised to accommodate an indifferent younger generation. The Half-Way Covenant of 1662, together with the Cambridge Platform printed below, represent two of the most important Puritan adjustments to seventeenth-century realities.

Chap. XVII. Of the Civil Magistrates power in Matters Ecclesiastical

It is lawfull, profitable. & necessary for christians to gather themselves into Church estate, and therin to exercise all the ordinances of christ according unto the word, although the consent of Magistrate could not be had therunto, because the Apostles & christians in their time did frequently thus practise, when the Magistrates being all of them Jewish or pagan, & mostly persecuting enemies, would give no countenance or consent to such matters.

2 Church-government stands in no opposition to civil govenment of common-welths, nor any intrencheth upon the authority of Civil Magistrates in their jurisdictions; nor any whit weakneth their hands in governing; but rather strengthneth them, & furthereth the people in yielding more hearty & conscionable obedience unto them, whatsoever some ill affected persons to the wayes of Christ have suggested, to alienate the affections of Kings & Princes from the ordinances of Christ; as if the kingdome of Christ in his church could not rise & stand, without the falling & weakning of their government, which is also of Christ: wheras the contrary is most true, that they may both stand together & flourish the one being helpfull unto the other, in their distinct & due administrations.

3 The powr & authority of Magistrates is not for the restraining of churches, or any other good workes, but for helping in & furthering therof; & therfore the consent & countenance of Magistrates when it may be had, is not to be sleighted, or lightly esteemed; but on the contrary; it is part of that honour due to christian Magistrates to desire & crave their consent & approbation therin: which being obtayned, the churches may then proceed in their way with much more encouragement, & comfort.

4 It is not in the powr of Magistrates to compell their subjects to become church-members, & to partake at the Lords table: for the priests are reproved, that brought unworthy ones into the sanctuarie: then, as it was unlawfull for the preists, so it is as unlawfull to be done by civil Magistrates. Those whom the church is to cast out if they were in, the Magistrate ought not to thrust into the church, nor to hold them therin.

Williston Walker, *The Creeds and Platforms of Congregationalism* (New York, Charles Scribner's Sons, 1893), pp. 194–197.

5   As it is unlawfull for church-officers to meddle with the sword of the Magistrate, so it is unlawfull for the Magistrate to meddle with the work proper to church-officers. the Acts of Moses & David, who were not only Princes, but Prophets, were extraordinary; therfore not imitable. Against such usurpation the Lord witnessed, by smiting Uzziah with leprosie, for presuming to offer incense

6   It is the duty of the Magistrate, to take care of matters of religion, & to improve his civil authority for the observing of the duties commanded in the first, as well as for observing of the duties commanded in the second table. They are called Gods. The end of the Magistrates office, is not only the quiet & peaceable life of the subject, in matters of righteousness & honesty, but also in matters of godliness, yea of all godliness. Moses, Joshua, David, Soloman, Asa, Jehoshaphat, Hezekiah, Josiah, are much commended by the Holy Ghost, for the putting forth their authority in matters of religion: on the contrary, such Kings as have been fayling this way, are frequently taxed & reproved by the Lord. & not only the Kings of Judah, but also Job, Nehemiah, the king of Niniveh, Darius, Artaxerxes, Nebucadnezar, whom none looked at as types of Christ, (thouh were it soe, there were no place for any just objection,) are commended in the book of God, for exercising their authority this way.

7   The object of the powr of the Magistrate, are not things meerly inward, & so not subject to his cognisance & view, as unbeleife hardness of heart, erronious opinions not vented; but only such things as are acted by the outward man; neither is their powr to be exercised, in commanding such acts of the outward man, & punishing the neglect therof, as are but meer inventions, & devices of men; but about such acts, as are commanded & forbidden in the word; yea such as the word doth clearly determine, though not alwayes clearly to the judgment of the Magistrate or others, yet clearly in it selfe. In these he of right ought to putt forth his authority, though oft-times actually he doth it not.

8   Idolatry, Blasphemy, Heresy, venting corrupt & pernicious opinions, that destroy the foundation, open contempt of the word preached, prophanation of the Lords day, disturbing the peaceable administration & exercise of the worship & holy things of God, & the like, are to be restrayned, & punished by civil authority.

9   If any church one or more shall grow schismaticall, rending it self from the communion of other churches, or shall walke incorrigibly or obstinately in any corrupt way of their own, contrary to the rule of the word; in such case, the Magistrate is to put forth his coercive powr, as the matter shall require. The tribes on this side Jordan intended to make warr against the other tribes, for building the altar of witness, whom they suspected to have turned away therin from following of the Lord.

THE CHRISTIAN CALLING

The idea of the Christian calling—to find some worldly role and pursue it well according to one's God-given talents, for the glory of God—was an important part of Puritan doctrine. It forms the basis for what has come to be called "the Protestant ethic." It could be and usually was conducive to a high degree of individualism. Each man, uncertain as to whether he was saved or damned, took success in worldly pursuits as a sign of God's favor. And so the Puritan pursued worldly success aggressively and competitively. This competitive spirit was one more factor that militated against the success of the original idea of the "holy community."

The selection below is from a sermon by John Cotton, one of the most important Puritan theologians.

JOHN COTTON ON PURITAN ECONOMIC AND SOCIAL IDEALS

Wee are now to speake of living by faith in our outward and temporall life: now our outward and temporall life is twofold, which wee live in the flesh. It is either a civill, or a naturall life, for both these lives we live, and they are different the one from the other: Civill life is that whereby we live, as members of this or that City, or Town, or Commonwealth, in this or that particular vocation and calling.

Naturall life I call that, by which we doe live this bodily life, I meane, by which we live a life of sense, by which we eate and drinke, by which we goe through all conditions, from our birth to our grave, by which we live, and move, and have our being. And now both these a justified person lives by faith; To begin with the former.

A true beleeving Christian, a justified person, hee lives in his vocation by his faith.

Not onely my spirituall life, but even my Civill life in this world, all the life I live, is by the faith of the Son of God: he exempts no life from the agency of his faith, whether he live as a Christian man, or as a member of this or that Church, or Commonwealth, he doth it all by the faith of the Son of God.

Perry Miller and Thomas Johnson, eds., *The Puritans* (New York, Harper and Row, 1963), pp. 319–324, 326. This document has been abridged in the present work as indicated by the ellipses.

Now for opening this point, let me shew you what are those severall acts of faith which it puts forth about our occasions, and vocations, that so we may live in Gods sight therein.

First, Faith drawes the heart of a Christian to live in some warrantable calling; as soone as ever a man begins to looke towards God, and the wayes of his grace, he will not rest, till he find out some warrantable Calling and imployment: An instance you have in the Prodigall son, that after he had received & spent his portion in vanity, and when being pinched, he came home to himself, & comming home to his Father, the very next thing after confession and repentance of his sin, the very next petition he makes, is, *Make mee one of thy hired servants;* next after desire of pardon of sin, then put me into some calling, though it be but of an hired servant, wherein he may bring in God any service; A Christian would no sooner have his sinne pardoned, then his estate to be setled in some good calling, though not as a mercenary slave, but he would offer it up to God as a free-will Offering, he would have his condition and heart setled in Gods peace, but his life setled in a good calling, though it be but of a day-labourer, yet make me as one that may doe thee some service. . . .

Now more particularly, faith doth warily observe the warrantablenesse of its calling.

Three things doth faith finde in a particular calling.

First, It hath a care that it be a *warrantable* calling, wherein we may not onely aime at our own, but at the publike good, that is a warrantable calling, *Seek not every man his owne things, but every man the good of his brother,* 1 Cor. 10. 24. Phil. 2. 4. Seek one anothers welfare; faith works all by love, *Gal.* 5. 6. And therefore it will not think it hath a comfortable calling, unlesse it will not onely serve his own turne, but the turn of other men. Bees will not suffer drones among them, but if they lay up any thing, it shall be for them that cannot work; he would see that his calling should tend to publique good.

Secondly, Another thing to make a calling warrantable, is, when God gives a man *gifts* for it, that he is acquainted with the mystery of it, and hath gifts of body and minde sutable to it: *Prov.* 16. 20. *He that understands a matter shall finde good;* He that understands his businesse wisely. God leads him on to that calling, 1 Cor. 7. 17. To shew you that when God hath called me to a place, he hath given me some gifts fit for that place, especially, if the place be sutable and fitted to me and my best gifts; for God would not have a man to receive five Talents, and gaine but two, he would have his best gifts improved to the best advantage.

Thirdly, That which makes a calling warrantable, is, when it is attained unto by warrantable and direct *meanes,* when a man enterprises not a calling, but in the use of such meanes as he may see Gods providence leading him to it. . . .

2. Another work of faith, about a mans vocation and calling, when faith hath made choyce of a warrantable calling, then he *depends* upon God for the quickning, and sharpning of his gifts in that calling, and yet depends not upon his gifts for the going through his calling, but upon God that gave him those gifts, yea hee depends on God for the use of them in his calling; faith saith not, Give me such a calling and turne me loose to it; but faith lookes up to heaven for skill and ability, though strong and able, yet it looks at all its abilities but as a dead work, as like braided wares in a shop, as such as will be lost and rust, unlesse God refresh and renue breath in them. . . .

Thirdly, We live by faith in our vocations, in that faith, *in serving God, serves men, and in serving men, serves God*. . . .

Fourthly, Another act of faith about a mans vocation is this; It *encourageth* a man in his calling to the most homeliest, and difficultest, and most dangerous things his calling can lead and expose himselfe to; if faith apprehend this or that to be the way of my calling, it encourages me to it, though it be never so *homely*, and *difficult*, and *dangerous*. . . .

Now there are three sorts of burthens that befall a man in his calling.

1. *Care about the successe of it*; and for this faith casts its care upon God. . . .

2. A second burthen, is *feare of danger* that may befall us therein from the hand of man. . . .

3. Another burthen, is the burthen of *injuries*, which befalls a man in his calling. . . .

Sixtly, Faith hath another act about a mans vocation, and that is, it takes *all successes* that befall him in his calling with *moderation*, hee equally beares good and evill successes as God shall dispense them to him. . . .

Seventhly, The last work which faith puts forth about a mans calling, is this, faith with boldnesse *resignes up* his calling into the hands of God or man; when ever God calls a man to lay downe his calling, when his work is finished, herein the sons of God farre exceed the sons of men; another man when his calling comes to bee removed from him, hee is much ashamed, and much afraid, but if a Christian man be to forgoe his calling, he layes it downe with comfort and boldnesse, in the sight of God and man. . . .

It is an Use of instruction to every Christian soule that desires to walke by faith in his calling, If thou wouldst live a lively life, and have thy soule and body to prosper in thy calling, labour then to get into a good calling, and therein live to the good of others; take up no calling, but that thou hast understanding in, and never take it unlesse thou mayest have it by lawfull and just meanes, and when thou hast it, serve God in thy calling, and doe it with cheerfulnesse, and faithfulnesse, and an heavenly minde; and in difficulties and dangers, cast thy cares and feares upon God, and see if he will not beare them for thee; and frame thy heart to this heavenly moderation in all successes to sanctifie Gods name; and if the houre and power of darknesse come, that thou beest to resigne up thy calling, let it bee enough that conscience may witnesse to thee, that thou hast not sought thy selfe, nor this world, but hast wrought the Lords workes; thou mayest then have comfort in it, both before God and men. . . .

THE PURITAN'S MORAL DECATHLON

The Puritan had to do more than simply follow his calling. Every day saw him in the throes of an inward struggle with his conscience, trying to be worthy of salvation but never quite sure that he was. If he could not attain "sainthood" by good works, he could at least prepare himself to attain salvation by repressing all evil tendencies within himself.

Repression is indeed the key word to describe Michael Wigglesworth. Most famous as the author of the sulfurous poem Day of Doom *(1662), Wigglesworth was a Harvard graduate and a teacher at that institution, and eventually refused the presidency of the College. Among his other works was the popular* Meat out of the Eater; or Meditations concerning the Necessity, End and Usefulness of Affections unto God's Children. All tending to Prepare them for and Comfort them under the Cross *(1669). Like many Puritans, he kept a diary in which he analyzed, blow by blow, his bouts with the devil of temptation. A selection from his diary is included below. One cannot help being struck by his sincere devotion to goodness against what, for him, must have been tremendous odds. In these selections Wigglesworth is to be seen variously involved in self-denigration and praying to God to forgive the backsliding of his Harvard students. He appears to have had a severe problem with "carnal lusts" to the point where he feared that God had taken vengeance upon him by inflicting him with a social disease. This problem he solved by the simple expedient of marriage, as described in the document below. Most interesting is his chart of sins, which reminds us of similar charts made by Benjamin Franklin nearly a century later. Though Puritan theology was in its death throes, Puritan morality and guilt were to persist far into the future of American life.*

MICHAEL WIGGLESWORTH'S DIARY

F. March. 1

On the lecture day the Lord discover'd to me more of the vileness of my whoarish departures from god and inordinate taking content in the creature and the secret weariness of my heart of that spiritual duty of meditation, when the Lord was giving me sweet communion with himself on the last sabbath day at night. My soul even trembles at the horribleness of those my iniquitys so fearfully aggravated. and I am sensible of my desert and therefore affraid that the Lord should forsake me, and leav me to my lusts, and sins and to dishonour him.

Ah! moreover I cannot seek after future settlement without carnal aimes. Lord that it might be possible with the (all things I know are possible) to pardon me the cheef of sinners, and to heal my backslidings O when shall it once be. Say amen to my groanings after thee, and strengthen me with strength in my soul that I may follow hard after thee. And let me see and enjoy, and rest satisfy'd with thee and thy love as a full portion: subdue this untowardness and unconquerable enmity of heart against thy will, that I may become one of thy willing people rejoycing to work righteousness and to endeavour that others may do so to.

[March 5] On the sabbath day morning I was somewhat affraid lest my soul never rested in christ, or took up satisfaction in christ alone. the Lord helpt me over these fears by reading in Mr shepard's sound Beleever, in that 1: I dayly war and wrestle against a heart that is resting any where but in christ. 2ly because my wandrings make for my further establishment and closer cleaving to christ; God sendeth vexation in the creature and maketh me to seek and find more abundant sweetness in himself. so that I concluded christ was mine, and all spiritual blessings in him according to Mr Oakes his text out of Ephesians 1.3. yet I found so much unbeleef that I could not make it real to me, and so much sensuality that I could not se the glory of this priviledge and rejoyce in it, as we were exhorted. I found also a multitude of vayn thoughts, and neglected to go and reprove some carnal mirth in the lowest Chamber til it was too late, which I pray god to pardon.

[March 6] Stil I find my whoarish affections forsaking the sweet fountain, setting light by him, and digging broken cisterns. Therefore the Lord goeth on to smite me, in the stubborness of my pupils after all the warnings given them; And I goe on frowardly; being quite overcome of anger when they came

Michael Wigglesworth, *The Diary of Michael Wigglesworth, 1653–1657*, Edmund Morgan, ed. (New York, Harper and Row, 1965), pp. 68–69, 76–77, 84–88. Reprinted by permission of the Colonial Society of Massachusetts. The selections originally appeared in Volume 35 of the Society's Publications. The footnotes are those of Edmund Morgan.

not to recite, almost out of patience. thus Lord I am that sinner that destroy's much good by adding sin to sin. I ly down in my shame before the, and acknowledge that the Lord is righteous; but O let not thy own work fall to ground, but turn their hearts, o Lord, who can do it as thou turnest the rivers of water.

[March 7] I was much perplexed in mind with many thoughts to and fro, about leaving the colledge, one while ready to resolv upon it almost, and quite another way; and I know not what to do, how to liue here and keep a good conscience because my hands are bound in point of reforming disorders; my owne weakness and pupils froward negligence in the Hebrew stil much exercise me. yet for all this trouble god hath bin with me in my personal studys; for this day I began and finished all that part of my synopsis which treats about method. Blessed be god whose strength is perfected in weakness.

[March 8] *Pride estrangement of heart from God and outgoing after the creature with some stirrings of carnal lusts this day which I am afraid of Notwithstanding   cant get my heart so to loathe as I would   O Lord leave me not to return with the sow to her wallowing in the mire   Let me not live rather than live in my lusts*

The thursday I went to Boston and from thens to Mr Butlers he being married. There I found my heart secretly departing from god hankering after the creature. but at Boston lecture and at a private meeting at Mr Butlers god did in some measure awaken and recal my straying affections . . .

[August 5] But ah how apt am I to kick with the heel Jesurun like and lightly to esteem the rock of my salvation? how soon haue I forgotten his wonderful works? A mind distracted with a thousand vanitys sabbath dayes and week days when I should be musing off the things of god But where is my sorrow and bitter mourning for these prophanations of gods ordinances? a thing so grievous to my God. It hath bin some grief to me that I am so unprofitable a servant, that I cannot serv god in my calling aiming at his glory, and doing it as his work. I haue begged this mercy but alas! I cannot attain it, but I lose myself and my love to god amidst my multitude of occasions. My heart is hurried now this way, now that way by divers lusts; one while anxiously sollicitous, another while pleasing my self with this or that creature, this or that project, but ah! where is my walking with god, and rejoycing in the light of his countenance? And now good Lord haue mercy on me! how unfit am I to sanctify a sabbath with such a carnal heart, such dead and dul affections, such distracting thoughts as posses and fill my mind, such a faint and feeble body? And how much more unfit to partake of a sacrament? I am affraid I shall abuse it: at least get no good by it, But the same carnal, secure, vain sensual, slouthful, proud, unbeleiving, unthankful, unfruitfull frame remain in me still. He also (even the sonns of God) is flesh; this is that which grieveth the Lord at the heart. such an one am I: oh! that I could relent and repent with hearty sorrow. And when shall it be otherwise good Lord! when shall it once be? Thy ordinances are of thyne own appointing and in them thou wilt be sought; and wilt thou not be found? Is it invain to come to sacraments and believ on, and feed upon christ as given by thy self? I know it is not invain: though my sins be not yet subdued, though my wounds are yet unhealed. faithful is he who hath promised and will perform it, though I be vile. I feel dayly a spirit of whoardom in the midst of me, a heart revolting from god to the other things. But yet verily Living and dying thou art my hope, o do not fail me utterly; forsake me not o my God; but uphold me by thy right hand in following hard after thee; and let me find that it is not invain to wait upon thee in ways of thy own appointment.

September 26.

upon examination before the Lord supper I find

1: A loose and common heart that loveth vanity and frothyness.

2. A prophane heart appearing in { Distracting thoughts in holy dutys / wearines of them through / slouth and carnality

3. A proud heart.
4. An unbelieving heart. which questeons Gods love, which cannot wait his time which cannot trust his providence without distracting cares and overwhelming disquietments.
5. An hard heart that cannot be so deeply affected with my sins and spiritual wants, as with my outward troubles this maketh me affraid.
6: A sensual. heart that sometimes can se no glory in heavenly things, no nor in heaven it self.
7ly An unthankful heart
8 A heart full of spiritual whoardoms revolting from the Lord to some vanity [or] other every day

[March 31, 1655] Much pride, A common heart (sitting loos from god, not savouring the service of god) carnal lusts stirring and prevalent, are the Plagues that discover themselves this week. I loath and abhor judge and condemn my self for these. I fear and tremble lest the Lord should depart away from me, as I deserv and then woe to me! when the Lord departs away, besides whom miserable comforters are all my comforts. But who is a god like thee? that pardons iniquity and passeth by &c oh Pardon all the multitudinous evils thou seest in me in the multitude of thy mercys. Pardon my inordinate affections to this world or any thing therein. Pardon my unbeleif and unnecessary disquieting cares. Pardon my distemper'd passions. Pardon my want of due watchfulnes and care against these or any other evils for thy sons sake. Amen. I receiv'd letters from Rowley this week wherein I perceiv that my friends there be wel, and the heart of my cousen (after myne received) is toward me as before. Blessed be the good name of my god who hath so far heard prayer, as to carry my letters safe thither, to giue them so good acceptance, to return me an answer, whereby I perceiv it is my way to go down speedily into the Bay. And what further to attend for the present I see not, but I hope the Lord wil direct when I come there. The Lord in mercy make me desirous as formerly to attend onely my duty and leav the rest to him. Lord increas my faith, and patience.

I got Mr Newton* to pray with me on thursday night after a relation of the present difficultys which surround me wherewith he was much affected. Lord hear in heaven and give answers of peace.

[April 4] At the lecture out of Job. 14.2. Many cordials being propounded to strengthen the hearts of gods people Against bodily infirmitys and death it self: Me thoughts I felt an unspeakable unwortynes of any intrest in god and his grace at such times of need, because of the unspeakable vilenes of my heart which I feel, o that I could feel it more. Ah pride! frothines I haue not matter for good discours, nor a heart unto it. it grieveth me to think of my folly and madnes. ah! I do serv my self and not my god in all I doe.

On the sabbath day morning, (having prepared to preach the 2 dayes before and fully intending it) I awaked with a very sore throat, so that I perceived my mouth was stop't for that day. Mr stow being in the town by a providence supply'd the place. It was a sacrament day and I ventured out (hooded) before noon, but afternoon *again* durst not. I kept hous all that week, being much pained in swallowing my spittle, and so overflowed with rhewm that If I forbare spitting my throat grew painful with drines. This ilnes marrd my stomack utterly, (especially by the nauseous tast of the fleum at the beginning and latter end thereof) mightily enfeebled my spirits, wasted my moysture and made me feaverish. I used principally burnt wine, which almost set me in a swoon divers times, yet I think did me good. At the latter end of the week growing something better I ventured out to wethersfield hooded. whence I had a hors brought me according to agreement on munday and [April 17] on Tuesday I set forth for the Bay. The motives that hasten'd me were these. 1. I found my ilnes continue and no means there to help me. 2ly I conceived journeying might do me good as much as physick, if I could keep from could. 3. To redeem the spring time for marrying or taking physick, or both. God brought me thorow comfortably in 2 dayes from springfield to Roxbury, much bettered (though wearied) with my journey. staying a day in the Bay and consulting with Mr Alcock (who advized to proceed with the busines of

---

* Roger Newton was minister at Farmington, Connecticut.

marriage In the 1st place) I reach't Rowley on the saturday. On munday ensueing I dined and discoursed with Mr Rogers about the great busines. He could by noe means concur with the other physicians in advizing first to marriage and afterward to taking physick, for many reasons by him alledged; but thought it meet 1. to rectify the habit of my body and afterward to proceed. I was distressed at the hearing of his opinion, because it stil made the case more difficult. I prayd to the god of heaven and such was his mercy to me, that after a little reasoning about the case, and fuller declaration of my ilness &c. Mr Rogers his mind was quite altered, and he declared himself free and ready to further the consummation thereof with all possible speed. And so he contrived the busines and wrought it with them whom it concerned, that it was then publish't, and I was to return again and be contracted the next friday sev'night. and so I left my friends with determination so to return. Yet after I was gone from thence. My own weakness (which formerly perplexed me at such times) setting in with Mr Rogers his scruples did much trouble me, and caus me to questeon, whither it were my way to marry, before the use of more means, and to run such a hazzard as that of my life and health without an apparent necessity, before I had tryed the utmost that physick could doe. I repaired to Mr Alcock with all speed again to speak with him and object unto him for my farther satisfaction.

1: He told me that he hoped my diseas might be cured by physick; but It would be a long and teadious and far more difficult cure, then he hoped it would be by marriage, and astringent cordials afterward. And he had no heart to go the farther way about when as he might haue a nearer way by providence offer'd him.

2: He told me divers experiences of the success of this cours in like distempers. An example of one just affected like my self before his marriage, who was grievously perplexed with it, yet went on with it and did very wel after, and hath divers children living at this day. And so of divers others who have taken this cours with good success.

3: He told me that mine was not vera Gon:* as he could prove nor the excretio (*which happened by the presence of such a friend*) seminis but quasi sudor partium genitatium: as a little alumn will caus the mouth to fil with water, so a little acrimony gathering there, causeth humours to flow thither amain, which might come away in great quantity, and yet there be plenty of veri seminis behind. And so I found it to be.

---

* The word intended here is obviously gonorrhea, but I have thought it best not to expand the abbreviation, because former accounts of Wigglesworth's life have professed to be mystified with regard to the disease of which Wigglesworth so frequently complains. It seems indisputable from the symptoms described and from this direct statement that Wigglesworth thought that he had gonorrhea. Whether his disease was actually gonorrhea, of course, no one can say.

4ly. He told me that which made me so fearful, made him fearles, and gave him the more hopes, that marriage would take away the caus of that distemper, which was naturalis impulsus seu instinctus irresistibilis.

These things together with the consideration. 1. of my unsettled condition wherein I cannot attend rules of Physick with any conveniency. 2ly off the great charge and expences I must be at for a continued cours of Physick and diet better than ordinary. 3ly of my inability with comfort and honesty to live long as I am single. 4ly off the little hopes to prevayl against rebellious nature, which is disquieted rather than overcome by physick in statu presenti. These things make it pretty clear to me that god calleth to a speedy change of my condition, which I therefore desire to attend as a duty that god calleth unto, leaving my life and health in his hands. And oh! that I had a meek spirit to submit to his good pleasure. A beleiving heart! and a judicious mind to see clearly that this is my way at all times

I went up at the time appointed and was contracted on friday (May   ) God made this journey more comfortable to me, refreshing me and cheering me among my dearest friends. yet with the admixture of the same affliction as formerly, though something moderated blessed be God! I was troubled to think that they were not willing to have the wedding before the election, and so to drive a month at least it may be two months because the magistrates would all be absent at that time. yet here again providence appeared sweetly in bowing their spirits to issue it within a fourtnight, and so before the Election; And all things we found conspiring to further our intendment, Taylors ready to do the work in time, merchants ready to take provisions for shopp commoditys, &c. blessed be god! who worketh all our works in us and for us. [May 18] oh! I am ashamed of my frothines and vanity and fruitless conversation, and sensuality and all those sins whereby I am offending so good a god. saturday. May

I was somewhat perplexed also at my return into the bay after my contraction, concerning the lawfulness of márrying with a Kinswoman, because the mothers sister is forbidden; now sister in scripture language is put for a Kinswoman sometimes. I spent some time about it and the Lord gaue me comfortable satisfaction in this point also, that my scruple was Invalid.

At the time appointed with fear and trembling I came to Rowley to be marryed. The great arguments unto me were, 1: Physicians counsel: 2ly the institution of marryage by god himself for the preservation of purity and chastity, which with most humble and hearty prayers I have begged and stil wil beg of the Lord. so that I went about the business which god call'd me to attend And consummated it now is by the will of god May 18. 1655. oh Lord! let my cry come up unto thee for all the blessings of a marryed estate, A heart sutable thereto, chastity especially thereby, and life and health if it be thy will. oh crown thy own ordinance with thy blessing, that it may appear it is not in vain to wait upon thee in the wayes of thy own appointment. *I feel the stirrings and strongly of my former distemper even after the use of marriage the next day which makes me exceeding afraid. I know not how to keep company with my dearest friend but it is with me as formerly in some days already.* oh pitty the poorest and vilest of thy creatures for the Lords sake, And let not thy servants be a curs each to other but a blessing in this new relation . . .

THE CHANGING NATURE OF NATURE

The latter half of the seventeenth century saw the emergence of a scientific revolution that culminated in the appearance of the Principia Mathematica of Sir Isaac Newton in 1687 and the publication just three years later of John Locke's Essay Concerning Human Understanding and his Two Treatises on Government. The cosmography of Newton helped sweep away the old Ramean and Platonic view of the world; it saw the universe not as emanations from the mind of God and his ever-present divine providence, but as a regularly working system of natural laws which the mind of a very astute man could discover.

Similarly Lockean psychology, posited on the idea of learning through empirical observation and the rational combination in the mind of facts derived by this process, helped turn the minds of men away from the mysterious and inscrutable mind of God to the regular laws of nature. One of these laws was deemed by Locke to be the natural rights of men. In his writings on natural rights, Locke was influenced by a German, Samuel von Pufendorf, whose Of Natural Law and Men (1672) Locke called "the best book of its kind." All these writings, from the scientific to the political, reinforced the tendencies which had been building for a long time toward individualism, or the idea of man as a discrete and irreducible natural unit. The impact of this kind of thinking, which helped to bring about the downfall of Puritanism, is nowhere better exemplified than in John Wise's A Vindication of the Government of New England's Churches published in 1717.

Wise was a minister in Ipswich, Massachusetts, and he wrote his treatise as part of his continuing struggle against the Mathers' hopeless efforts to regain centralized control over the churches of New England. Though his work was published long after the end of the seventeenth century, Wise, influenced by Pufendorf rather than by Locke, had fought a continuing battle against the attempts at political control of the churches by the Royal Governor, Sir Edmund Andros, and against the counterforce of the Mathers' ecclesiastical control since the end of the 1680's. His arguments reveal one more factor that brought about the downfall of New England Puritanism.

JOHN WISE AND NATURAL LAW

1. I shall disclose several Principles of Natural Knowledge; plainly discovering the Law of Nature; or the true sentiments of Natural Reason, with Respect to Mans Being and Government. And in this Essay I shall peculiarly confine the discourse to two heads, viz
    1. Of the Natural [in distinction to the Civil] and then,
    2. Of the Civil Being of Man. And I shall Principally take Baron *Puffendorff* for my Chief Guide and Spokes-man.
    1. I shall consider Man in a state of Natural Being, as a Free-Born Subject under the Crown of Heaven, and owing Homage to none but God himself. It is certain Civil Government in General, is a very Admirable Result of Providence, and an Incomparable Benefit to Man-kind, yet must needs be acknowledged to be the Effect of Humane Free-Compacts and not of Divine Institution; it is the Produce of Mans Reason, of Humane and Rational Combinations, and not from any direct Orders of Infinite Wisdom, in any positive Law wherein is drawn up this or that Scheme of Civil Government. Government [says the Lord *Warrington*] is necessary—in that no Society of Men can subsist without it; and that Particular Form of Government is necessary which best suits the Temper and Inclination of a People. Nothing can be Gods Ordinance, but what he has particularly Declared to be such; there is no particular Form of Civil Government described in Gods Word, neither does Nature prompt it. The Government of the *Jews* was changed five Times. Government is not formed by Nature, as other Births or Productions; If it were, it would be the same in all Countries; because Nature keeps the same Method, in the same thing, in all Climates. If a Common Wealth be changed into a Monarchy, is it Nature that forms, and brings forth the Monarch? Or if a Royal Family be wholly Extinct

John Wise, *A Vindication of the Government of New England's Churches*, Perry Miller, ed., facsimile edition [Scholars' Facsimiles and Reprints, Gainesville, Fla., 1958), pp. 32–36.

[as in *Noah's* Case, being not Heir Apparent from Descent from *Adam*] is it Nature that must go to work [with the King Bees, who themselves alone preserve the Royal Race in that Empire] to Breed a Monarch before the People can have a King, or a Government sent over them? And thus we must leave Kings to Resolve which is their best Title to their Crowns, whether Natural Right, or the Constitution of Government settled by Humane Compacts, under the Direction and Conduct of Reason. But to proceed under the head of a State of Natural Being, I shall more distinctly Explain the State of Humane Nature in its Original Capacity, as Man is placed on Earth by his Maker, and Cloathed with many Investitures, and Immunities which properly belong to Man separately considered. As,

1. The Prime Immunity in Mans State, is that he is most properly the Subject of the Law of Nature. He is the Favourite Animal on Earth; in that this Part of Gods Image, *viz.* Reason is Congenate with his Nature, wherein by a Law Immutable, Instampt upon his Frame, God has provided a Rule for Men in all their Actions, obliging each one to the performance of that which is Right, not only as to Justice, but likewise as to all other Moral Vertues, the which is nothing but the Dictate of Right Reason founded in the Soul of Man. . . . That which is to be drawn from Mans Reason, flowing from the true Current of that Faculty, when unperverted, may be said to be the Law of Nature; on which account, the Holy Scriptures declare it written on Mens hearts. For being indowed with a Soul, you may know from your self, how, and what you ought to act, Rom. 2. 14. *These having not a Law, are a Law to themselves.* So that the meaning is, when we acknowledge the Law of Nature to be the dictate of Right Reason, we must mean that the Understanding of Man is Endowed with such a power, as to be able, from the Contemplation of humane Condition to discover a necessity of Living agreeably with this Law: And likewise to find out some Principle, by which the Precepts of it, may be clearly and solidly Demonstrated. The way to discover the Law of Nature in our own state, is by a narrow Watch, and accurate Contemplation of our Natural Condition, and propensions. Others say this is the way to find out the Law of Nature. *scil.* If a Man any ways doubts, whether what he is going to do to another Man be agreeable to the Law of Nature, then let him suppose himself to be in that other Mans Room; And by this Rule effectually Executed. A Man must be a very dull Scholar to Nature not to make Proficiency in the Knowledge of her Laws. But more Particularly in pursuing our Condition for the discovery of the Law of Nature, this is very obvious to view, *viz.*

1. A Principle of Self-Love, & Self-Preservation, is very predominant in every Mans Being.

2. A Sociable Disposition.

3. An Affection or Love to Man-kind in General. And to give such Sentiments the force of a Law, we must suppose a God who takes care of all Man-

kind, and has thus obliged each one, as a Subject of higher Principles of Being, then meer Instincts. For that all Law properly considered, supposes a capable Subject, and a Superiour Power; And the Law of God which is Binding, is published by the Dictates of Right Reason as other ways: Therefore says *Plutarch, To follow God and obey Reason is the same thing.* But moreover that God has Established the Law of Nature, as the General Rule of Government, is further Illustrable from the many Sanctions in Providence, and from the Peace and Guilt of Conscience in them that either obey, or violate the Law of Nature. But moreover, the foundation of the Law of Nature with relation to Government, may be thus Discovered.

"THERE SHALL BE A STINK"

As the seventeenth century wore on, and especially after the restoration of Charles II in 1660 caused an influx of court favorites into New England, it became more and more difficult for orthodox congregationalism in Massachusetts to maintain its identity and its discipline over the lives of church members. While increased social, economic, and political ties with England threatened the power of the orthodoxy in commercial Boston, Puritan pioneers were also moving out into the wilderness to establish frontier communities beyond the direct control of the Bay leaders. The frontier movement led to conflict with the Indians, who in three years of hideous raids destroyed twenty towns, massacring the settlers and making captives of a number of Puritan women. In 1675–1676, almost simultaneously with Bacon's campaigns in Virginia, the Puritans, full of vengeance, all but annihilated the Wampanoags and their allies in a bloody conflict called "King Philip's War" after the name of the slain Indian leader. The Reverend Increase Mather, regarded as one of Puritanism's leaders, used the war as an occasion to deliver one of his most powerful sermons. Speaking from his pulpit at the Second Congregational Church of Boston, Mather in 1676 delivered a jeremiad which reveals clearly his fears of moral backsliding and internal dissension within the church. It also includes some strictures against too extended an "errand" into the wilderness. As Puritanism began to disintegrate in the latter half of the century, the jeremiad, or "fire and brimstone" sermon, became an ever more common form of Puritan oratory.

The following is an excerpt from Mather's famous sermon.

INCREASE MATHER DELIVERS A JEREMIAD
ON THE OCCASION OF KING PHILIP'S WAR

Quest. But what shall be done that so there may be such a Reformation as God may approve of?

Text. I. *Those Evills which have been confessed before the Lord, and which are manifest let them be reformed.* In that Order before mentioned respecting a day of publick humiliation appointed by *Authority* there are many Evills instanced in[;] as the matter of Confession and Humiliation before the Lord, let those sins be repented of, and turned from. We shall here take notice of some of them.

1. *Manifold abuses of Peace and the Blessings of God in this good land.* Alas when we have had peace from enemies, we would not be at peace among our selves. And as the Calamity which is come upon us is General, so *Contention* is a sin which all sorts of men have been too guilty of: and now we see the bitter fruit of it, whilst the Sheep (yea the shepherds too some of them) have been contending one with another, God hath let loose Wolves upon us all. And how have the Blessings of God been abused to serve *Baal?* The Plenty, which our Peace hath been attended with hath been abused unto great Sensuality, and many **Professors and Church** Members have been shamefully guilty in that respect. How common hath it been with them to *haunt Taverns;* and squander away precious hours, nay dayes in publick houses, which if but half that time had been spent in Meditation, Secret Prayer and Self Examination it had been happy for them, and it may be for others for their sakes. When as our Fathers were *Patterns of Sobriety,* they did not drink a cup of wine nor strong drink, more than should suffice nature, and conducent to their health, men of latter time would transact no business, nor hardly ingage in any discourses but it must be over a pint of wine or a pot of beer, yea so as that Drunkenness in the sight of man is become a common Sin, but how much more that is Drunkenness in the sight of God. And how have the Blessings of God been abused to nourish *pride?* There have been no small Provocation before the

Increase Mather, *An Earnest Exhortation To The Inhabitants of New England, To harken to the voice of God in his late and present Dispensation as ever they desire to escape another Judgement, seven times greater than anything which as yet hath been* (Boston, John Foster, 1676), pp. 6–7.

Courtesy of Allan I. Ludwig.

Detail of a New England gravestone: the Joseph Tapping stone, 1678, King's Chapel, Boston, Massachusetts.

Lord in that thing, yea as to *Pride in respect of Apparel*. People in this land
have not carryed it, as it becometh those that are in the Wilderness, especially
when it is such an humbling time as of late years hath been. And none more
guilty than the poorer sort of people, who will needs go in their Silks and
Bravery as if they were the best in the Land. Though it be also too true that the
rich and the honourable have many of them greatly offended by strange Apparel, especially here in *Boston*. A proud Fashion no sooner comes into the
Country, but the *haughty Daughters of Zion* in this place are taking it up, and
thereby the whole land is at last infected. What shall we say when men are
seen in the streets with monstrous and horrid *Perriwigs*, and Women with
their *Borders and False Locks* and such like whorish Fashions, whereby the
anger of the Lord is kindled against this sinful Land! And now behold how
dreadfully is God fulfilling the third chapter of Isaiah. *Moreover the Lord
saith* (if the Lord say it who dare slight what is said) *because the Daughters
of Zion are haughty*, therefore he will discover their Nakedness. Hath not the
Lord fulfilled this threatning, when the *Indians* have taken so many and
stripped them naked as in the day that they were born. *And instead of a Sweet
Smell there shall be a Stink*, Is not this verified when poor Creatures are carried away Captive into the Indians filthy and stinking *Wigwams*, yea when so
many English are faign to crowd together till it becomes loathsome and un-
savoury? *And burning instead of Beauty*, is it not so when poor creatures are
exposed to the burning heat of the sun, and burnt and tauned therby till they
become of an hue like unto these Indians? *Thy men shall fall by the Sword, &
Thy Mighty by the War*. Hath not that word been fulfilled upon us when so
many have fallen by the Sword, yea so many Captains in this War, and this is
because of the pride of the Daughters of Zion. Oh then let that sin be reformed
and repented of.

THE DEVIL AMONGST THEM

The last desperate stand of Puritan orthodoxy came in 1692 with the witch-craft trials at Salem. Cotton Mather was an intensely interested student of witchcraft delusion, and some of his speculations appear in the documents that follow. Though Mather's studies of witchcraft contributed to the Salem hysteria, he himself opposed the execution of the "witches." Samuel Sewall was a judge at the trials. When they were over, nineteen "witches" had been convicted on fabricated and hearsay evidence and hanged. One poor wretch who refused to plead either innocent or guilty had been executed by being pressed to death between two stones. Soon the entire community felt a revul-sion at what had been done, and five years later, in 1697, Samuel Sewall posted a public apology. In one last, long, hideous excess the Puritan ortho-doxy had condemned itself.

The selections that follow include some of Mather's speculations, exam-ples of two witchcraft "examinations," and Sewall's apology.

COTTON MATHER ON WITCHCRAFT AND THE WITCHCRAFT TRIALS TOGETHER WITH JUDGE SAMUEL SEWALL'S PROFOUND APOLOGY

1. *Cotton Mather on Witchcraft*

In all the *Witchcraft* which now Grievously Vexes us, I know not whether anything be more unaccountable, than the Trick which the Witches have to render themselves, and their Tools *Invisible*. *Witchcraft* seems to be the Skill of Applying the *Plastic Spirit* of the World, unto some unlawful purposes, by means of a Confederacy with *Evil Spirits*. Yet one would wonder how the *Evil Spirits* themselves can do some things; especially at *Invisibilizing* of the Grossest Bodies. I can tell the Name of an Ancient Author, who pretends to show the *way*, how a man may come to walk about *Invisible*, and I can tell the

Cotton Mather, *The Wonders of the Invisible World. Being an Account of the Tryals of Several Witches Lately executed in New England* (London, John Russell Smith, 1862), pp. 161–163. Witch-craft trials in *Historical Collections of the Essex Institute*, III, pp. 68–69; II, pp. 51–55. Sewall's apology in Stedman and Hutchinson, eds., *A Library of American Literature from the Earliest Settlement to the Present Time*, II, p. 188.

Name of another Ancient Author, who pretends to Explode that way. But I will not speak too plainly Lest I should unawares Poison some of my *Readers*, as the pious *Hemingius* did one of his *Pupils*, when he only by way of Diversion recited a *Spell*, which, they had said, would cure *Agues*. This much I will say; The notion of procuring *Invisibility*, by any *Natural Expedient*, yet known, is I Believe, a meer Plinyism; How far it may be obtained by a *Magical Sacrament*, is best known to the Dangerous Knaves that have try'd it. But our *Witches* do seem to have got the knack: and this is one of the Things, that makes me think, *Witchcraft* will not be fully understood, until the day when there shall not be one Witch in the World.

There are certain people very *Dogmatical* about these matters; but I'll give them only these three Bones to pick.

First, One of our bewitched people, was cruelly assaulted by a *Spectre*, that, she said, ran at her with a *Spindle*: tho' no body else in the Room, could see either the *Spectre* or the *spindle*. At last, in her miseries, giving a snatch at the *Spectre*, she pull'd the *spindle* away, and it was no sooner got into her hand, but the other people then present, beheld, that it was indeed a Real, Proper, Iron *spindle*, belonging they knew to whom; which when they lock'd up very safe, it was nevertheless by *Demons* unaccountably stole away, to do further mischief.

Secondly, another of our bewitched people, was haunted with a most abusive *Spectre*, which came to her, she said, with a *sheet* about her. After she had undergone a deal of Teaze, from the Annoyance of the *Spectre*, she gave a violent snatch at the sheet, that was upon it; wherefrom she tore a corner, which in her hand immediately became *Visible* to a Roomful of Spectators; a palpable Corner of a Sheet. Her Father, who was now holding her, catch'd that he might keep what his Daughter had so strangely siezed, but the unseen *Spectre* had like to have pull'd his hand off, by endeavouring to wrest it from him; however he still held it, and I suppose has it, still to show; it being but a few hours ago, namely about the beginning of this *October*, that this Accident happened; in the family of one *Pitman*, at *Manchester*.

Thirdly, A young man, delaying to procure Testimonials for his Parents, who being under confinement on suspicion of *Witchcraft*, required him to do that service for them, was quickly pursued with odd Inconveniences. But once above the Rest, an Officer going to put his *Brand* on the Horns of some *Cows*, belonging to these people, which tho he had siez'd for some of their debts, yet he was willing to leave in their possession, for the subsistance of the poor Family; this young man help'd in holding the Cows to be thus branded. The three first *Cows* he held well enough; but when the hot Brand was clap'd upon the Fourth, he *winc'd* and *shrunk* at such a Rate, as that he could hold the Cow no longer. Being afterwards Examined about it, he confessed, that at that very instant when the *Brand* entered the *Cow's Horn*, exactly the like burning *Brand* was clap'd upon his own Thigh; where he has exposed the lasting marks of it, unto such as asked to see them.

Unriddle these Things,—*Et Eris mihi magnus Apollo.* . . .

2. The Examination and Confession of Ann Foster at Salem Village, 15 July 1692

after a while Ann ffoster conffesed that the devil apered to her in the shape of a bird at several Times, such a bird as she neuer saw the like before; & that she had had this gift (viz. of striking ye afflicted downe with her eye euer since) & being askt why she thought yt bird was the diuill she answered because he came white & vanished away black & yt the diuill told her yt she should haue this gift & yt she must beliue him & told her she should haue prosperity & she said yt he had apeared to her three times & was always as a bird, & the last time was about half a year since, & sat upon a table had two legs & great eyes & yt it was the second time of his apearance that he promised her prosperity & yt it was Carriers wife about three weeks agoe yt came & perswaded her to hurt these people.

16 July 1692. Ann ffoster Examined confesed yt it was Goody Carrier yt made her a witch yt she came to her in person about Six yeares agoe & told her if she would not be a witch ye diuill should tare her in peices & carry her away at wch time she promised to Serve the diuill yt she had bewitched a hog of John Loujoys to death & that she had hurt some persons in Salem Vilage, yt goody Carier came to her & would have her bewitch two children of Andrew Allins & that she had then two popets made & stuck pins in them to bewitch ye said children by which one of them dyed ye other very sick, that she was at the meeting of the witches at Salem Villige, yt Goody Carier came & told her of the meeting and wonld haue her goe, so they got upon Sticks & went said Jorny & being there did see Mr Buroughs ye minister who spake to them all, & this was about two months agoe that there was then twenty five persons meet together, that she tyed a knot in a Rage & threw it into the fire to hurt Tim. Swan & that she did hurt the rest yt complayned of her by Squesing popets like them & so almost choaked them.

18. July 1692. Ann ffoster Examined confesed yt ye deuil in shape of a man apeared to her wth Goody carier about six yeare since when they made her a witch & that she promised to serve the diuill two years, upon which the diuill promised her prosperity and many things but neuer performed it, that she & martha Carier did both ride on a stick or pole when they went to the witch meeting at Salem Village & that the stick broak: as they were caried in the aire aboue the tops of the trees, & they fell but she did hang fast about the neck of Goody Carier & ware presently at the vilage, that she was then much hurt of her Leg, she further saith that she heard some of the witches say that there

was three hundred & fiue in the whole Country & that they would ruin that place ye Vilige, also saith ther was present att that meetting two men besides Mr Burroughs ye minister & one of them had gray haire, she saith yt she formerly frequented the publique metting to worship god. but the diuill had such power ouer her yt she could not profit there & yt was her undoeing: she saith yt about three or foure yeares agoe Martha Carier told her she would bewitch James Hobbs child to death & the child dyed in twenty four hours. 21. July 92. Ann ffoster Examined Owned her former conffesion being read to her and further conffesed that the discourse amongst ye witches at ye meeting at Salem village was that they would afflict there to set up the Diuills Kingdome. This confesion is true as witness my hand.———

Ann ffoster Signed & Owned the aboue Examination & Conffesion before me

Salem 10th Septembr 1692.   John Higginson, Just Peace.

Now follows the examination or confession of Mary Lacey, *daughter* of Ann Foster:

21 July 1692. A part of Goody Laceyes 2d Examination and confession to be added to the first. [The *first* not now to be found.]

Before majr Gedney, Mr. Hawthorn & Mr Corwin.

When Goodey foster was upon examination the second tyme, Goody Lacey was brought in also, who said to her mother foster. We haue forsaken Jesus Christ, and the devil hath got hold of us. how shall we get cleare of this evil one.

She confeses that her mother foster, Goody Carryer & herself rid upon a pole to Salem Village meeting, and that the pole broke a little way off from the village, she saith further that about 3 or 4 years agoe she saw mistress Bradbury Goody How and Goody nurse baptised by the old Serpent at newbury falls. And that he dipped theire heads in the water and then said they were his and he had power over them, she sayes there wer Six baptised at that tyme who were some of the chieff or heigher powers, and that there might be neare about a hundred in company at that tyme. It being asked her, after what manner she went to Newbury falls, answered the devil carryed her in his arms. And sayth further that if she doe take a ragg, clout or any such thing and Roll it up together, And Imagine it to represent such & such a persone, Then whatsoever she doth to that Ragg or clout so rouled up, The persone represented thereby will be in lyke manner afflicted.

It being againe asked her if what she had said was all true, She answer affimatively, confessing also that Andrew Carryer was a witch.

She confesses that she afflicted Timothy Swan in compa with mistress Bradbury Goody Carryer, Richard Carryer and her own daughter mary lacey.

They afflicted him with an Iron spindle and she thinks they did once with a tobacco pipe.

She said she was in Swans chamber and it being ask't which way she got in answered the devil helpt her in at the window;

She also remembers the afflicting of Ballards wife, and yt Richd Carryer was yr also.

She said further the devil take away her memory and will not let her remember.

3. The Examination of George Jacobs, Sr., and Margaret Jacobs

WARRANT V. GEO. JACOBS SR.

To The Constables in Salem.

You are in theire Majests names hereby required to apprehend and forth-with bring before vs George Jacobs Senr of Salem And Margaret Jacobs, the daughter of George Jacobs Junr of Salem, Singlewoman, Who stand accused of high suspition of sundry acts of witchcraft by them both Committed on sundry persons in Salem to theire great wrong and Injury and hereof faile not. (Dated Salem, May 10th, 1692.)

John Hathorne, }
Jonathan Corwin, } Assists.

To constable Joseph Neale.

(May ye 10th, 1692.) Then I apprehended the Bodyes of George Jacobs Senr and Margaret Jacobs, daughter of George Jacobs Junr, Both of Salem, According to the Tenor of the Aboue warrant p me.

(Joseph Neale Constable In Salem.)

COMPLAINT V. GEO. JACOBS SR.

Salem, May the 14th, 1692.

Lt Nathanill Ingersoll and Sergt Thomas Putnam, yeoman, both of Salem Village, personally appeared before vs and made complaint in behalfe of theire Majests against Daniell Andrew of Salem Village Bricklayer, George Jacobs Junr of Salem Village, husbandman, And ———— Jacobs the wife of said George Jacobs, ———— Buckley the wife of Wm Buckley of Salem Village cordwayner, and Mary Withridge of Salem Village, daughter of said Buckley, ———— Hart the wife of Isaac Hart of Lynn Husbandman, Thomas ffarrer senr of Lynn husbandman, Elizabeth Colson of Reding singlewoman, And Bethia Carter of onburne, daufter of Widdow Carter of sd Towne for Suspition of

Sundry Acts of witchcrafts by them Committed or Donne lately on the body of Ann Putnam, Marcy Lewis, Mary Walcott and Abigail Williams and others of Salem Village, wherebye much hurt is done to their bodyes, therefore Craues Justice.

Nathaniel Ingersoll,
Thomas Putnam.

INDICTMENT V. GEO. JACOBS SR.

Essex: ss.

(The Jurors for our Sovereigne Lord and Lady the King and Queen pesents, That George Jacobs Senr of Salem in ye County of Essex, the 11th day of May in the fourth Year of the Reigne of our Sovereigne Lord and Lady William and Mary by the Grace of God of England, Scottland, ffrance and Ireland King and Queen Defendrs of the ffaith &c., and Divers other Dayes and times as well before as after certaine Detestable Arts called Witchcrafts and sorceries Wickedly and ffelloniously hath vsed Practised and Exercised at and within the Township of Salem in the county of Essex aforesaid, in upon and agt one Marcy Lewis of Salem village singlewoman, by which said Wicked arts the said Marcy Lewis the 11th Day of May in the fourth year abovesaid and Divers other Dayes and times as well before as after was and is Tortured, Afflicted, Pined, Consumed, wasted and Tormented and also for sundry other acts of witchcraft by said George Jacobs Committed and Done before and since that time agt the Peace of our Sovereigne Lord and Lady the King and Queen their Crowne and Dignity and agt the forme of the Statutes in that Case made and provided.

Witnesses {	Marcy Lewis,	Eliz. Hubbard,
	Mary Walcott,	Sarah Churchill.

EXAMINATION OF GEO. JACOBS SR.

(The Examination of Geo. Jacobs Senr., 10 May, 1692.
Here are them that accuse you of acts of Witchcraft.
Well, let us hear who are they and what are they.
Abigail Williams. Jacobs laught.
Because I am falsely accused. Your worships all of you do you think this is true?
Nay, what do you think?
I never did it.
Who did it.
Don't ask me.
Why should we not ask you? Sarah Churchwell accuseth you, there she is.

I am as innocent as the Child born-to-night. I have lived 33 yeare here in Salem.

What then?

If you can prove that I am guilty I will lye under it.

Sarah Churchwell said last night I was afflicted at Deacon Ingersoll's and Mary Walcott said it was a man with 2 staves, it was my master.

Pray do not accuse me. I am as clear as your worships—you must do right judgments.

What book did he bring you Sarah?

The same that the other woman brought.

The Devill can go in any shape.

Did he not he appear on the other side of the river and hurt you—did not you see him?

Yes he did.

Look there, she accuseth you to your face, she chargeth you that you hurt her twice. Is it not true?

What would you have me say? I never wronged no man in word nor deed. Here are 3 evidences.

You tax me for a wizard, you may as well tax me for a buzard. I have done no harm.

Is it no harm to afflict these?

I never did it.

But how comes it to be in your appearance?

The Devil can take any likeness.

Not without their consent.

Please your worship it is untrue. I never showed the book. I am silly about these things as the child born last night.

That is your saying; you argue you have lived so long; but what then Cain might live long before he killed Abel, and you might live long before the Devill had so prevailed on you.

Christ hath suffered 3 times for me.

What three times.

He suffered the crosse and Gall.

You had as good confesse (said Sarah Churchwell) if you are guilty.

Have you heard that I have any witchcraft?

I know you live a wicked life.

Let her make it out.

Doth he ever pray in his family?

Not unless by himself.

Why do you not pray in your family?

I cannot read.

Well, but you may pray for all that. Can you say the Lord's prayer? Let us hear you.

He might in severall parts of it and could not repeat it right after Mary Mialls.

Sarah Churchwell, when you wrote in the book you was showed your master's name you said.

Yes, Sir.

If she say so, if you do not know it what will you say?

But she saw you or your likeness tempt her to write.

One in my likeness, the Devil may present my likeness.

Were you not frighted Sarah Churchwell when the representation of your master came to you?

Yes.

Well! burn me, or hang me, I will stand in the truth of Christ. I know nothing of it.

Do you know nothing of getting your son George and his daughter Margaret to signe?

No, nothing at all.

The 2d Examination of said George Jacobs, 11 May, 1692.

The bewitched fell into most grevious fits and screkings when he came in.

Is this the man that hurts you?

Abig. Williams cryed out this is the man and fell into a violent fit.

Ann Putnam said this is the man, and he hurts and brings the book to her and would have her write in the book and she should be as well as his Grand-daughter.

Mercy Lewis, is this the man?

This is the man, (after much interruption by fits,) he almost kills me.

Eliz. Hubbard said this man never hurt her till to-day he came upon the Table.

Mary Walcot, is this the man?

After much interruptions by fits she said this is the man; he used to come with two staves and beat her with one of them.

What do you say, are you not a witch?

No, I know it not, if I were to dye presently.

Mercy Lewis went to come near him but fell into great fits.

Mercy Lewis testimony read. What do you say to this?

Why it is false. I know not of it any more than the child that was born to-night.

Ann Putnam said yes, you told me so, that you had been so this 40 yeares.

Ann Putnam and Abigail Williams had each of them a pin stuck in their hands and they said it was this old Jacobs.

Abigail Williams Testimony read.

Are not you the man that made disturbance at a Lecture in Salem?
No great disturbance. Do you think I use witchcraft?
Yes, indeed.
No, I use none of them.

On the 12th of May, 1692, George Jacobs, sen., of Salem Village, was committed to Boston jail for witchcraft, and remained there six weeks and a few days. On the fifth day of August, the same year at a Court of Oyer and Terminer held at Salem, he was tried with five others—the Rev. Geo. Burroughs, a former minister of Salem Village, John Proctor and his wife Elizabeth, John Willard and Martha Carryer of Andover, who were all brought in by the jury guilty of the crime of Witchcraft.

They were all executed on the nineteenth of August, with the exception of Elizabeth Proctor, on Gallows Hill in Salem.

The witnesses in these trials were Margaret Jacobs, grand-daughter of George Jacobs, Mary Wolcott, Elizabeth Hubbard, Ann Putnam, Mercy Lewis and Mary Warren.

It is probable that Margaret Jacobs testified against her grandfather and Mr. Burroughs to save her own life, for she acknowledged to Mr. B., the day before the execution, that she had belied him and begged his forgiveness, who not only forgave her, but also prayed with and for her. The day after their execution she wrote the following letter to her father, George Jacobs, jr.:

From the dungeon in Salem Prison.

August 20th, 1692.

Honoured Father:—After my humble duty remembered to you, hoping in the Lord of your good health, as blessed be God I enjoy, though in abundance of affliction, being close confined here in a loathsome dungeon; the Lord look down in mercy upon me, not knowing how soon I shall be put to death, by means of the afflicted persons, my grandfather having suffered already, and all his estate seized for the king. The reason of my confinement is this: I having through the magistrates' threatenings, and my own vile and wretched heart, confessed several things contrary to my conscience and knowledge, though to the wounding of my soul, (the Lord pardon me for it!) but oh! the terrors of a wounded conscience who can bear? But, blessed be the Lord, he would not let me go on in my sins, but in mercy, I hope, to my soul, would not suffer me to keep it any longer; but I was forced to confess the truth of all before the magistrates, who would not believe me, but it is their pleasure to put me in here, and God knows how soon I shall be put to death. Dear Father, let me beg your prayers to the Lord on my behalf, and send us a joyful and happy meeting in heaven. My mother, poor woman, is very crazy, and remembers her kind love to you and to uncle viz.: D. A. So leaving you to the protection of the Lord, I rest your dutiful daughter.

Margaret Jacobs

4. Samuel Sewall: The Judge's Confession

Copy of the Bill I put up on the Fast day; giving it to Mr. Willard as he pass'd by, and standing up at the reading of it, and bowing when finished; in the Afternoon.

Samuel Sewall, sensible of the reiterated strokes of God upon himself and family; and being sensible, that as to the Guilt contracted upon the opening of the late Commission of Oyer and Terminer at Salem (to which the order for this Day relates) he is, upon many accounts, more concerned than any that he knows of, Desires to take the Blame and shame of it, Asking pardon of men, And especially desiring prayers that God, who has an Unlimited Authority, would pardon that sin and all other his sins; personal and Relative: And according to his infinite Benignity, and Sovereignty, Not Visit the sin of him, or of any other, upon himself or any of his, nor upon the Land: But that He would powerfully defend him against all Temptations to Sin, for the future; and vouchsafe him the efficacious, saving Conduct of his Word and Spirit.

[Date, January 14, 1697]